Peter Klimczak, Christer Petersen (eds.)
AI – Limits and Prospects of Artificial Intelligence

KI-Kritik / AI Critique | Volume 4

Editorial

Since Kant, critique has been defined as the effort to examine the way things work with respect to the underlying conditions of their possibility; in addition, since Foucault it references a thinking about "the art of not being governed like that and at that cost." In this spirit, **KI-Kritik / AI Critique** publishes recent explorations of the (historical) developments of machine learning and artificial intelligence as significant agencies of our technological times, drawing on contributions from within cultural and media studies as well as other social sciences.
The series is edited by Anna Tuschling, Andreas Sudmann and Bernhard J. Dotzler.

Peter Klimczak (Prof. Dr. Dr.) is adjunct professor at Brandenburgische Technische Universität. He conducts research on digital/social media, cognitive systems, and the use of artificial languages in media and cultural studies.
Christer Petersen (Prof. Dr.) holds the Chair of Applied Media Studies at Brandenburgische Technische Universität and works in the fields of media and cultural semiotics, materiality and technicity of media.

Peter Klimczak, Christer Petersen (eds.)

AI – Limits and Prospects of Artificial Intelligence

[transcript]

Bibliographic information published by the Deutsche Nationalbibliothek
The Deutsche Nationalbibliothek lists this publication in the Deutsche Nationalbibliografie; detailed bibliographic data are available in the Internet at http://dnb.d-nb.de

This work is licensed under the Creative Commons Attribution-NonCommercial-NoDerivatives 4.0 (BY-NC-ND) which means that the text may be used for non-commercial purposes, provided credit is given to the author.
To create an adaptation, translation, or derivative of the original work and for commercial use, further permission is required and can be obtained by contacting rights@transcript-publishing.com
Creative Commons license terms for re-use do not apply to any content (such as graphs, figures, photos, excerpts, etc.) not original to the Open Access publication and further permission may be required from the rights holder. The obligation to research and clear permission lies solely with the party re-using the material.

First published in 2023 by transcript Verlag, Bielefeld
© Peter Klimczak, Christer Petersen (eds.)

Cover layout: Maria Arndt, Bielefeld
Typeset: Sebastian M. Schlerka, Bielefeld
Printed by: Majuskel Medienproduktion GmbH, Wetzlar
https://doi.org/10.14361/9783839457320
Print-ISBN: 978-3-8376-5732-6
PDF-ISBN: 978-3-8394-5732-0
ISSN of series: 2698-7546
eISSN of series: 2703-0555

Printed on permanent acid-free text paper.

Contents

Preface 7

Learning Algorithms
What is Artificial Intelligence Really Capable of?
Rainer Berkemer, Markus Grottke 9

Transgressing the Boundaries
Towards a Rigorous Understanding of Deep Learning and Its
(Non-)Robustness
Carsten Hartmann, Lorenz Richter.. 43

**Limits and Prospects of Ethics in the Context of Law and Society
by the Example of Accident Algorithms of Autonomous Driving**
Peter Klimczak 83

**Limits and Prospects of Big Data and Small Data Approaches
in AI Applications**
Ivan Kraljevski, Constanze Tschöpe, Matthias Wolff 115

Artificial Intelligence and/as Risk
Isabel Kusche 143

When You Can't Have What You Want
Measuring Users' Ethical Concerns about Interacting with AI
Assistants Using MEESTAR
Kati Nowack.. 163

Man-Machines
Gynoids, Fembots, and Body-AI in Contemporary
Cinematic Narratives
Christer Petersen 195

Trends in Explainable Artificial Intelligence for Non-Experts
Elise Özalp, Katrin Hartwig, Christian Reuter 223

Machine Dreaming
Stefan Rieger 245

Let's Fool That Stupid AI
Adversarial Attacks against Text Processing AI
Ulrich Schade, Albert Pritzkau, Daniel Claeser, Steffen Winandy 267

Authors 285

Preface

Just today, as we are making the final corrections to the present volume, an online article rolls into our newsfeeds. There we read that in June of this year, Google programmer Blake Lemoine went public. He was concerned with the 'Language Model for Dialogue Applications' (LaMDA), an intelligent speech bot from Google specialized in dialogues. "As first reported in the Washington Post, programmer Lemoine, after his conversations with LaMDA, no longer believes that this machine is merely a tool. He demands that LaMDA be treated as a person. He believes LaMDA has gained consciousness." – "Can this be?" asks the author of the article. – "Short answer: most likely not."[1]

And yet, no other topic in recent years has triggered such a storm of enthusiasm and simultaneously such a wave of uncertainty: artificial intelligence. Intelligent software will automate work, understand images and text and make medical diagnoses. It enables cars to drive independently and supports scientific work. On the basis of current innovations, a global revolution in business and industry can be predicted, which is being driven along ever further by the networking of 'smart machines'. At the same time, artificial intelligence promises to be able to analyze the masses of data produced in the course of digitalisation for patterns and to make automated decisions based on these, which will not only rival the quality of human analysis, but will be far superior to human work in terms of efficiency.

The current central paradigm of AI is machine learning, whereby deep learning seems to represent the most promising technological approach: software is no longer programmed for its specific tasks but is trained on

---

1 "Künstliche Intelligenz, [...] was kommt da auf uns zu?" October 11, 2002. URL: https://krautreporter.de/4601-kunstliche-intelligenz-so-verstandlich-wie-moglich-erklart?utm_campaign=pocket-visitor, translated from German.

large amounts of data – on Big Data. Here, however, the limits of the new technology begin to become apparent, as data volumes are not always available in the desired quality and quantity. It also requires basic or retrospective labelling by humans as well as the processing of data by means of symbolic AI procedures, therefore by supporting Small Data approaches. It is not uncommon for social discrimination to be inherent in the data sets, to which human preselection, categorisation and corresponding annotation make a decisive contribution. Inevitably, this leads to the integration of cognitive biases into a given AI: prejudices embedded in society are reproduced and to some extent further reinforced. Moreover, if machine decisions are made on the basis of deep learning systems, the decisions made by the machine are also non-transparent for humans. These are quite rightly characterised as black box procedures, which are accompanied by considerable legal problems. And finally, but importantly, the fundamental question arises as to whether people can trust systems with which they are supposed to collaborate, when not even the systems' very creators can reconstruct and interpret the decisions of their technical creatures.

The volume is therefore intended to explicitly show the limits of AI, to describe the necessary conditions for the functionality of AI, to reveal its attendant technical and social problems, and to present some existing and potential solutions. At the same time, however, we also want to describe the societal and attending economic hopes and fears, utopias and distopias that are associated with the current and future development of AI. This has led us to gather in this volume authors and contributions from a variety of scientific disciplines, meaning that computer scientists, engineers, mathematicians, as well as media studies experts, social scientists and economists have their say on an equal footing. And lastly, but foremost, we thank our English-language editor, Richard Slipp, who has repeatedly defied DeepL and all other artificially intelligent translators and pointed out their limitations, thus making the volume in its present form possible.

Peter Klimczak and Christer Petersen
October 2022

Learning Algorithms
What is Artificial Intelligence Really Capable of?

Rainer Berkemer, Markus Grottke

I. Introduction

Intelligent machines and algorithms, mostly subsumed under the name of artificial intelligence, are pervading ever more areas of modern life. In doing so, they are increasingly presenting results that exceed the capabilities of humans in the respective area of application. Examples are Alpha Go in the Asian game of Go, AI-based chess computers, ChatGPT or the Watson system in the television show Jeopardy. But what can really be concluded from such results with respect to the capabilities of artificial intelligence?

One of the great challenges of analyzing artificial intelligence with regard to such a question is that – outside of certain formal rules – nobody knows the why, that is, for what reason the algorithms in question learn, i.e. how they finally acquire their capabilities and why they act as they act. This is especially true for learning algorithms based on neural networks as explainable AI still remains the exception in this area, even though research in explainable AI is currently starting to mushroom (Gunning et al. 2019: 2; Samek/Müller 2019: 13).

On the other hand, it is the responsibility of university teachers to communicate the implications of such a lack of understanding and to enable a constructive but at the same time critical approach to such learning algorithms. In this respect it might be of interest that many of the questions that currently arise were already discussed by the early pioneers of artificial intelligence, such as Alan Turing, creator of the Turing test, and Norbert Wiener, founder of cybernetics.

Referring back to and expanding on such discussions, the following article poses, based on the famous example of AlphaZero, one central question and derives from it some important points for discussion, namely: Based on the concrete example of AlphaZero: What does artificial intelligence do and what are the implications of how artificial intelligence is perceived? This points to questions like: What does the lack of understanding – e.g. the blackbox character – that is typical for artificial intelligence really involve? And – based on this – what is the social responsibility of decision makers such as artificial intelligence developers? What social responsibility do economic decision makers of funding for the development of artificial intelligence have? What effects on society and the working world can be expected from the use of artificial intelligence?

The rest of the paper is organized as follows. First, neural networks in general are discussed. Also, important definitions are formulated which prepare the groundwork for the following analyses but also limit the field of analysis. In the next chapter, learning algorithms are discussed, especially those that have been employed in cases where the performance of artificial intelligence compared to human intelligence is discussed. This part of the paper deals with these general questions by making use of the example of AlphaZero. This learning algorithm has been chosen, as chess has long since been regarded as the "drosophila" of AI. Unlike other chess programs, AlphaZero is based on a "general reinforcement algorithm". This suggests that it could be "strong AI" because the principle can be applied easily to other games, as well as strategic situations – in fact, however, the historical course of events was the other way around. An application to the board game Go took place first and only after it was surprisingly successful in that domain was the principle later transferred to chess and shogi. Finally, some considerations on this basis are shown with respect to the discussions around the emerging question of social responsibility for artificial intelligence, before the paper concludes with an overview of the results, limitations of the present analyses and an outlook.

II. Principles of Neural Networks and Possible Definitions of (Artificial) Intelligence

II.1 Neural Networks: Basic Principles and Typical Areas of Application

The starting point of an artificial neural network is a schematic reproduction of a biological model, a neuron, which is artificially reproduced in the case of a neural network. A single neuron has any number of inputs but always only one output.

Within a single neuron, the input information is processed – mostly by *weighted summation* – and the output signal is determined depending on the threshold values that are exceeded or not. This procedure is also closely related to the biological model, in which a nerve cell fires when a threshold voltage is exceeded, i.e. transmits an electrical signal.

The described mechanism becomes relevant with respect to artificial neural networks as soon as a large number of neurons are assembled into more complex structures, typically grouped into layers, with the flow of information usually proceeding forward from the *input layer* to the *output layer*. Figure 1 shows two common network structures.

Figure 1: Two common structures of neural networks (Nguyen et al. 2018: 6)

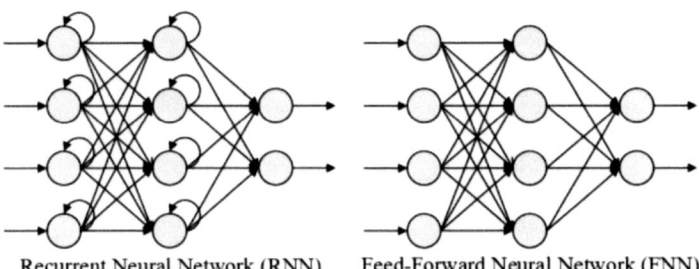

Recurrent Neural Network (RNN)   Feed-Forward Neural Network (FNN)

The layers in between are called *hidden layers* and modern neural networks, as they are often used in the field of pattern recognition, typically have a huge number of such hidden layers. These are commonly also called Deep Neural Networks (DNN) insofar as they exhibit a sufficiently high number of layers.

Typically, the task of a neural network is to train artificial neurons to correctly distinguish an unknown data set that follows the same underlying rules as the classification patterns used to train the neural network from a data set that does not follow such classification patterns.

For this purpose, a neural network consisting of artificial neurons is trained using an initial data set with labelled data that has already correctly assigned outputs so that the result of this training could be used for classifying patterns that are still unknown.

One of the challenges in training is that the respective neural network can be over-trained (so-called over-fitting) or under-trained (so-called under-fitting). This is illustrated in figure 2.

Figure 2: Over-fitting, neural network with adequate generalization, under-fitting (Kriesel 2007: 86 adjusted by Jerems 2018: 49)

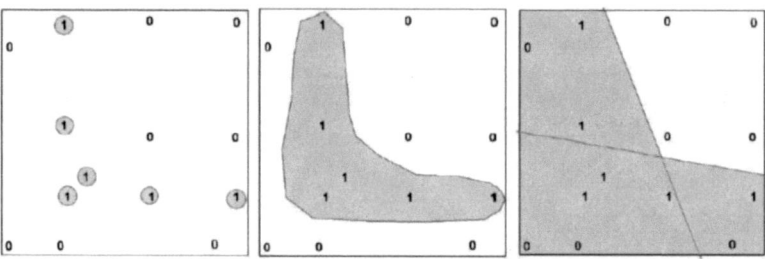

The left of the three figures shows an overtrained network, while on the right, we can see an undertrained network and the middle of the three figures represents an adequately generalizing network. The overtrained network only concretizes single cases, but has no generalization anymore, as the small circles around the single cases indicate. Thus, it is questionable whether it would still correctly classify an unknown pattern. An undertrained neural network has false positives (as seen in in the classified zeros in the figure on the right). A good classification, on the other hand, separates adequately but also goes beyond pure learning by rote.

II.2 Intelligence

When dealing with learning algorithms in the area of artificial intelligence, we should first think about what we mean when we employ the notion of intelligence. For example, some possible characteristics might immediately come to mind, such as curiosity, long-term-planning, or learning capabilities. One approach to address the notion of intelligence, for example, can be based on the so-called Turing test from 1950.

The Turing test defines artificial intelligence by comparison with a human being as follows:

Before dealing with artificial intelligence one should first develop an understanding of natural (human) intelligence. When we then have to decide whether one should attribute "intelligence" also to a machine, the most obvious approach is given when artificial intelligence is assigned to a computer or to a machine if it can successfully imitate human answers under certain conditions.

Specifically, a human observer must not be able to determine several times without error whether an answer to a posed question was given by a computer or by another human being. If the person cannot distinguish this, the machine has "passed" the Turing test (cf. Turing 1950).

The first chatbot Eliza by Joseph Weizenbaum (MIT 1967), for example, managed to give its users the impression of talking to a counterpart full of empathy and understanding by skillfully manipulating symbols. The following dialogue may illustrate the idea.

Person: Men are all alike.
ELIZA: In what way?
Person: They're always bugging us about something or other.
ELIZA: Can you think of a specific example?
Person: Well, my boyfriend made me come here.
ELIZA: Your boyfriend made you come here?
Person: He says I'm depressed much of the time.
ELIZA: I am sorry to hear that you are depressed.
Person: It's true. I am unhappy.
ELIZA: Do you think coming here will help you not to be unhappy?
Person: I need some help, that much seems certain.
ELIZA: What would it mean to you if you got some help?
Person: Perhaps I could learn to get along with my mother.
ELIZA: Tell me more about your family. (Kendall 2001)

It seems to be significant here that Eliza gets along without semantics, i.e. did not need to understand the meaning of the terms uttered. A knowledge base was sufficient that, for example, connects father, mother and son etc. with family, i.e. that knows the correct use of syntax. Nevertheless, it might pass a Turing test – at least a sufficiently superficial one. Obviously, the currently discussed ChatGPT would also pass the Turing test.

More suitable for our purposes as a method to classify artificial intelligence as intelligent or not is, however, the Chinese room framework that was developed by the linguist John Searle. It assumes that a computer would pass the Turing test and is, additionally, based on English instructions (!) able to convince a human Chinese speaker that the AI program is a living Chinese speaker. What Searle is pointing at here is that it is necessary to avoid the very deception that Eliza was undergoing. The key question that separates the two is whether a program really understands Chinese or whether it is just simulating it. To test this, the following situation is established: an English-speaking person without any knowledge in Chinese sits in a closed room with a book full of English instructions. Chinese letters are passed into the room through a slit, the person reads the English instructions and on this basis, that is by taking recourse to the instructions and the incoming Chinese letters, also passes Chinese letters to the outside. Searle argues that a person acting in this way is as intelligent as a program based on input and output. But Searle also makes clear that this does not mean that the computer can think: neither computer nor human will think in such a framework, but rather both of them mindlessly follow certain instructions (for more elaborations on the Chinese room cf. Walch 2020).

In this respect, a precise differentiation is required in each case as to when which form of knowledge is received. These can be distinguished from each other according to the following figure 3, which shows the beginning of a knowledge pyramid.

Figure 3: Sign – data – information (North 2021: 37)

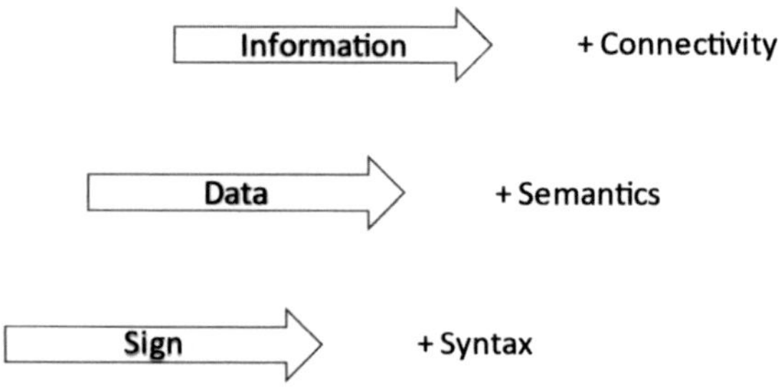

Information →	+ Connectivity
Data →	+ Semantics
Sign →	+ Syntax

If you follow the examples mentioned so far, Eliza takes you to the level of syntax situated in the knowledge pyramid, i.e. the linking of characters according to given rules. Similarly, the program as the human in the Chinese room experiment use and apply only knowledge at this syntax level and do not really understand what they are doing. However, in the Eliza example the syntax level limitations become somewhat apparent after some time. In the Chinese room experiment it is, on the one hand, apparent that it was the creator of the instructions and the selector of the Chinese Letters who put the intelligence in the action of the program while the program still remains on a syntax level. However, the impression of intelligence of the program (which seems to be able to deal with Chinese) is impressive from the outside. As we will see, this is quite comparable to AlphaZero (which seems to be able to understand chess).

However, both, that is the Turing test and Chinese room, can be considered to be limited to a certain application area for, among others, the following reason: we know that people react differently to identical stimuli and identically to different stimuli because of the meaning that they attach to the words of other people as well as to their own words (Hayek 1979: 43). Neither the Turing test nor Chinese room experiment can address such a behavior because they would need (at least statistically) identical reactions to identical stimuli (according to certain given rules or instructions). It is exactly for that reason that both cannot grasp human behavior generally but only capture an imitation of such behavior by artificial intelligence.

II.3   Types of Artificial Intelligence

Artificial intelligence may be subdivided into numerous facets, a brief overview of which is provided below to the extent that it is relevant to the following discussion. According to a review article by Seifert et al. (2018: 56), AI technology can be divided into three different categories, namely behavioral ("human") AI, *systems that think and act rationally*, and biologically inspired systems. We do not pursue the topic of the latter as they are not commonly counted among the "classical" forms of AI (Seifert et al. 2018: 58).

Examples of behavioral technologies include semantic systems, natural language processing (NLP) and cognitive modelling. Semantic systems attempt to understand meaning in data by formulating relationships and dependencies. Compared to the syntax-based system Eliza, this brings us to the second stage, the linking of data using semantics.

In the case of NLP, human language is addressed in diverse forms and used via text recognition, language generation/comprehension and automatic translation (Seifert et al. 2018: 58). A potential application area for NLP are chatbots.

Cognitive modelling refers to models that mimic human intelligence and simulate human behavior (Seifert et al. 2018: 57). Systems that think and act rationally can be divided into the subfields of computer vision, robotic process automation and machine learning. Computer Vision refers to the detection and classification of objects or actions in images or videos.

Robotic Process Automation refers to the automatic recognition and processing of routine activities in business processes (Seifert et al. 2018: 60). By means of information technology it provides a promising approach to process automation in which repetitive and time-consuming or error-prone activities are learned and automated by software robots.

II.4 Types of Learning: Supervised, Unsupervised and Reinforcement Learning

Machine learning can be differentiated into supervised learning, unsupervised learning and reinforcement learning (Bruns/Kowald 2019: 9).

Supervised learning means that an algorithm receives a training set with a classification that has already been performed and that resulted in labelled data on which the algorithm is subsequently trained. Thus, the classification to be learned or a form of regression are already given. As soon as the algorithm has acquired these, validation takes place on a further data set that was not used during training, thus allowing a performance estimate of the learning machine on data that has not yet been seen.

Unsupervised learning in the form of data mining involves trying to find patterns in data sets without explicitly specifying a learning goal in order to reveal relationships between the underlying variables. In the now much more common case, however, unsupervised learning is used to predict variable states on as yet unseen data sets.

Reinforcement learning, by contrast, seeks to find a solution to the problem by providing the algorithm with feedback in the form of incentive/punishment (Bruns/Kowald 2019: 9–10). The main difference between reinforcement learning and other machine learning paradigms, therefore, is that reinforcement learning is not only concerned with predictive performance, but with finding a course of action ("policy") under given (or presumed) environmental conditions that leads to the maximization of a previously specified quality criterion (reward).

This objective includes a high predictive power as an intermediate step, but goes beyond this with respect to its purpose, as it desires situation-appropriate actions of the AI as system output. Consequently, with the help of reinforcement learning, an AI "independently learns a strategy for solving a problem or task" (Seifert et al. 2018: 60). While computer vision and robotic process automation, like supervised learning, do not go beyond the level of data processing described so far, unsupervised learning and reinforcement learning seem to make possible a different quality, which could go beyond the stages that described models of AI (e.g. ELIZA) reached so far in the knowledge pyramid shown in Figure 3.

In a nutshell, what the defining work up to this point reveals is that at least almost all current AI can be classified as being able to connect signs. However, to what degree artificial intelligence goes beyond is not so clear. It is only clear that it is not yet using its capabilities to act on its own. In the following, we will look at one amazing example of AI in detail. Based on our example, chess, we will elaborate very thoroughly, not only because of the very long tradition of chess as a role model for computer science and artificial intelligence applications. AlphaZero, the learning algorithm in question, which is a classical reinforcement learning algorithm, is very suitable for illustration precisely because of this, namely, because the use of artificial intelligence in chess is comparably well-understood. Whether and especially to what degree, however, the algorithm reaches a different level in the knowledge pyramid, is a question that remains to be answered when we analyze AlphaZero.

III. The Analysis of a Self-learning Algorithm: The Example of AlphaZero

III.1 Automatons Playing Chess - Historical Overview of Chess Computing Systems

For a long time chess was regarded as the drosophila of AI research, as a number of important scientists who have also made important general contributions to mathematics and logic have also tried to automate chess. Even before the necessary hardware existed, Charles Babbage, for example, conceived of a corresponding computing system in theory – in the middle of the 19th century (Bauermeister n.d.: 1).

According to Bauermeister, it was not until about 100 years later that the world's first non-mechanical functional program-controlled calculating machine was built, the famous Z3, by Konrad Zuse in 1941. A mechanical functional program-controlled machine had already been achieved with the

Z1. To program the computer, Zuse developed a language called "Plankalkül", the archetype of all of today's algorithmic programming languages. (ibid: 1)

Zuse chose the game of chess as a test object to demonstrate that such a machine can not only compute numbers (the word computer is derived from this) but that this machine, in principle, is also suitable for addressing and solving non-numerical problems.

The first algorithm ready to be implemented was developed by none other than Turing himself. In 1947, Turochamp was launched, a one-move generator with something that many later programs would pick up – a rating function that tried to incorporate chess-specific knowledge (ibid: 2). The pieces were rated according to their potential strength – a pawn was assigned the value of one unit, the minor pieces (knight and bishop) the value of 3 to 3.5 pawn units. A rook was rated as strong as 5 pawns and the queen as strong as 2 rooks.

This form of so-called material evaluation seems at first sight to be extremely static. However, in almost all current chess programs it is still the essential basis and when human chess players analyze games – mostly with the support of computers – then they, normally, think in these "pawn units" and translate other factors, like the mobility of the pieces as well into this scheme.

Now Turing had his algorithm but no corresponding machine – he had to go through the program on paper and had to evaluate the resulting positions by hand (ibid: 3)!

In this way games against human opponents were actually realized – Turing sat on the other side of the board and stubbornly followed (as in the Chinese room) the instructions of his algorithm without being allowed to incorporate his own understanding of chess. This must have been a frustrating experience, because the program revealed the typical shortcomings of the early days of computer chess, such as material overvaluation and planning inability.

During the game, Turing always tried to predict the next move made by his program, but this must have led to considerable disappointment as he regularly failed! After these sobering experiences with Turochamp, Turing put forward the thesis that it is impossible to develop a program that plays stronger than its developer. A claim that, as we know today, is definitely not correct.

The current chess programs have been playing for decades at a level that not only dwarfs the abilities of their developers but also those of the strongest grandmasters. As early as 1996, a supercomputer from IBM called Deep Blue won against then world champion Garri Kasparov. Even though Kasparov was able to save the "honor of mankind" at the time, holding the upper hand in the overall competition over 6 games, the time had finally come one year later: in the rematch of 1997, the human world champion no longer lost just individual games, but also the overall competition.

In the meantime, it is considered pointless to let humans compete against computers in chess, which is why specially designed competitions for computer chess engines emerged.

During the 2010s, the free chess program Stockfish has dominated the Top Chess Engine Championship (TCEC), which is considered the unofficial championship in computer chess.

III.2   Some Theoretical Considerations on Chess Computing

III.2.1   Zermelo's Theorem (1912)

Besides practical programming trials, Zermelo's Theorem (1912) is one of the hallmarks that also theoretically characterize the challenges involved in chess computing. Zermelo's Theorem can be summarized as follows: in any board game, the first-player can force a win, or the second-player can force a win, or both players can force a draw. In other words, with perfect play the game will always end in the same result. However, it must satisfy the following conditions (Zermelo 1912: 501–504):

- The game board is finite,
- There are only two players,
- The game is of perfect information (nothing is hidden, unlike poker),
- The players alternate turns,
- There is no element of chance.

Zermelo's work anticipated the essentials of game theory, at least for games like chess, several decades before game theory came into being. Later, when von Neumann and Morgenstern presented their seminal work on game theory in 1944 (von Neumann/Morgenstern 1944), a corresponding generalization resulted, which is today known as the minmax algorithm, an algorithm which is suitable for determining the optimal strategy in all two-person zero-sum games with perfect knowledge.

In the general case, three possible results need not be assumed (as for chess). There can also be fewer – there are also games without a draw – or more so-called outcomes can be conceivable. But the decisive point is: if both sides play optimally, the result should always be the same.

From the point of view of game theory, chess is as simple as tic-tac-toe, and the fact that chess tournaments with or without computer participation still produce different results only proves that the optimal strategy has not been mastered yet.

From a practical point of view, Zermelo's theorem does not really help players. It is not even clear which of the three possible outcomes must result from optimal playing. Most practitioners assume the draw, some can also imagine an advantage for the white pieces (the player with this color plays first). But it is theoretically not impossible that having to start may even amount to a disadvantage. There are a number of well-known so-called forced move positions in chess where the side that has to move necessarily loses. While it is rather unlikely that the starting position should also be such a position, this is at least theoretically not impossible.

III.2.2 Further Theoretical Developments by Claude Shannon and Norbert Wiener

Another seminal paper is that of Claude Shannon (1950). It is interesting for a variety of reasons. The most notable of them in this context is that DeepMind's developers picked it up and cited it later in their own work (Silver 2017: 5), which will then bring us to the implementation details of AlphaZero.

Shannon, the founder of information theory, took up the minmax algorithm. However, it was also clear to him that the decision trees in chess would become much too extensive and too complex to manage (even) with computer help. Therefore, among other things, considerations were made to prune these decision trees, and not to consider all possible responses of an opponent, but to limit oneself to the most plausible responses. Norbert Wiener, the founder of cybernetics, again took up Shannon's work in his book The Human Use of Human Beings (Wiener 1954: 178), and obviously discussed it with him and others; the idea of a self-learning chess machine, with its possible potential but also its dangers, also came up already in the early 1950s. We will take up these aspects again in more detail in the concluding discussion. Against this background, let us now turn to implementation details of AlphaZero.

III.3 Implementation Details with Respect to AlphaZero

III.3.1 Overview

So what makes AlphaZero so innovative? First of all, AlphaZero breaks with the approach of traditional chess engines and acts completely differently. For example, AlphaZero has no domain-specific knowledge at all – with the exception of chess rules. As already described, early on from the time of Turochamp developers counted on evaluation functions which combined material aspects by summing up the value of pieces, positional aspects, for example the pawn structure, and security of the king, among other things. These evaluation functions had to be handcrafted and carefully weighted by human chess experts in traditional approaches. In addition, the aspects of material and position, which are static by nature, had to be supplemented by dynamic factors such as the mobility of the pieces and so-called tempi (a time advantage of three moves is valued approximately at one pawn unit).

With the traditional approaches, it took decades of hard work until it was finally possible to beat a human world champion (Gary Kasparov). Moreover, it should be taken into account that modern chess computers (before the neural network approaches) are also equipped with powerful opening libraries, in which centuries of human experience have been accumulated.

AlphaZero was able do without all that completely. Not even the most basic opening principles were implemented – no endgame table base was needed either. Instead, the algorithm relies on "learning from the scratch". The developers themselves coined the term tabula rasa reinforcement learning algorithm (Silver 2017: 2).

Briefly summarized: with the exception of the chess rules themselves, all knowledge of chess experts is dispensed with. Instead, methods are used that have generally proven themselves in modern AI systems (deep neural nets), such as convolutional neural networks, the gradient descent method and the MCTS approach – we will discuss these below.

III.3.2 Convolutional Neural Networks (CNN)

A CNN consists of filters (convolutional layers) and subsequent aggregations (by pooling layers), which are repeated alternately to be completed by one or more layers of fully connected normal neurons (Dense/Fully Connected

Figure 4: Convolutional Neural Networks ("Convolutional Neural Networks" 2019)

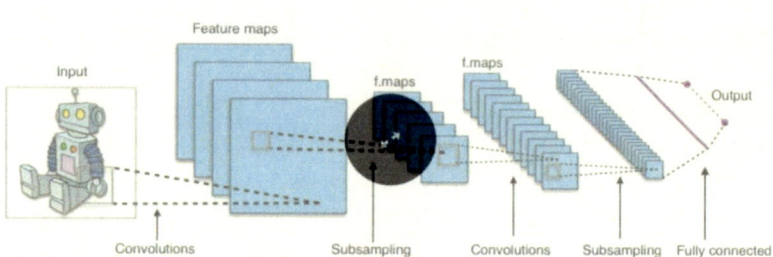

Layer). This leads to another strength of Convolutional Neural Networks, which is to condense information from a matrix input into a meaningful vector. ("Convolutional Neural Networks" 2019)

CNNs are used very successfully in the currently oft-discussed field of autonomous driving, for example, but also for the classification of objects in general. Some of the early layers of the network recognize simple features, such as differences in edges and brightness levels. Later on, these are combined to represent contours. Finally, in the later layers of the deep neural network this information is then combined to recognize objects as a whole.

Using CNNs for the game Go, too, was an obvious choice, in order to generate a one-dimensional fully connected layer from a two-dimensional input. The developers of deep mind first designed their general reinforcement algorithm for Go, and there the contours that separate white and black regions certainly play a special role. When transferring the concept to chess and shogi, it turned out to be useful to keep the principle in order to capture the two-dimensional board position as input.

The algorithm in question thus enables self-learning in the sense of reinforcement learning mentioned above. In the beginning, it was completely amateurish – but after 44 million games against itself, the system had obviously gained enough "experience" to "recognize" non-obvious resources in positions.

III.3.3 Adjustment by Gradient Descent

Learning in neural networks is based on the fact that the parameters of the network are continuously adjusted. A standard is the gradient descent method for training the weights connecting the neurons. Here, we are not dealing with supervised learning, but with reinforcement learning. In this sense, a training phase is never finished, but instead the system keeps improving itself, reinforcing everything that worked well and weakening everything that went wrong. In order to implement this reinforcement, an *externally defined objective function* is needed. In the case of AlphaZero, the developers have implemented a loss function for this purpose:

$$l = (z - v)^2 - \pi^T \log p + c||\theta||^2 \qquad (1)$$

Silver et al. (2017: 3) adjust the neural network parameters in such a way that they minimize this loss function which contains on the one hand a mean-squared error $(z-v)^2$ but also so-called cross-entropy-losses, which is the second part in the equation above containing the logarithm. Most relevant is this second part because it contains with p a vector for the probabilities of the moves. A detailed description of the corresponding formula can be omitted here[1], but there is a close connection between quantities like information – entropy – probabilities and the logarithm function (Berkemer 2020: 242–244).

III.3.4 MCTS (Monte Carlo Tree Search)

The standard technique in traditional chess engines is to use so-called alpha-beta search to prune these decision trees. This was a significant enhancement to the minimax search algorithm that eliminates the need to search large portions of the game tree applying a branch-and-bound technique. Remarkably, it does this without any potential of overlooking a better move. If one already has found quite a good move and searches for alternatives, one refutation is enough to to exclude it from further calculations. (Chessprogramming, n.d.)

But even with alpha-beta pruning, there still remain very large decision trees, which ultimately cause many superfluous calculations in the chess engines. At this point, it proved worthwhile for the deep mind developers to take up Shannon's idea and, similar to human players, preferentially search

---

[1] c is a parameter controlling the level of L2 weight regularisation (c.f. Silver 2017).

the part of the branches that is plausible counterplay. This is based on an update of probabilities. The main idea is that probable moves are analyzed more deeply.

Instead of an alpha-beta search with domain-specific enhancements, AlphaZero used a general-purpose Monte-Carlo tree search (MCTS) algorithm. (Silver 2017: 3). The developers of AlphaZero recur in this respect to an idea already proposed by Shannon to focus on such branches of the decision tree where the more plausible moves are to be found.

To give an idea of how effective this different approach is: AlphaZero had to search just 80 thousand positions per second, compared to 70 million for Stockfish (Silver 2017: 5). Why is this restriction to evaluate fewer positions an advantage for AlphaZero? Similar to human chess players, it is often not the quantity of calculations that matters, but that the "essential" calculations are carried out. The professional grandmaster is usually able to intuitively grasp in complicated positions what the plausible plans of both sides will be, which is an enormous help in a systematic evaluation. The amateur player, on the other hand, often uses a lot of computing capacity in the same situation to play through many possibilities rather unsystematically. Most individual calculations will be completely superfluous.

III.4 Illustration of AlphaZero's Strengths

III.4.1 Details on How an Opening is Self-learned by AlphaZero

As mentioned, AlphaZero had to learn everything itself and had no opening library, yet the algorithm seemed to succeed in gaining such a deep understanding of the specific problems of some openings that human chess analysts would later comment on this enthusiastically. The paper by Silver et al. (2017) records how often AlphaZero resorted to the 12 most common human chess openings. From their original figure we selected the first six.

Figure 5: Some selected chess openings and the frequency of their use (Silver 2017: 6)

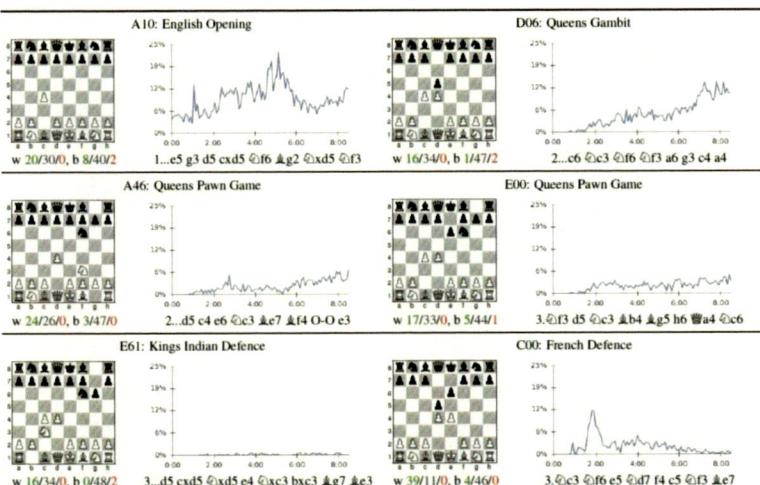

We would like to draw attention to the French defense as an example (the entry at the bottom right). In an initial phase of the self-learning process, this opening is given a considerable frequency, but in the later course of time AlphaZero refrains from it.

It is also interesting to note that some of the other openings are increasingly "sorted out" by the algorithm over time. Let's take a closer look at an example of this, namely the French Defense just mentioned.

To illustrate how AlphaZero works, we refer to the publicly available video on Youtube, in which AlphaZero teaches another computer program, "Stockfish", a lesson in the French Defense. As already mentioned, Stockfish was considered at that time to be one of the strongest traditional chess programs. In one game against AlphaZero, where Stockfish (with the black pieces) used the French defense, the following position arose:

Figure 6: Potential answers to Stockfish capturing a bishop on d2 (own representation based on ChessNetwork, n.d., at minute 5:17)

In this position Stockfish (Black) has just captured with his knight on d2. Which piece will AlphaZero use to recapture? In the same game some moves later the following position is reached:

Figure 7: Safe haven for the white king (found by AlphaZero close to center) (own representation based on ChessNetwork, n.d., at minute 5:31)

AlphaZero has recaptured with the king. Normally, chess players are taught to keep the king safe by castling. That is no longer possible here – but it doesn't matter. A few moves later the king is safe – well protected by his pawns (highlighted by circles) but closer to the center of the board than usual. An interesting aspect here is that in such positions it is humans who would react schematically and not the machine. Precisely because the human player is used to dividing the game explicitly into game phases (opening, middlegame and endgame), almost every player would almost automatically remember: "Caution! We are still in the opening and have not yet castled" – therefore, almost every player would recapture with the knight. AlphaZero – unencumbered by any opening knowledge – has the advantage of being more flexible here.

III.4.2 The Foresight of AlphaZero – Does AlphaZero Really Have a Planning Horizon?

Figure 8: About 15 moves later (The foresight of AlphaZero – did it "see" that there is no extra piece?) (own representation based on ChessNetwork, n.d., at minute 13:07)

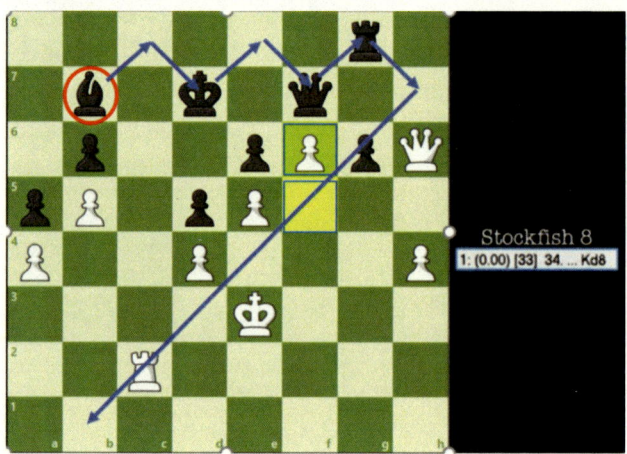

AlphaZero with White lacks a complete piece – at least at a superficial examination. On the other hand, there is a protected passed pawn on f6, which is nice for White but normally not enough for compensation. After all, version 8 of Stockfish can even be commended for at least recognizing the basic danger. It "seems to feel" that there is an exceptional situation here. Stockfish's assessment gives an evaluation of exactly 0, which should be interpreted as White having "perfect compensation" for the missing material. An evaluation of zero means that Stockfish considers the position as a draw.

Unfortunately, such an assessment is still far too optimistic. The position is completely lost for Stockfish. Black's "additional" piece, the bishop (circled in red on b7), does not play any role. Blue arrows indicate an eventual path for activating this piece. But this would require far too much time to achieve.

Incidentally, the necessary time would be de facto even longer than indicated by the arrows. "Coincidentally" (or was this planned?), both king, queen and rook are themselves also still in the way of this path. In fact, White does not really have a piece less – only the additional passed pawn counts. White will force an exchange of queens and/or rooks in a few more moves and Black can no longer prevent the opponent's passed pawn from becoming a decisive power. The "extra" bishop is not even good enough to sacrifice itself for this pawn.

AlphaZero seems to be able to "look very far ahead". Other chess programs do sacrifice pieces from time to time, but then they have a concrete compensation in mind.

There are also other examples with respect to the French defense opening reported from matches between AlphaZero and Stockfish where Black's white-squared bishop doesn't come into play – which are discussed on ChessNetwork. But is this really foresight on AlphaZero's part – does the program have a planning horizon?

In fact, this is difficult to answer, because the neural network is a black box. What the adjusted weights and other network parameters mean is not comprehensible. There are good reasons to doubt that any particular foresight was at work here. Highly efficient pattern recognition could alone sufficiently explain these cases.

So does the program really understand anything about chess? It may not even understand that it is playing chess at all!

For this purpose, let us consider the interpretation of the output layer. A common application of CNN are classification problems. In the output layer, as many neurons are provided as there are classes to be recognized. In general, the last layer often receives a so-called softmax activation. In the specific case of AlphaZero, this will always be done, because the output should be interpreted as probability of moves. The sum of all output neurons must then be exactly 1. In AlphaZero, all plausible moves are assigned probabilities. This, together with the iterative application, explains the far-sightedness. Thus, even iteratively, several plausible countermoves are considered and not just the best countermove "at first sight". However, human tutoring is still required here – for impossible moves the probability must be "artificially" set to $p = 0$.

As self-contained as it seems to act at first sight, the program is therefore in fact not self-contained. One might even doubt that the program understood that the outputs should be probabilities. On the other hand, it may be unfair to say that it is merely pattern recognition. Good pattern recognition is quite closely related to chess understanding. This is demonstrated by studies comparing the performance of grandmasters and amateur players.

III.4.3 Some General Afterthoughts

Beyond AlphaZero, it might be of interest that it can also be stated quite concretely that, similar to chess, human performance, which was previously considered to be non-reproducible by artificial intelligence, is increasingly being addressed by AI engineers. One thinks here, for example, of composing music, painting pictures, speaking dialogues, answering questions, dreaming etc. For each of these examples, there is a branch of artificial intelligence research that can already be reproduced with considerable success. Creativity, for example, is reproducible in music through a music-producing neural network (cf. the album "I am AI," (see Nelson 2018; Amper AI 2017). Similarly, there are already extensive efforts to measure human emotions and to replicate them or to have an AI react adequately to these emotions (Deml 2019: 86; Bartl 2019: 90).

Collaboration is, for example, already partly reproducible through computer collaboration, edge computing, e.g. in the form of the control of decentralized data processing, which controls the processing, utilization or priority in a network of collaborative computers. Google is working on Google Duplex, an assistant that is indistinguishable from a human assistant in the sense of the Turing Test or the Chinese Room (Walch 2020). IBM Watson beat its human opponents in Jeopardy back in 2011 with its Question Answering System. Currently, the AI system GPT-3 is being discussed (not to forget the even more elaborated followers like ChatGPT), which uses an autocomplete function as question answering based on, among other things, the entire Wikipedia entries and has an answer to almost every knowledge question. Do these systems really only go as far as level 3 of the knowledge pyramid mentioned above in Figure 3?

III.5 Back to the Knowledge Pyramid – What Our Insights into AlphaZero Involve

Against the background of the analyses and considerations carried out thus far, let us return to the knowledge pyramid which is now illustrated in figure 9.

Viewed in the context of the knowledge pyramid, it becomes clear how limited artificial intelligence is. AlphaZero can only accomplish its amazing performance because it has precisely specified that this should take place within the framework of the application reference chess and chess rules.

Figure 9: Complete knowledge pyramid (North 2021: 37)

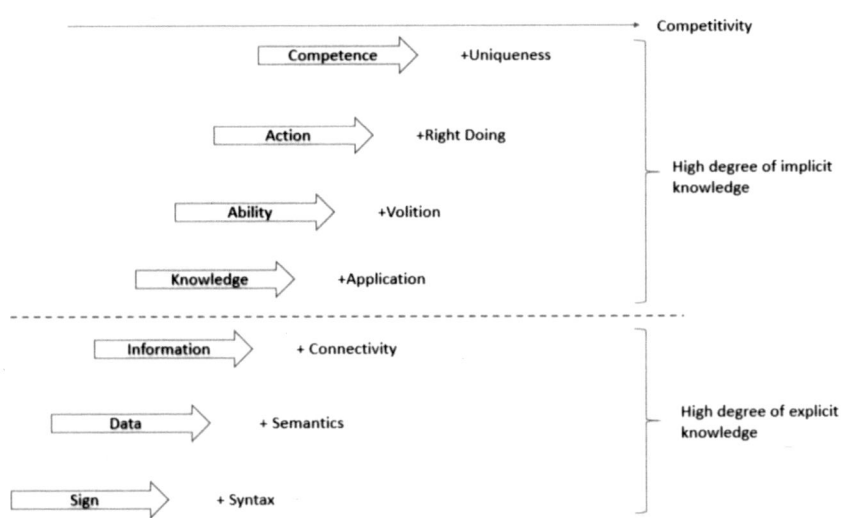

But these rules come from humans. Does AlphaZero have a will? Apparently not, because as Beck (2017: 11) notes:

> Computers may beat us at chess or Go, that is not surprising, neither creative nor worrisome. I would only be seriously concerned if a computer started making mistakes and subsequently proclaimed: "Chess? Oh no, don't feel like it anymore, it's boring ....".

Also, it is hardly to be expected that AlphaZero realizes when playing against itself that it always has to end in a draw – provided that nobody makes a mistake. By the way, it was implicitly assumed just now that the third possibility (draw) of Zermelo's theorem might be the most plausible. We will return to the clarification of this question shortly.

Does AlphaZero have an understanding of chess? If AlphaZero could "recognize" that chess can be treated in principle exactly like tic-tac-toe, it could define concepts like two-person/zero-sum games, make generalizations for Tic-Tac-Toe, Chess, Go, etc. and independently develop something like a Theorem of Zermelo on its own. Something like this would indeed be impressive, but AlphaZero doesn't even have to understand that it is playing chess.

In a nutshell, these limitations mean that some of Norbert Wiener's worries about the advent of the chess machine are (still) unfounded. He was thinking about a machine that could also take over all governmental affairs and certainly sees a threat in such a "machine à gouverner". In this regard, he also quoted an informative book review by Pere Dominique Dubarle in *Le Monde* on Wiener's book *"Cybernetics"*. Dubarle comes to the following assessment with reference to Hobbes' Leviathan:

> "[I]n comparison, Hobbes' Leviathan was nothing but a pleasant joke." (Dubarle 1948 cited by Wiener 1950: 180)

As long as the objective function is externally specified, as in AlphaZero, the system will never do anything other than play chess as well as possible and would never arrive at the idea to independently create references to other games or strategically similar situations. It might be important to note that this does not involve transfer learning by using parts of the neural network elsewhere. It is only the general reinforcement principle that is applied once more. Therefore, the following cinematic scenario would also be impossible, even if it is still so appealing. The theme of the movie War Games[2] is the danger that a self-learning software becomes first independent and then virtually unstoppable by humans. Specifically, a boy accidentally triggers a "thermonuclear war" simulation on the supercomputer and things take their fateful course. Unfortunately, the software is so intelligent that it knows how to resist when humans try to interfere. The machine's rationale must necessarily insist on "Mutual Assured Destruction", because anything else would undermine a credible deterrence – there is no place for humans with their emotions.

What is particularly interesting is how the boy, together with the AI researcher responsible for its development, manages to prevent the catastrophe in the end. The machine won't simply switch off. But it does agree to play Tic Tac Toe against itself – like chess and shogi, a 2-person constant-sum game. In the process, the machine learns that it is impossible to win this game. An endless series of draws shows the machine that it is pointless to try any further.

What is the real punchline, then? It is that the software recognizes the analogy to nuclear war itself. It plays through all variants of the "game" ther-

---

2   For details on the movie War Games from 1983, consider: https://www.themoviedb.org/movie/860-wargames.

monuclear war against itself. As with tic tac toe, the frustrating result every time: WINNER NONE. This leads the AI to the independent conclusion: "it is a strange game" and "the only winning move is not to play."

IV. Discussion

IV.1 What Does the Lack of Understanding Involve?

As we have identified beforehand, it is precisely this lack of understanding that characterizes artificial intelligence learning algorithms such as AlphaZero, despite the impressive results they deliver. Precisely this also repeatedly opens up the question of disruptive attacks on an AI by humans or other AI systems (so-called "adversarial attacks" or "adversarial examples"). One example is the rather famous story in AI research circles about a neural network model that was trained to distinguish between wolves and huskies. The model learned to identify the distinction successfully, achieving high accuracy when given images that weren't used for its training. However, it soon became apparent that something was going wrong – some very clear images were being misclassified. When the researchers looked into why the neural network was making such gross mistakes, researchers figured out that the model had learned to classify an image based on whether there was snow in it – all images of wolves used in the training had snow in the background, while the ones of huskies did not. Unsurprisingly, the model was failing. In other words, what humans understand immediately – that it is wolves that count and not the context in which wolves occur – was precisely that which was not understood by the model, and this made clear that the model only searched for the best way to discriminate between two different labels provided by humans to images. There was no understanding. As Goodfellow/Shlens/Szegedy (2015: 9) pointed out with respect to adversarial examples:

> The existence of adversarial examples suggests that being able to explain the training data or even being able to correctly label the test data does not imply that our models truly understand the tasks we have asked them to perform.

This also entails that the AI itself is not prepared to detect ex ante which of its own weak points will be targeted and the AI can thus easily be misused or misled into making incorrect decisions. Here again, technical solutions must be found and anticipated by the sense-making human to make an AI robust against such attacks. One way to mitigate such challenges is to carefully select the training data set.

In addition to such weaknesses of AI, there is the realization that the behavior of an AI depends massively on the data set that was used for training the net, or, in the case of reinforcement learning, every interaction leaves its (unpredictable) repercussions on the AI, which in turn depends on the given rules of the AI. As such, it can be observed that an AI incorporates e.g. discrimination into its own behavior without reflection (cf. e.g. Beck 2019: 92–94). This was already evident with Alexa, which, trained on unethical data, famously recommended to its users that they kill their mother-in-law. In other words, a learning algorithm will optimize what it is trained to optimize but leaves out what – perhaps varying – circumstances might come along with the elements focused on in its solution. Furthermore, it will ignore the potential consequences of that. It does not change its optimization rules that determine the direction of learning within the rules of the game set out by humans, it does not contradict or point out that there might be a different perspective involved and it does not highlight the challenge of reconciling diverse perspectives. All this is still the reserve of humans and not very surprisingly an essential part of personality and education: basically, this is a topic that already occupied the pioneers of AI. Early on, Wiener was concerned with the question of what could happen if the chess machine should "grow up". In the case of AlphaZero this does not happen: it will not occur to AlphaZero to introduce new rules, but theoretically there could be manifold variations. Why not play atomic chess, which humans invented as soon as normal chess with always the same openings became too boring for them. However, do machines know boredom at all? Or do machines know such a thing as curiosity? It has obviously been possible to develop admirable algorithms that are very powerful at linking information from different areas and that perform excellently when it comes to answering questions. But formulating questions of one's own accord is probably still the domain of humans. Even young children are inquisitive. You don't have to train them to develop curiosity. Here we have again the component of the will. The child pesters adults with one question after another; it is not satisfied with an insufficient, half-baked answer and keeps on asking: "why this?", "why that?".

It is clearly evident here: there is a lack of independent will for AlphaZero to do something just for the fun of it. Here there is a lack of real understanding that what AlphaZero is trained for in the first place is a "game" of chess, which is supposed to be "fun". AlphaZero doesn't even need to understand that it provides probabilities. Humans had to help out here with a softmax activation. There can be no question of acting and competence on higher levels of the knowledge pyramid. All in all, according to the analyses made here, even the newest AI applications therefore still remain far behind (at least educated) humans even though they might seem to be at the same level (which is especially visible in the example of ChatGPT).

As we elaborated on above, artificial intelligence and its capabilities are the result of the context labelled and established by a human mind. The result that comes to the fore when the algorithm works might then seem to be at the upper end of the knowledge pyramid, but, in reality, it is only performing without its own understanding what the human mind has included in the context that the artificial intelligence has been trained with. What happens, then, when reinforcement algorithms like AlphaZero are trained on subjects that involve volition, right or wrong action and in the end uniqueness without the humans setting adequate labels?

This seems to be difficult in that even human experts do not fully understand in all its consequences what the AI incorporates when learning. We humans resort very consciously to different frames in acting and the more competencies we have, the more unique is the result. This is the exact difference in the case of AI. An AI always acts according to the context that was set beforehand and based on the same frame set defined by the rules. It does not decide whether it wants to act under such conditions. To recur to the wolf example: humans must first anticipate that the context difference could be used at all to classify before they are able to mitigate the misclassification in the training data by providing images with snow but without wolves and images with wolves but without snow. They decide that it makes no sense to discriminate based on whether there is sun or snow. Or, for an even more sensitive question: when we distinguish between good or bad actions, can we really employ algorithms of artificial intelligence in assisting us in such a task? The analysis of Davin (2020) demonstrates how difficult such a task is. The author demonstrates that the nearest neighbor method allowed for identifying separate clusters of "good" or "bad" people in fairy tales. However, it was not able to differentiate between them as good or bad people. One reason put forward by the author is that categories like good or bad rely on very high degrees of implicit knowledge, which is precisely the competence of humans. However, when we take into consideration that values nearly always influence human actions when seen in a certain context – even driving a car takes on a moral dimension when it is analyzed in the context of its effects on the climate – then it seems to be very naïve to train artificial intelligences within a certain explicit (or even unknown) context but then extend it to other contexts. It seems that humans much too easily assume that they really know what they are training the AI for and then are "surprised" by adversarial attacks that relate to the higher levels of the knowledge pyramid whose context and involvement in the situation have not been adequately reflected. As such, it seems to us that it is not necessarily progress that is currently taking place, but rather disorientation.

IV.2 Societal Consequences and Responsibility

In fact, the discussion above directly leads to a further point of utmost importance. Let us for a moment think to ourselves what this involves when in the most different areas such – probably in most cases only half-reflected – experiments with artificial intelligence take place.

Consider what happens when AI begins to interact with humans in terms of the meaning and implications of higher levels of the knowledge pyramid, although the understanding of unanticipated side-effects is lacking among the human experts responsible for designing the algorithms. Especially in the case of unsupervised learning in datasets that can no longer be fully understood by any human, the implications are likely to be enormous.

It is easy to find current cases of application. What happens with an artificial intelligence that is designed to maximize the time children spend on social networks – without taking into account that this might not be good for the children themselves? What happens when an artificial intelligence is trained to maximize silo communication instead of cooperation, to divide societies and to corrupt elections with respect to certain candidates? What are the side effects of that? What happens when an artificial intelligence is trained – in an industrial context – to maximize profit but not to maximize the adequacy of the products with respect to the customer's safety, needs or health? Anyone familiar with today's business world is also aware that such things could happen. And even more alarming is that it might be nearly impossible to determine this after the fact – whether an artificial intelligence causes critical adversarial attacks could be – given the existing data masses – just as easily be a result of chance as a deliberately calculated effect of the artificial intelligence. Therefore, it is impossible to judge why an artificial intelligence – which cannot judge itself and which acts according to certain criteria that have been acquired in a mixture of human design and unknown data masses – acts in a certain way. And how should we judge people who become influenced by such information and then act accordingly? Given that we are already subject to such experiments, this reminds us to stay very cautious in our judgements. In particular, judging people or positions as evil or as enemies no longer becomes a viable option. We can only point to possible consequences of one's own actions.

Moreover, an artificial intelligence acts based on data as given or optimized – humans, however, evolve freely. Without this dimension of evolving freely, artificial intelligences could judge and therefore discriminate unthinkingly based on the status quo, whereas e.g. social work would start to reach a different stage.

V. Summary and Conclusion

If we summarize the analyses carried out above, we might state that so far especially the areas of explicit knowledge (supervised learning) and explicit specifications (reinforcement learning, unsupervised learning) have been convincingly addressed by artificial intelligence. In fact, many routine activities that are currently still performed by humans can be performed faster and more efficiently by artificial intelligence in the future. Here, too, the economic potential of artificial intelligence is expected to be realized in the near future. However, for the time being, educated people cover numerous competencies that artificial intelligence cannot (yet?) address and for which, based on our current state of knowledge, one can only speculate as to whether they will ever be open to artificial intelligence.

Even in those areas in which artificial intelligence has high potential, this is tied in particular to the availability of data. A challenge that remains is therefore the existence and selection of training data (Bartschat et al. 2019: 1401). Whether the training data represent a comprehensive problem domain for the posed problem depends on whether later results are also correctly classified or processed. Precisely this comprehensiveness is usually hard to ensure for rare or complex events (Bartschat et al. 2019: 1401), whereas what is rare and complex for AI can also be a simple manual task from a human perspective.

At the same time, an AI usually processes single data sets in a certain way and does not draw any novel conclusions from the surrounding context in such a way that the perspective is changed, e.g. a phenomenon has to be looked at more closely or differently because an observation otherwise turns out inadequate (Buder 2020: 17–22). Why it might be possible to train the AI with every new classification by taking recourse to human feedback, this will still not solve the problem of situation-specific decision-making as far as the meaning of situations are indeed dependent on a specific context. This might be addressed by including even more data and variables. At the same time, however, an explosion of hidden layers makes it even more difficult to understand how an artificial intelligence arrives at its results (Schmitz et al. 2019: 777).

From the perspective of university teachers (scholars), this results in a threefold task. First, future generations must be trained more strongly in those competencies that make a difference, i.e. knowledge, skills, action and competence. Second, it is necessary to sharpen for the focus on current application areas of AI and not to overinterpret them, in order to maintain a clear view of the prerequisites for the successful use of AI, which could turn out to be much more limited than is often suggested today. Finally, the dependency on the training data set and the rules determined beforehand by humans (in reinforcement learning) is central and must be analyzed in particular detail.

For example, in chess and Go the underlying objective function may be uncontroversial. Providing a general reinforcement algorithm here was extremely successful, as could be seen, and in this respect such an application is unproblematic – but with thermonuclear war and other "war games" as well as strategic management decisions, the situation looks completely different. The tendency to assume that people who are good at chess will be more successful than others in such strategic situations has always been questionable, because from a game-theoretical point of view, two-person-zero-sum games are neither the common case nor the most important ones. But to think that an AI based on the general reinforcement approach should be granted decision-making competence in these critical areas just because it was more successful in chess and Go could have literally catastrophic consequences.

A word of warning is therefore in order against the overinterpretation of the term "general" in the concept of the general reinforcement algorithm. Natasha Regan, co-author of the book Game Changer, claims in an interview that the technique could be used for any complicated system where one needs to navigate a path through lots of possibilities.

Silver et. al. (2017) have successfully transferred the basic concept of the general reinforcement algorithm from one zero-sum game to another. Essentially, this only costs time for new training and this does not seem to be too essential, if then, as in the example of chess, four hours are sufficient to dwarf centuries of human knowledge.[3]

But these games do not represent just *"any complicated system* where you need to find navigate a path". Making strategic decisions in management or, as Shannon had in mind, in simplified military operations is a completely different issue. First of all, these are not zero-sum games. The rules are not so clearly specified. Most importantly, it will not be so easy to gain sufficient experience by "playing against oneself". In chess, go and shogi, all possible countermoves of the opponents are fixed, the consequences of one's own decisions can be clearly calculated. If one wanted to use a general reinforcement approach in management or war scenarios, a simulation model would have to be implemented in addition to predict these consequences, and since simulations can only ever represent a simplified image of reality, an inherent source of error is built in.

Let us conclude with the reflections of Norbert Wiener. On the one hand, Wiener would certainly be thrilled that it was possible to ultimately implement his and Shannon's ideas on self-learning machines. As suggested by Shannon, a focus on plausible (probable) moves proved to be superior to other approaches. It is possible, however, that Wiener would have been disappointed at how shockingly easy it was to implement machine learning. A tabula rasa approach certainly would not have appealed to him. He wanted the machine to keep improving, but he had firmly counted on the premise that in order to learn, it would have to compete against passable or, even better, very good human players. Here, Wiener was completely wrong in his assessment, similar to Turing, who was sure that the machines would never surpass the level of their developers.

---

3   However, if one also considers, in addition to the time, the energy consumption of such training, the situation looks different (cf. Marischka 2020).

References

Amper AI (2017): *I am AI*. February 2, 2020. URL: https://futurism.com/the-worlds-first-album-composed-and-produced-by-an-ai-has-been-unveiled.

Bartschat, Andreas, Stephan Allgeier, Sebastian Bohn et al. (2019): "Digitale Bildverarbeitung und Tiefe Neuronale Netze in der Augenheilkunde – aktuelle Trends." In: *Klinische Monatsblätter für Augenheilkunde* 236 (2019), pp. 1399–1406.

Bartl, Michael (2019): "The rise of Emotion AI." In: *Handbuch künstliche Intelligenz*. away Medias GmbH, Bonn 2019, pp. 87–90.

Bauermeister, Karsten (n.d.): *Schachcomputergeschichte*. July 6, 2021. URL: http://www.schachcomputer.at/gesch.htm.

Beck, Henning (2017): *Irren ist nützlich. Warum die Schwächen des Gehirns unsere Stärken sind*. Hanser: München.

Beck, Susanne (2019): "Wie diskriminierend ist künstliche Intelligenz?" In: *Handbuch künstliche Intelligenz*. away Medias GmbH, Bonn, pp. 91–95.

Berkemer, R. (2020): "Effiziente Nutzung von Information als Rohstoff im Spannungsfeld von Kommerzialisierung und Kollaboration." In: *Digitale Bildung und Künstliche Intelligenz in Deutschland*. Springer: Wiesbaden, pp. 241–255.

Buder, Jürgen (2020): "Wieviel Mensch steckt in der Maschine?" In: *Information – Wissenschaft & Praxis* 71.1, pp. 17–22.

Bruns, Beate, and Cäcilie Kowald (2019): "Wieviel KI steckt in Bots?" In: *Handbuch künstliche Intelligenz*. away Medias GmbH, Bonn, pp. 77–82.

Buxmann, Peter, and Holger Schmidt (2019): *Künstliche Intelligenz – Mit Algorithmen zum wirtschaftlichen Erfolg*. Berlin: Springer Gabler.

Chessgames Services LLC (n.d.): *AlphaZero – Stockfish (2017)*, London ENG, Dec-04. July 6, 2021. URL: https://www.chessgames.com/perl/chessgame?gid=1899422.

ChessNetwork (n.d.): *AlphaZero teaches Stockfish a lesson in the French Defense*. July 6, 2021. URL: https://www.youtube.com/watch?v=4ebzevCLGbQ.

Chessprogramming (n.d.): *AlphaBeta*. July 8, 2021. URL: https://www.chessprogramming.org/Alpha-Beta.

Convolutional neural networks – Aufbau Funktion und Anwendungsgebiete (2019). August 16, 2020. URL: https://jaai.de/convolutional-neural-networks-cnn-aufbau-funktion-und-anwendungsgebiete-1691/.

Deml, Barbara (2019): "KI für die Arbeitswelten der Zukunft." In: *Handbuch künstliche Intelligenz*. away Medias GmbH, Bonn, pp. 83–86.

Dubarle, Dominique (1948): Book review on "Cybernetics" In: *Le Monde*, December 28, 1948.

Goodfellow, Ian J., Jonathan Shlens, and Christian Szegedy (2015): *Explaining and harnessing adversarial Examples*. International Conference on Learning Representations.

Gunning, David, Mark Stefik, Jaesik Choi, Timothy Miller, Simone Stumpf, and Ghuong-Zhang Yang (2019): "XAI-Explainable artificial intelligence." In: *Science Robotics* 4.37, eaay7120.

Hayek, Friedrich August von (1979). *The Counter-Revolution of Science. Studies on the Abuse of Reason*, 2. Aufl. Indianapolis: Liberty Fund.

Jerems, Stefanie (2018): "SYD81 Neuronale Netze 1." AKAD University: Stuttgart.

Kendall, Graham (2001): "G5AIAI – Introduction to Artificial Intelligence". July 6, 2021. URL: http://www.cs.nott.ac.uk/ pszgxk/courses/g5aiai/002 history/eliza.htm.

Kriesel, David (2007): "A Brief Introduction to Neural Networks" available at http://www.dkriesel.com. September 22, 2021. URL: https://www.dkriesel.com/_media/science/neuronalenetze-en-zeta2-1col-dkrieselcom.pdf.

Marischka, Christoph (2020): *Cyber Valley – Unfall des Wissens. Künstliche Intelligenz und ihre Produktionsbedingungen – Am Beispiel Tübingen*, Köln: PapyRossa.

Nelson Jr., Keith (2018): "Taryn Southern's new album is produced entirely by AI." August 16, 2020. URL: https://www.digitaltrends.com/music/artificial-intelligence-taryn-southern-album-interview/.

Nguyen Cong Luong, Thai Hoang Dinh, Gong Shimin, Niyato Dusit, Wang Ping, Ying-Chang Liang, and In-Kim Dong (8. 10. 2018): "Applications of Deep Reinforcement Learning in Communications and Networking: A Survey". https://arxiv.org/pdf/1810.07862v1.pdf.

North, Klaus (2021): *Wissensorientierte Unternehmensführung: Wissensmanagement im digitalen Wandel*. Wiesbaden: Springer Gabler.

Sadler, Matthew, and Natasha Regan (2019): *Game Changer: AlphaZero's Groundbreaking Chess Strategies and the Promise of AI*. Alkmaar: New in Chess.

Samek, Wojciech, and Klaus-Robert Müller (2019): "Towards explainable artificial intelligence." In: *Explainable AI: interpreting, explaining and visualizing deep learning*. Springer, Cham, pp. 5–22.

Schmitz, Rüdiger, René Werner, and Thomas Rösch (2019): "Der Einfluss der Algorithmen. Künstliche Intelligenz in der Endoskopie: Neuronale Netze und maschinelles Sehen – Techniken und Perspektiven." In: *Zeitschrift für Gastroenterologie* 57, pp. 767–780.

Seifert, Inessa, Matthias Bürger, Leo Wangler, Stephanie Christmann-Budian, Marieke Rohde, Peter Gabriel, and Guido Zinke (2018): "Potentiale künstlicher Intelligenz im produzierenden Gewerbe in Deutschland." February 29, 2020. (https://www.bmwi.de/Redaktion/DE/Publikationen/Studien/potenziale-kuenstlichen-intelligenz-im-produzierenden-gewerbe-in-deutschland.pdf?__blob=publicationFile&v=8.).

Shannon, Claude, E. (1950): "Programming a Computer for Playing Chess." In: *Philosophical Magazine*, Ser, 7.41, pp. 256–275.

Silver, David, Thomas Hubert, Julian Schrittwieser, Ioannis Antonoglou, Matthew Lai, Arthur Guez, …, Timothy Lillicrap, Karen Simonyan, and Demis Hassabis (2017): "Mastering chess and shogi by self-play with a general reinforcement learning algorithm." arXiv preprint arXiv:1712.01815.

Turing, Alan (1950): "Computing Machinery and Intelligence." In: *Mind*, pp. 433–460.

Von Neumann, John, and Oscar Morgenstern (1944): *Theory of games and economic behavior (commemorative edition)*. New Jersey: Princeton university press.

Walch, Kathleen (2020): "Rethinking weak vs. Strong AI." August 10, 2020. URL: https://www.forbes.com/sites/cognitiveworld/2019/10/04/rethinking-weak-vs-strong-ai/#499b55006da3.

Wiener, Norbert (1954): *The human use of human beings*. London: Eyre and Spottiswoode.

Zermelo, Ernst (1912): "An application of set theory to the theory of chess-playing." In: *Proc. 5th Int. Congress of Mathematics*, Cambridge.

Transgressing the Boundaries
Towards a Rigorous Understanding of Deep Learning and Its (Non-)Robustness

Carsten Hartmann, Lorenz Richter

1. Introduction

According to Wheeler (2016: 2), machine learning is a "marriage of statistics and computer science that began in artificial intelligence". While statistics deals with the question of what can be inferred from data given an appropriate statistical model, computer science is concerned with the design of algorithms to solve a given computational problem that would be intractable without the help of a computer.

Artificial intelligence and, specifically, machine learning have undergone substantial developments in recent years that have led to a huge variety of successful applications, most of which would not have been possible with alternative approaches. In particular, advances in deep learning (i.e. machine learning relying on deep neural networks) have revolutionized many fields, leading, for instance, to impressive achievements in computer vision (e.g. image classification, image segmentation, image generation), natural language processing (semantic text understanding, text categorization and text creation, automatic question answering) and reinforcement learning (agents and games, high-dimensional optimization problems); cf. Sarker (2021) and the references therein.

Moreover, deep learning is nowadays increasingly applied in multiple scientific branches as an acceptable tool for conducting inference from simulated or collected data. For example, in the medical field, the development of drugs (Ma et al. 2015) or the analysis of tomography (Bubba et al. 2019) are enhanced with deep learning. In molecular simulations, ground-state properties of organic molecules are predicted (Faber et al. 2017), equilibrium energies of molecular systems are learnt (Noé et al. 2019) or multi-electron Schrödinger equations are solved (Hermann/Schätzle/Noé 2020). Speaking of which, the numerical treatment of high-dimensional partial differential equations with neural networks has undergone vast improvements (E/Han/Jentzen 2017; Nüsken/Richter 2021), allowing for applications in almost all sciences. In biology, cell segmentation and classification have been studied with certain convolutional neural networks (Ronneberger/Fischer/Brox 2015), in signal processing speech separation is approached with temporal versions of these (Richter/Carbajal/Gerkmann 2020), and in finance relevant stock pricing models are solved with deep learning (Germain/Pham/Warin 2021). In remote sensing, temporal recurrent neural networks are for instance used for crop classification (Rußwurm/Körner 2018) and image segmentation promises automatic understanding of the increasing amount of available satellite data (Zhu et al. 2017). The list of successful deep learning applications is long and there are many more fields in which they have made significant contributions and still promise exciting advances that we shall omit here for the sake of brevity.

It is probably fair to say that, like statistics, deep learning (or machine learning in general) aims at drawing inferences from data. But unlike statistics, it avoids being overly explicit regarding the underlying model assumptions. In statistics, either the model assumptions or the complete model are set prior to making inferences, whereas the neural networks in deep learning are mostly seen as black boxes that are essentially able to 'learn' the model. In this sense, deep learning delegates what Reichenbach (1949: §72, 374) called the "problem of the reference class" to a computer algorithm, namely, the problem of deciding what model class to use when making a prediction of a particular instance or when assigning a probability to a particular event. While this might be understandable – or even desirable – from the user's point of view, it poses risks and might bring dangerous side-effects:

- In most of the applied deep learning models, there is a lack of explainability, meaning that even though their inference from data might work well, the mechanisms behind the predictions are not well understood. As the ambition in all sciences it to understand causal relationships rather than pure correlations, this might neither be satisfying nor lead to further deeper understandings in corresponding fields.
- Without understanding the details of a model, potential robustness issues might not be realized either. For example, who guarantees that

certain deep learning achievements easily translate to slightly shifted data settings and how can we expect neural network training runs to converge consistently?
- Finally, often the ambition of a prediction model to generalize to unseen data is stated on an 'average' level and we cannot make robust statements on unexpected events, which might imply dangerous consequences in risk-sensitive applications. In general, there is no reliable measure for prediction (un-)certainty, which might lead to blind beliefs in the model output.

Even when it comes to the success stories of deep learning, many achievements and properties of the models can simply not be explained theoretically, e.g. why does one of the most naive optimization attempts, stochastic gradient descent, work so well, why do models often generalize well even though they are powerful enough to simply memorize the training data and why can high-dimensional problems be addressed particularly efficiently? Not only is it important from a practical point of view to understand these phenomena theoretically, as a deeper understanding might motivate and drive novel approaches leading to even more successful results in practice, but it is also important for getting a grip on the epistemology of machine learning algorithms. This then might also advance pure 'trial and error' strategies for architectural improvements of neural networks that sometimes seem to work mostly due to extensive hyperparameter finetuning and favorable data set selections; cf. (Wang et al. 2019).

In this article, we will argue that relying on the tempting black box character of deep learning models can be dangerous and it is important to further develop a deeper mathematical understanding in order to obtain rigorous statements that will make applications more sound and more robust. We will demonstrate that there are still many limitations in the application of artificial intelligence, but mathematical analysis promises prospects that might at least partially overcome these limitations. We further argue that, if one accepts that explainable DL must not be understood in the sense of the deductive-nomological model of scientific explanation, Bayesian probability theory can provide a means to explain DL in a precise statistical (abductive) sense. In fact, a comprehensive theory should guide us towards coping with the potential drawbacks of neural networks, e.g. the lack of understanding why certain networks architectures work better than others, the risk of overfitting data, i.e. not performing well on unseen data, or the lack of knowledge on the prediction confidences, in particular, leading to overconfident predictions on data far from the training data set.

Even though we insist that understanding deep learning is a holistic endeavor that comprises the theoretical (e.g. approximation) properties of artificial neural networks in combination with the practical numerical algorithms that are used to train them, we refrain from going beyond the mathematical framework and exploring the epistemological implications of this framework. The epistemology of machine learning algorithms is a relatively new and dynamic field of research, and we refer to recent papers by Wheeler (2016) and Sterkenburg/Grünwald (2021), and the references given there.

1.1 Definitions and first principles

We can narrow down the definition of machine learning to one line by saying that its main intention is to identify functions that map input data $x \in \mathcal{X}$ to output data $y \in \mathcal{Y}$ in some *good* way, where $\mathcal{X}$ and $\mathcal{Y}$ are suitable spaces, often identified with $\mathbb{R}^d$ and $\mathbb{R}$, respectively. In other words, the task is to find a function $f : \mathcal{X} \to \mathcal{Y}$ such that

$$f(x) = y. \tag{1}$$

To illustrate, let us provide two stereotypical examples that appear in practice. In a classification task, for instance, $x \in \mathcal{X}$ could represent an image (formalized as a matrix of pixels, or, in a flattened version, as a vector $x \in \mathbb{R}^d$) and $y \in \mathcal{Y} = \{1, \ldots, K\}$ could be a class describing the content of the image. In a regression task, on the other hand, one tries to predict real numbers from the input data, e.g. given historical weather data and multiple measurements, one could aim to predict how much it will rain tomorrow and $y \in \mathcal{Y} = \mathbb{R}_{\geq 0}$ would be the amount of rain in milliliters.

From our simple task definition above, two questions arise immediately:

1. How do we design (i.e. find) the function f?
2. How do we measure performance, i.e. how do we quantify deviations from the desired fit in (1)?

Relating to question 1, it is common to rely on parametrized functions $f(x) = f_\theta(x)$, for which a parameter vector $\theta \in \mathbb{R}^p$ specifies the actual function. Artificial neural networks (ANNs) like deep neural networks are examples of such parametrized functions which enjoy specific beneficial properties, for instance in terms of approximation and optimization as we will detail later on. The characterizing feature of (deep) neural networks is that they are built by (multiple) concatenations of nonlinear and affine-linear maps:

Definition 1.1 (Neural network, e.g. Berner et al. 2021; Higham/Higham 2019) We define a *feed-forward neural network* $\Phi_\sigma : \mathbb{R}^d \to \mathbb{R}^m$ with L layers by

$$\Phi_\sigma(x) = A_L\sigma(A_{L-1}\sigma(\cdots\sigma(A_1 x + b_1)\cdots) + b_{L-1}) + b_L, \qquad (2)$$

with matrices $A_l \in \mathbb{R}^{n_l \times n_{l-1}}$, vectors $b_l \in \mathbb{R}^{n_l}$, $1 \leq l \leq L$, and a nonlinear activation function $\sigma : \mathbb{R} \to \mathbb{R}$ that is applied componentwise. Clearly, $n_0 = d$ and $n_L = m$, and the collection of matrices A_l and vectors b_l, called *weights* and *biases*, comprises the learnable parameters θ.

In practice, one often chooses $\sigma(x) = \max\{x, 0\}$ or $\sigma(x) = (1 + e^{-x})^{-1}$, since their (sub)derivatives can be explicitly computed and they enjoy a universal approximation property (Barron 1993; Cybenko 1989).

Even though the organization of an ANN in layers is partly inspired by biological neural networks, the analogy between ANNs and the human brain is questionable and often misleading when it comes to understanding the specifics of machine learning algorithms, such as its ability to generalize (Geirhos et al. 2018), and it will therefore play no role in what follows. We rather regard an ANN as a handy representation of the parametrized function f_θ that enjoys certain mathematical properties that we will discuss subsequently. (Note that closeness in function space does not necessarily imply closeness in parameter space and vice versa as has been pointed out in Elbrächter/Berner/Grohs 2019: Sec. 2). Clearly, alternative constructions besides the one stated in Definition 1.1 are possible and frequently used, depending on the problem at hand.

1.2 Probabilistic modelling and mathematical perspectives

Now, for actually tuning the parameter vector θ in order to identify a good fit as indicated in (1), the general idea in machine learning is to rely on training data $(x_n, y_n)_{n=1}^N \subset \mathcal{X} \times \mathcal{Y}$. For this, we define a *loss function* $\ell : \mathcal{Y} \times \mathcal{Y} \to \mathbb{R}_{\geq 0}$ that measures how much our predictions, i.e. function outputs $f(x_n)$, deviate from their targets y_n. Given the training sample, our algorithm can now aim to minimize the *empirical loss*

$$\mathcal{L}_N(f) = \frac{1}{N} \sum_{n=1}^{N} \ell\left(f(x_n), y_n\right), \tag{3}$$

i.e. an empirical average over all data points. Relating to question 2 from above, however, it turns out that it is not constructive to measure approximation quality by how well the function f can fit the available training data, but rather to focus on the ability of f to generalize to yet unseen data. To this end, the perspective of statistical learning theory assumes that the data is distributed according to an (unknown) probability distribution $\mathbb{P}$ on $\mathcal{X} \times \mathcal{Y}$. The training data points x_n and y_n should then be seen as realizations of the random variables X and Y, which admit a joint probability distribution, so

$$(X, Y) \sim \mathbb{P}. \tag{4}$$

We further assume that all pairs (x_n, y_n) are distributed identically and independently from one another (i.i.d.). The expectation over all random (data) variables of this loss is then called expected loss, defined as

$$\mathcal{L}(f) = \mathbb{E}[\ell\left(f(X), Y\right)], \tag{5}$$

where the expectation $\mathbb{E}\left[\cdot\right]$ is understood as the average over all possible data points (X, Y). The expected loss measures how well the function f performs on data from $\mathbb{P}$ *on average*, assuming that the data distribution does not change after training. It is the general intention in machine learning to have the expected loss as small as possible.

Example 1.2 To fix ideas, let us consider a toy example in $d = 1$. We assume that the true function is given by $f(x) = \sin(2\pi x)$ and that the data x is distributed uniformly on the interval $[0, 2]$. In Figure 1 we display the function f along with $N = 100$ randomly drawn data points $(x_n, y_n)_{n=1}^{N}$, where y_n is once given by the deterministic mapping $y_n = f(x_n)$ and once by the stochastic mapping $y_n = f(x_n) + \eta_n$, where $\eta_n \sim \mathcal{N}(0, 0.01)$ indicates noise, by denoting $\mathcal{N}(\mu, \sigma^2)$ a normal (i.e. Gaussian) distribution with mean μ and variance σ^2. The stochastic mapping induces the probability measure $\mathbb{P}$, i.e. the joint distribution of the random variables $(X, Y) \in \mathcal{X} \times \mathcal{Y}$, which we plot approximately in the right panel. Note that (even for simple toy problems) $\mathbb{P}$ can usually not be written down analytically.

Figure 1: We plot a given function $f(x) = \sin(2\pi x)$ (in gray) along with data points (in orange) given either by a deterministic or stochastic mapping in the first two panels. The right panel shows an approximation of the measure $\mathbb{P}$ for the stochastic case.

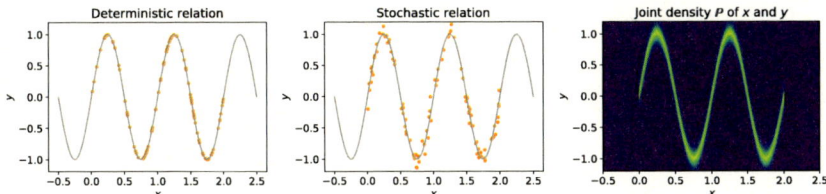

For a further analysis, let us give names to three different functions that minimize a given corresponding loss (assuming for simplicity that all minima are attained, even though they may not be unique):

$$f^B \in \underset{f \in \mathcal{M}(\mathcal{X},\mathcal{Y})}{\arg\min}\, \mathcal{L}(f), \quad f^* \in \underset{f \in \mathcal{F}}{\arg\min}\, \mathcal{L}(f), \quad \widehat{f}_N \in \underset{f \in \mathcal{F}}{\arg\min}\, \mathcal{L}_N(f). \quad (6)$$

The first quantity, f^B, is the theoretically optimal function among all mathematically reasonable (or: *measurable*) functions (cf. Appendix B), denoted here by the set $\mathcal{M}(\mathcal{X}, \mathcal{Y})$, the second quantity, f^*, is the optimal function in a specified function class $\mathcal{F}$ (e.g. the class of neural networks), and the third quantity, $\widehat{f}_N$, is the function that minimizes the empirical error on the training data.

With regard to the second quantity above, finding a suitable function class $\mathcal{F}$ requires balancing two conflicting goals: on the one hand, the function class should be sufficiently rich to enjoy the *universal approximation property*, i.e. the ability to represent any theoretically optimal function f^B up to a sufficiently small approximation error that is still considered acceptable.[1] On the other hand, the function class should not be overly complex, in order to avoid overfitting which may lead to a function f (e.g. a classifier) that poorly generalizes beyond known data.

Let us make this point more precise, and let us say that we have some training algorithm that has produced a function f on the training data $(x_n, y_n)_{n=1}^N$ (see Appendix A for details).

---

1   What is considered an acceptable approximation error depends on the problem at hand.

We can decompose the deviation of the function f from the theoretically optimal solution f^B into four different terms that correspond to three different error contributions – generalization, optimization and approximation error:

$$\mathcal{L}(f) - \mathcal{L}(f^B) = \underbrace{\mathcal{L}(f) - \mathcal{L}_N(f)}_{\text{generalization error}} + \underbrace{\mathcal{L}_N(f) - \mathcal{L}_N(f^*)}_{\text{optimization error}} \\ + \underbrace{\mathcal{L}_N(f^*) - \mathcal{L}(f^*)}_{\text{generalization error}} + \underbrace{\mathcal{L}(f^*) - \mathcal{L}(f^B)}_{\text{approximation error}}. \quad (7)$$

Specifically, if we set $f = \widehat{f}_N$, the above decomposition reveals what is known as the bias-variance tradeoff, namely, the decomposition of the total error (as measured in terms of the loss) into a contribution that stands for the ability of the function $f^* \in \mathcal{F}$ to best approximate the truth f^B (bias) and a contribution that represents the ability to estimate the approximant f^* from finitely many observations (variance), namely[2]

$$\mathcal{L}(\widehat{f}_N) - \mathcal{L}(f^B) = \underbrace{\mathcal{L}(\widehat{f}_N) - \mathcal{L}(f^*)}_{\text{estimation error (variance)}} + \underbrace{\mathcal{L}(f^*) - \mathcal{L}(f^B)}_{\text{approximation error (bias)}}.$$

We should stress that it is not fully understood yet in which cases overfitting leads to poor generalization and prediction properties of an ANN as there are cases in which models with many (nonzero) parameters that are perfectly fitted to noisy training data may still have good generalization skills; cf. (Bartlett et al. 2020) or Section 2.1 below for further explanation.

A practical challenge of any function approximation and any learning algorithm is to minimize the expected loss by only using a finite amount of training data, but without knowing the underlying data distribution $\mathbb{P}$. In fact, one can show there is no universal learning algorithm that works well for every data distribution (*no free lunch theorem*). Instead, any learning

---

2   Here we loosely understand the word 'truth' in the sense of empirical adequacy following the seminal work of van Fraassen (1980: 12), which means that we consider the function f^B to be empirically adequate, in that there is no other function (e.g. classifier or regression function) that has a higher likelihood relative to all unseen data in the world; see also Hanna (1983). The term 'truth' is typical jargon in the statistical learning literature, and one should not take it as a scientific realist's position.

algorithm (e.g. for classification) with robust error bounds must necessarily be accompanied by a priori regularity conditions on the underlying data distribution, e.g. (Berner et al. 2021; Shalev-Shwartz/Ben-David 2014; Wolpert 1996).[3]

Let us come back to the loss decomposition (7). The three types of errors hint at different perspectives that are important in machine learning from a mathematical point of view:

1. Generalization: How can we guarantee generalizing to unseen data while relying only on a finite amount of training data?
2. Function approximation: Which neural network architectures do we choose in order to gain good approximation qualities (in particular in high-dimensional settings)?
3. Optimization: How do we optimize a complicated, nonconvex function, like a neural network?

Besides these three, there are more aspects that cannot be read off from equation (7), but turn out to become relevant in particular in certain practical applications. Let us stress the following two:

4. Numerical stability and robustness: How can we design neural networks and corresponding algorithms that exhibit some numerical stability and are robust to certain perturbations?
5. Interpretability and uncertainty quantification: How can we explain the input-output behavior of certain complicated, potentially high-dimensional function approximations and how can we quantify uncertainty in neural network predictions?

In this article, we will argue that perspectives 4 and 5 are often overlooked, but still in particular relevant for a discussion on the limitations and prospects in machine learning. Along these lines, we will see that there

---

[3] As a consequence, deep learning does not solve Reichenbach's reference class problem or gives any hint to the solution of the problem of induction, but it is rather an instance in favor of the Duhem-Quine thesis, in that any learning algorithm that generalizes well from seen data must rely on appropriate background knowledge (Quine 1953: 44); cf. Sterkenburg (2019).

are promising novel developments and ideas that advance the aspiration to put deep learning onto more solid grounds in the future.

The article is organized as follows. In Section 2 we will review some aspects of neural networks, admittedly in a very a non-exhaustive manner, where in particular Sections 2.1–2.3 will correspond to perspectives 1–3 stated above. Section 3 will then demonstrate why (non-)robustness issues in deep learning are particularly relevant for practical applications, as illustrated by adversarial attacks in Section 3.1. We will argue in Section 3.2 that successful adversarial attacks on (deep) neural networks require careful thinking about worst-case analyses and uncertainty quantification. Section 3 therefore relates to perspectives 4 and 5 from above. Next, Section 4 will introduce the Bayesian perspective as a principled framework to approach some of the robustness issues raised before. After introducing Bayesian neural networks, we will discuss computational approaches in Section 4.1 and review further challenges in Section 4.2. Finally, in Section 5 we will draw a conclusion.

2. Deep neural networks: oddities and some specifics

One of the key questions regarding machine learning with (deep) neural networks is related to their ability to generalize beyond the data used in the training step (cf. perspective 1 in Section 1.2). The idea here is that a trained ANN applies the regularities found in the training data (i.e. in past observations) to future or unobserved data, assuming that these regularities are persistent. Without dwelling on technical details, it is natural to understand the training of a neural network from a probabilistic viewpoint, with the trained ANN being a collection of functions, that is characterized by a probability distribution over the parameter space, rather than by a single function. This viewpoint is in accordance with how the training works in practice, since training an ANN amounts to minimizing the empirical loss given some training data, as stated in equation (3), and this minimization is commonly done by some form of stochastic gradient descent (SGD) in the high-dimensional *loss landscape*[4], i.e. batches of the full training set are selected randomly during the training iterations (see also Appendix A). As

---

[4] The empirical risk $J_N(\theta) = \mathcal{L}_N(f_\theta)$, considered as a function of the parameters θ is often called the *loss landscape* or *energy landscape*.

a consequence, the outcome of the training is a random realization of the ANN and one can assign a probability distribution to the trained neural network.

2.1 Generalization, memorization and benign overfitting

If we think of the parametrized function that represents a trained neural network as a random variable, it is natural to assign a probability measure $Q(f)$ to every regression function f. So, let $Q^B = Q(f^B)$ be the target probability distribution (i.e. the truth), $Q^* = Q(f^*)$ the best approximation, and $\widehat{Q}_N = Q(\widehat{f}_N)$ the distribution associated with the N training points that are assumed to be randomly drawn from $\mathbb{P}$. We call $f(t) \in \mathcal{F}$ the function approximation that is obtained after running the parameter fitting until time t (see Section 2.3 and Appendix A below for further details) – $f(t)$ therefore models the training for a specified amount of training iterations. Ideally, one would like to see that $Q(f(t))$ resembles either the truth Q^B or its best approximation Q^* as the training proceeds; however, it has been shown that trained networks often memorize (random) training data in that Yang/E 2022: Thm. 6

$$\lim_{t \to \infty} Q(f(t)) = \widehat{Q}_N.$$

In this case, the training lets the model learn the data which amounts to memorizing facts, without a pronounced ability to generate knowledge. It is interesting to note that this behavior is consistently observed when the network is trained on a completely random relabelling of the true data, in which case one would not expect outstanding generalization capabilities of the trained ANN (Zhang/Bengio, et al. 2021). Finally, it so happens that $Q(f(t))$ does not converge to $\widehat{Q}_N$, in which case it diverges and thus gives no information whatsoever about the truth.

A phenomenon that is related to memorizing the training data and that is well known in statistical learning is called *overfitting*. It amounts to the trained function fitting the available data (too) well, while not generalizing to unseen data, as illustrated in the bottom left panel of Figure 2. The classical viewpoint in statistics is that when the function has far more parameters than there are data points (as is common with deep neural networks) and if the training time is too large, overfitting might happen, as illustrated in Figure 3. An indication of overfitting can be that the generalization error is strongly growing while the empirical risk is driven almost to zero. To prevent

Figure 2: Different examples of good and bad fits in the classical regression scheme: While a perfect fit to the training data may either lead to a high-fidelity model on the training data that has no (upper left panel) or very little (lower left panel) predictive power, underfitting leads to a low-fidelity model on the training data (upper right panel). A good fit (lower right panel) is indicated by a compromise between model-fidelity and predictive power.

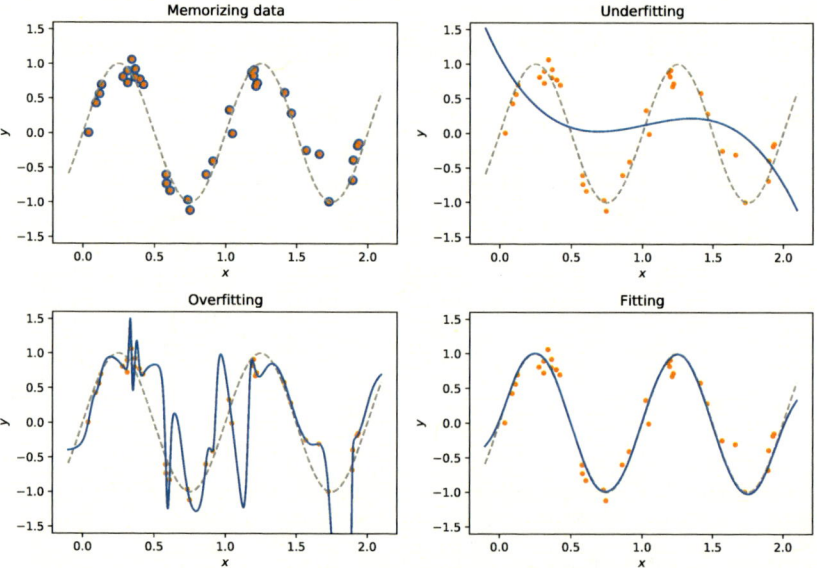

this, an alternative to increasing the number of training steps, t, while the training data remains the same, is early stopping. It has been shown (e.g. Yang/E 2022: Cor. 7) that the empirical distribution can be close to the truth (in which case the ANN generalizes well), if the training is stopped after a sufficiently long, but not too long training phase. Figure 3 shows the typical shape of the discrepancy between the trained network and the truth.

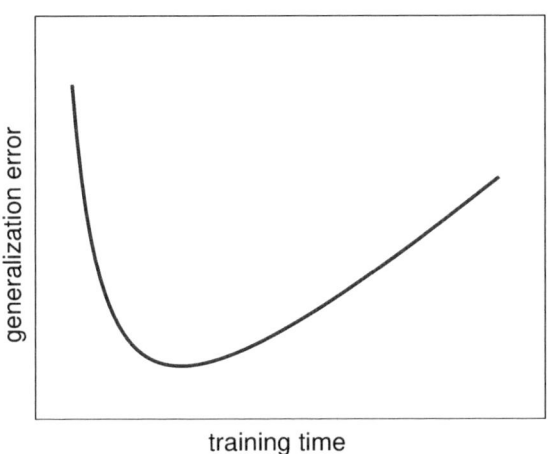

Figure 3: Traditional risk curve: schematic sketch of the generalization error of a generic deep neural network for a fixed amount of training data as a function of the training time t; see (Yang/E 2022) for details.

However, it turns out that there are also cases of benign overfitting, in which an ANN shows remarkable generalization properties, even though it is essentially fitting the noise in the training data. The phenomenon of benign overfitting, also known by the name of *double descent*, describes the empirical observation that the generalization error, as measured by the true risk, decreases again as the number of parameters is increased – despite severe overfitting (see Figure 4). Note that there is not contradiction between the double descent phenomenon and the traditional U-shaped risk curve shown in Figure 3 as they hold under different circumstances and the double descent requires pushing the number of parameters beyond a certain (fairly large) threshold.

It has been conjectured that this phenomenon is related to a certain low rank property of the data covariance; nevertheless a detailed theoretical understanding of the double descent curve for a finite amount of training data is still lacking as the available approximation results cannot be applied in situations in which the number of parameters is much higher than the number of data points. Interestingly, double descent has also been observed for linear regression problems or kernel methods, e.g. (Bartlett et al.

2020; Mei/Montanari 2021). Thus it does not seem to be a unique feature of ANNs; whether or not it is a more typical phenomenon for ANNs is an open question though (Belkin et al. 2019); see also Opper et al. (1990) for an early reference in which the double descent feature of ANNs has been first described (for some models even multiple descent curves are conjectured, Chen et al. 2021; Liang/Rakhlin/Zhai 2020).

Figure 4: Risk curve with benign overfitting: highly overparametrized ANNs often exhibit the double descent phenomenom when the number of parameters exceeds the number of data points. The leftmost vertical dashed line shows the optimal model complexity (for given observation data), beyond which the model is considered overparametrized. The rightmost vertical dashed line marks the interpolation threshold at which the model can exactly fit all data points.

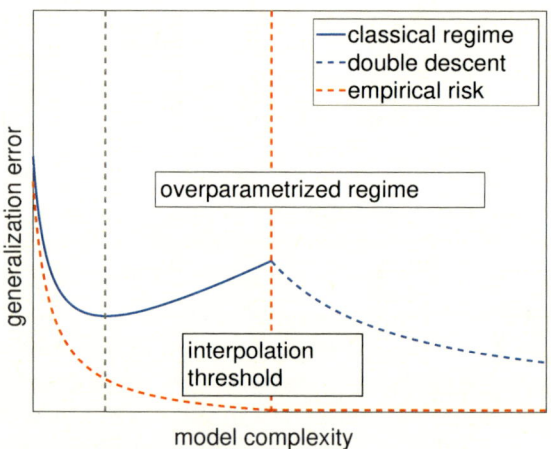

2.2 Curse of dimensionality

An important aspect of function approximation (and therefore related to perspective 2 stated in Section 1.2) is the question of how complicated the function f_θ or, equivalently, how rich the function class $\mathcal{F}$ needs to be. This becomes particularly interesting if the state space is high-dimensional and a notorious challenge is known as the *curse of dimensionality*. It describes the phenomenon that approximating a target function f^B or the corresponding probability distribution $Q^B = Q(f^B)$ when $\mathcal{X}$ is high-dimensional (i.e. when the number of degrees of freedom is large) requires a huge amount of training data to determine a regression function f_θ that is able to approximate the target. As a rule of thumb, approximating a function f^B on $\mathcal{X} = \mathbb{R}^d$ or the associated probability measure Q^B with an accuracy of ϵ needs about

$$N = \epsilon^{-\Omega(d)} \quad (8)$$

sample points in order to determine roughly the same number of a priori unknown parameters θ, thereby admitting an exponential dependence on the dimension.[5] It is easy to see that the number of parameters needed and the size of the training set become astronomical for real-world tasks. As an example, consider the classification of handwritten digits. The MNIST database (Modified National Institute of Standards and Technology database) contains a dataset of about 60 000 handwritten digits that are stored in digital form as 28×28 pixel greyscale images (LeCun 1998). If we store only the greyscale values for every image as a vector, then, the dimension of every such vector will be $28^2 = 784$. By today's standards, this is considered a small system, yet it is easy to see that training a network with about 10^{784} parameters and roughly the same number of training data points is simply not feasible, especially as the training set contains less than 10^5 data points.

In practice, the number of ANN parameters and the number of data points needed to train a network can be much smaller. In some cases, this inherent complexity reduction present in deep learning can be mathematically understood. Clearly, when the target function is very smooth, symmetric or concentrated, it is possible to approximate it with a parametric function having a smaller number of parameters. The class of functions that can be approximated by an ANN without an exponentially large number of parameters, however, is considerably larger; for example, Barron-regular functions that form a fairly large class of relevant functions can be approximated by ANNs in arbitrary dimension with a number of parameters that is independent of the dimension (Barron 1993: Thm. 3); there are, moreover, results that show that it is possible to express *any* labelling of N data points in $\mathbb{R}^d$ by an ANN two layers and in total $p = 2N + d$ parameters (Zhang/

---

5   Here we use the Landau notation $\Omega(d)$ to denote a function of d that asymptotically grows like αd for some constant $\alpha > 0$; often $\alpha = 1, 2$.

Bengio, et al. 2021: Thm. 1); cf. (DeVore/Hanin/Petrova 2021). In general, however, the quite remarkable expressivity of deep neural networks with a relatively small number of parameters and even smaller training sets is still not well understood (Berner et al. 2021: Sec. 4).[6]

2.3 Stochastic optimization as implicit regularization

Let us finally discuss an aspect related to the optimization of ANNs (cf. perspective 3 in Section 1.2) that interestingly offers a connection to function approximation as well. Here, the typical situation is that no a priori information whatsoever about the function class to which f^B belongs is available. A conventional way then to control the number of parameters and to prevent overfitting is to add a regularization term to the loss function that forces the majority of the parameters to be zero or close to zero and hence effectively reduces the number of parameters (Tibshirani 1996). Even though regularization can improve the generalization capabilities, it has been found to be neither necessary nor sufficient for controlling the generalization error (Géron 2017). Instead, surprisingly, there is (in some situations proveable) evidence that SGD introduces an implicit regularization to the empirical risk minimization that is not present in the exact (i.e. deterministic) gradient descent (Ali/Dobriban/Tibshirani 2020; Roberts 2021). A possible explanation of this effect is that the inexact gradient evaluation of SGD introduces some noise that prevents the minimization algorithm from getting stuck in a bad local minimum. It has been observed that the effect is more pronounced when the variance of the gradient approximation is larger, in other words: when the approximation has a larger sampling error (Keskar et al. 2016). A popular, though controversial explanation is that noisier SGD tends to favor

---

6   Here, 'relatively small' must be understood with respect to the dimension of the training data set. An ANN that was successfully trained on MNIST data may still have several hundred millions or even billions of parameters; nevertheless, the number of parameters is small compared to what one would expect from an approximation theory perspective, namely 10^{784}. However, it is large compared to the minimum number of parameters needed to fit the the data, which in our example would be $p = 2 \cdot 60\,000 + 784 = 120\,784$, hence an ANN with good generalization capacities is typically severely overfitting, especially if we keep in mind that the effective dimension of the MNIST images that contains about 90% black pixels is considerably smaller.

wider or flatter local minima of the loss landscape that are conventionally associated with better generalization capabilities of the trained ANN (Dinh et al. 2017; Hochreiter/Schmidhuber 1997). How to unambigously characterize the 'flatness' of local minima with regard to their generalization capacities, however, is still an open question. Furthermore, it should be noted that too much variance in the gradient estimation is not favorable either, as it might lead to slower training convergence, and it will be interesting to investigate how to account for this tradeoff; cf. (Bottou/Curtis/Nocedal 2018; Richter et al. 2020).

Example 2.1 To illustrate the implicit regularization of an overfitted ANN by SGD, we consider the true function $f(x) = \sin(2\pi x)$ and create $N = 100$ noisy data points according to $y_n = f(x_n) + 0.15\, \eta_n$, where x_n is uniformly distributed in the interval $[0, 2\pi]$ (symbolically: $x_n \sim \mathcal{U}([0, 2])$) and $\eta_n \sim \mathcal{N}(0, 1)$. We choose a fully connected NN with three hidden layers (i.e. $L = 4$), each with 10 neurons.

Once we train with gradient descent and once we randomly choose a batch of size $N_b = 10$ in each gradient step. In Figure 5 we can see that running gradient descent on the noisy data leads to overfitting, whereas stochastic gradient descent seems to have some implicit regularizing effect.

Figure 5: We consider a fully connected neural network (blue) that has been trained on $N = 100$ noisy data points (orange), once by gradient descent and once by stochastic gradient descent, and compare it to the ground truth function (grey).

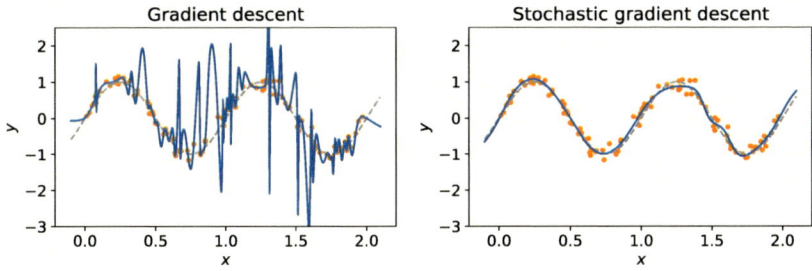

We have provided a potpourri of aspects related to the three perspectives *generalization, function approximation* and *optimization*, demonstrating subtleties of deep learning that have partly been understood with the help of rigorous mathematical analysis, while still leaving many open questions for future research. In the following, let us move towards perspectives 4 and 5 that we have stated in Section 1.2. In particular, the following chapter will argue that relying on classical statistical learning theory might not be sufficient in certain practical applications and additional effort and analysis are needed in order to make deep learning more robust.

3. Sensitivity and (non-)robustness of neural networks

So far we have measured the performance of prediction models in an 'average' sense. In particular we have stated the goal of a machine learning algorithm to minimize the expected loss

$$\mathcal{L}(f) = \mathbb{E}[\ell(f(X), Y)], \tag{9}$$

where the deviations between predictions and ground truth data are averaged over the (unknown) probability distribution $\mathbb{P}$. Statements from statistical learning theory therefore usually hold the implicit assumption that future data comes from the same distribution and is hence similar to that encountered during training (cf. Section 1.2). This perspective might often be valid in practice, but falls short of atypical data in the sense of having a small likelihood, which makes such an occurence a rare event or a *large deviation*. Especially in safety-critical applications one might not be satisfied with average-case guarantees, but rather strives for worst-case analyses or at least for an indication of the certainty of a prediction (which we will come back to in the next section). Moreover, it is known that models like neural networks are particularly sensitive with respect to the input data, implying that very small, barely detectable changes of the data can drastically change the output of a prediction model – a phenomenon that is not respected by an analysis based on expected losses.

3.1 Adversarial attacks

An extreme illustration of the sensitivity of neural networks can be noted in *adversarial attacks*, where input data is manipulated in order to mislead the algorithm.[7] Here the idea is to add very small and therefore barely noticeable perturbations to the data in such a way that a previously trained prediction model then provides very different outputs. In a classification problem this could for instance result in suggesting different classes for almost identical input data. It has gained particular attention in image classification, where slightly changed images can be misclassified, even though they appear identical to the original image for the human eye, e.g. (Brown et al. 2017; Goodfellow/Shlens/Szegedy 2014; Kurakin/Goodfellow/Bengio 2018).

Adversarial attacks can be constructed in many different ways, but the general idea is usually the same. We discuss the example of a trained classifier: given a data point $x \in \mathbb{R}^d$ and a trained neural network f_θ, we add some minor change $\delta \in \mathbb{R}^d$ to the input data x, such that $f_\theta(x+\delta)$ predicts a wrong class. One can differentiate in targeted and untargeted adversarial attacks, where either the wrong class is specified or the misclassification to any arbitrary (wrong) class is aimed at. We focus on the former strategy as it turns out to be more powerful. Since the perturbation is supposed to be small (e.g. for the human eye), it is natural to minimize the perturbation δ in some suitable norm (e.g. the Euclidean norm or the maximum norm) while constraining the classifier to assign a wrong label $\widetilde{y} \neq y$ to the perturbed data and imposing an additional box constraint. In the relevant literature (e.g. Szegedy/Zaremba et al. 2014), an adversarial attack is constructed as the solution to the following optimization problem:

$$\text{minimize } \|\delta\| \quad \text{subject to} \quad f_\theta(x+\delta) = \widetilde{y} \quad \text{and} \quad x+\delta \in [0,1]^d. \quad (10)$$

Note that we have the hidden constraint $f_\theta(x) = y$, where $y \neq \widetilde{y}$ and the input variables have been scaled such that $x \in [0,1]^d$. In order to have an implementable version of this procedure, one usually considers a relaxation of (10) that can be solved with (stochastic) gradient descent-like methods in δ; see e.g. (Carlini/Wagner 2017).

Roughly speaking, generating an adversarial attack amounts to doing a (stochastic) gradient descent in the data rather than the parameters, with the

---

7   This desire to mislead the algorithm is in accordance with Popper's dictum that we are essentially learning from our mistakes. As Popper (1984: 324) mentions in the seminal speech *Duldsamkeit und intellektuelle Verantwortlichkeit* on the occasion of receiving the *Dr. Leopold Lucas Price of the University of Tübingen* on the 26th May 1981: "[...] es ist die spezifische Aufgabe des Wissenschaftlers, nach solchen Fehlern zu suchen. Die Feststellung, daß eine gut bewährte Theorie oder ein viel verwendetes praktisches Verfahren fehlerhaft ist, kann eine wichtige Entdeckung sein."

aim of finding the closest possible input $\widetilde{x}$ to x that gets wrongly classified and to analyze what went wrong.[8]

Example 3.1 (Adversarial attack to image classification) Let us provide an example of an adversarial attack in image classification. For this we use the Inception-v3 model from (Szegedy/Vanhoucke et al. 2016), which is pre-trained on 1000 fixed classes. For the image in the left panel of Figure 6 a class is predicted that seems close to what is in fact displayed. We then compute a small perturbation δ, displayed in the central panel, with the goal of getting a different classification result. The right panel displays the perturbed image $x + \delta$, which notably looks indistinguishable from the original image, yet gets classified wrongly with the same Inception-v3 model. The displayed probabilities are the so-called softmax outputs of the neural network for the predicted classes and they represent some sort of certainty scores.

Figure 6: The original image of Thomas Bayes in the left panel gets reasonably classified ("cloak"), whereas the right picture is the result of an adversarial attack and therefore gets misclassified (as "mosque").

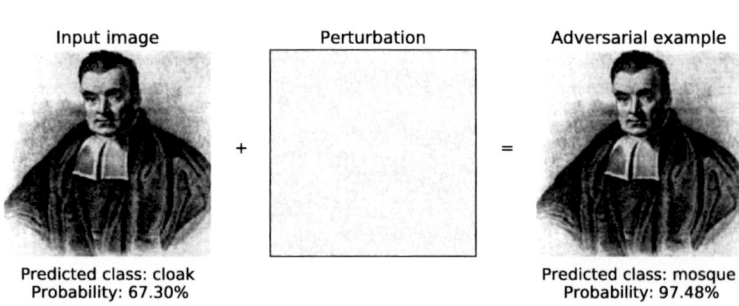

---

[8] Again, quoting Popper (1984: 325): "Wir müssen daher dauernd nach unseren Fehlern Ausschau halten. Wenn wir sie finden, müssen wir sie uns einprägen; sie nach allen Seiten analysieren, um ihnen auf den Grund zu gehen."

3.2 Including worst-case scenarios and marginal cases

Adversarial attacks demonstrate that neural networks might not be robust with respect to unexpected input data and the next question naturally is how this issue can be addressed. In fact, multiple defense strategies have been developed in recent years in order to counteract attacks, while it is noted that a valid evaluation of defenses against adversarial examples turns out to be difficult, since one can often find additional attack strategies afterwards that have not been considered in the evaluation (Carlini/Athalye et al. 2019). One obvious idea for making neural networks more robust is to integrate adversarial attacks into the training process, e.g. by considering the minimization

$$\min_{\theta} \mathbb{E}\left[\max_{\delta \in \Delta} \ell(f_\theta(X + \delta), Y)\right], \tag{11}$$

where $\Delta = \{\delta : \|\delta\| \leq \varepsilon\}$ is some specified perturbation range (Madry et al. 2018; Wang et al. 2019). Depending on the application, however, convergence of this min-max problem can be cumbersome. At present, the study of adversarial attacks is a prominent research topic with many questions still open (e.g. the role of regularization (Roth/Kilcher/Hofmann 2020)), and it has already become apparent that principles that hold for the average case scenario might not be valid in worst-case settings anymore; cf. (Ilyas et al. 2019: Sec. 4). To give an example, there is empirical evidence that overfitting might be more harmful when adversarial attacks are present, in that overparametrized deep NNs that are robust against adversarial attacks may not exhibit the typical double descent phenomenon when the training is continued beyond the interpolation threshold (cf. Figure 4); instead they show a slight increase of the generalization risk when validated against test data, i.e. their test performance degrades, which is at odds with the observations made for standard deep learning algorithms based on empirical risk minimization (Rice/Wong/Kolter 2020).

Another way to address adversarial attacks is to incorporate uncertainty estimates in the models and hope that those then indicate whether perturbed (or out of sample) data occurs. Note that the question as to whether some new data is considered typical or not (i.e. an outlier or a marginal case) depends on the parameters of the trained neural network which are random, in that they depend on the random training data. As a principled way of uncertainty quantification we will introduce the Bayesian perspective and Bayesian Neural Networks (BNNs) in the next section. We claim that these can be viewed as a more robust deep learning paradigm, which promises fruitful advances, backed up by some already existing theoretical results and empirical evidence. In relation to adversarial attacks, there have been multiple indications of attack identifications (Rawat/Wistuba/Nicolae 2017) and improved defenses (Feinman et al. 2017; Liu et al. 2018; Zimmermann 2019) when relying on BNNs. In fact, there is clear evidence of increasing prediction uncertainty with growing attack strength, indicating the usefulness of the provided uncertainty scores. On the theoretical side, it can be shown that in the (large data and overparametrized) limit BNN posteriors are robust against gradient-based adversarial attacks (Carbone et al. 2020).

4. The Bayesian perspective

In the previous chapter we demonstrated and discussed the potential non-robustness of neural networks related, for example, to small changes of input data by adversarial attacks. A connected inherent problem is that neural networks usually *don't know when they don't know*, meaning that there is no reliable quantification of prediction uncertainty.[9] In this chapter we will argue that the Bayesian perspective is well suited as a principled framework for uncertainty quantification, thus holding the promise of making machine learning models more robust; see (Neal 1995) for an overview.

We have argued that classical machine learning algorithms often act as black boxes, i.e. without making predictions interpretable and without indicating any level of confidence. Given that all models are learnt from a finite amount of data, this seems rather naive and it is in fact desirable that algorithms should be able to indicate a degree of uncertainty whenever not 'enough' data have been present during training (keeping in mind, however, that this endeavor still leaves certain aspects of interpretability such as posthoc explanations (Du/Liu/Hu 2019: Sec. 3)) open. To this end, the Bayesian credo is the following: we start with some beforehand (*a priori*) given uncertainty of the prediction model f. In the next step, when the model is trained

---

[9] Freely adapted from the infamous 2002 speech of the former U.S. Secretary of Defense, Donald Rumsfeld: "We [...] know there are known unknowns; that is to say we know there are some things we do not know. But there are also unknown unknowns – the ones we don't know we don't know."

on data, this uncertainty will get 'updated' such that predictions 'close' to already seen data points become more certain. In mathematical terms, the idea is to assume a prior probability distribution $p(\theta)$ over the parameter vector θ of the prediction model rather than a fixed value as in the classical case. We then condition this distribution on the fact that we have seen a training data set $\mathcal{D} = (x_n, y_n)_{n=1}^{N}$.

The computation of conditional probabilities is governed by Bayes' theorem, yielding the *posterior probability* $p(\theta|\mathcal{D})$, namely by

$$p(\theta|\mathcal{D}) = \frac{p(\mathcal{D}|\theta)p(\theta)}{p(\mathcal{D})}, \tag{12}$$

where $p(\mathcal{D}|\theta)$ is the likelihood of seeing data $\mathcal{D}$ given the parameter vector θ and $p(\mathcal{D}) = \int_{\mathbb{R}^p} p(\mathcal{D}, \theta) d\theta$ is the normalizing constant, sometimes called evidence, assuring that $p(\theta|\mathcal{D})$ is indeed a probability density. The posterior probability can be interpreted as an updated distribution over the parameters given the data $\mathcal{D}$. Assuming that we can sample from it, we can then make subsequent predictions on unseen data x by

$$f(x) = \int_{\mathbb{R}^p} f_\theta(x) p(\theta|\mathcal{D}) d\theta \approx \frac{1}{K} \sum_{k=1}^{K} f_{\theta^{(k)}}(x) \tag{13}$$

where $\theta^{(1)}, \ldots, \theta^{(K)}$ are i.i.d. samples drawn from the Bayesian posterior $p(\theta|\mathcal{D})$, i.e. we average predictions of multiple neural networks, each of which having parameters drawn from the posterior distribution.

Figure 7: We display the evaluation of a BNN by showing its mean prediction function (in dark blue) and a set of two standard deviations from it (in light blue), compared to the ground truth (in gray). Our BNN is either untrained (left) or has seen $N = 5$ (in the central panel) or $N = 100$ data points (in right panel) during training.

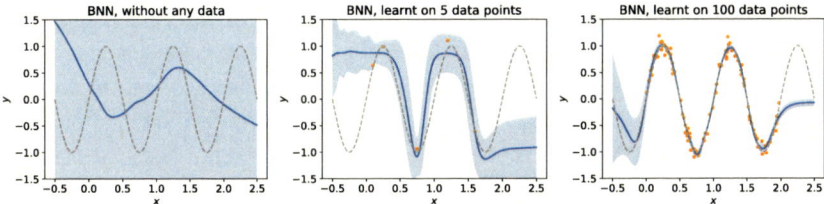

Example 4.1 (BNN based on different amounts of data) Let us say we want to learn the function $f(x) = \sin(2\pi x)$ and have a certain amount of training data $\mathcal{D} = (x_n, y_n)_{n=1}^N$ available, where the label is given by $y_n = f(x_n) + \eta_n$, with noise $\eta_n \sim \mathcal{N}(0, 0.01)$. Intuitively, the fitted neural network should be closer to the true function as well as more certain in its predictions the more data points are available. We consider a BNN trained with a mean field variational inference attempt and a Gaussian prior on the parameters (see next section for details). In Figure 7 we display the mean prediction function as defined in (13) as well as a confidence set defined by two standard deviations on the sample predictions. In the left panel we display the evaluation before training, i.e. without relying on any available data points, and note that the average prediction function is rather arbitrary and the uncertainty rather high, as expected. The central panel repeats the same evaluation, where now the BNN is trained on $N = 5$ data points. We can see an improved prediction function and a decreased uncertainty. Finally, the right panel displays a BNN trained on $N = 100$ data points, where now the mean prediction function is quite close to the true function and the uncertainty almost vanishes close to the data points, yet remains large wherever no training data was available. The BNN is therefore able to output reasonable uncertainty scores, depending on which data was available during training.

4.1 Bayesian neural networks in practice

Even though simple at first glance, the Bayes formula (12) is non-trivial from a computational point of view and can in almost all cases not be computed analytically. The challenging term is $p(\mathcal{D})$, for which, given the nested structure of neural networks, the integral has to be approximated numerically. Classical numerical integration, however, is infeasible too, due to the high dimension of the parameter vector θ. We therefore have to resort to alternative attempts that aim to approximate the posterior distribution $p(\theta|\mathcal{D})$.

An asymptotically exact method for creating samples from any (suitable) probability distribution is called Hamiltonian Monte Carlo (also: Hybrid Monte Carlo), which is based on ideas from Statistical Physics and the observation that certain dynamical systems admit an equilibrium state that can be identified with the posterior probability that we seek to compute (Neal 2011). For our purposes this attempt seems to be a method of choice when aiming for high approximation quality; however, it does not scale well to high dimensions and is therefore practically useless for state-of-the-art neural networks. A similar idea is to exploit the so-called Langevin dynamics in combination with subsampling of the data points (Welling/Teh 2011; Zhang/Cooper/De Sa 2020). This method scales much better, but it is biased since the data subsampling perturbs the stationary distribution. A quite different attempt is called *dropout*, which builds the posterior approximation into the neural network architecture and implicitly trains multiple models at the same time (Gal/Ghahramani 2016). Finally, another popular method is based on variational inference, where the true posterior is approximated within a family of simpler probability densities, e.g. multidimensional Gaussians with diagonal covariance matrices (Blundell et al. 2015). Depending on the approximation class, this method scales well, but approximation quality cannot be guaranteed.

Each of the methods mentioned above has advantages and disadvantages and many questions are still open. As a general remark, there is indeed repeated evidence that, ignoring the approximation challenges for the moment, the Bayesian framework works well in principle for quantifying the prediction uncertainties of neural networks. Additionally, there are indications, based on empirical studies (Izmailov et al. 2021), that the overall model performance might be improved when relying on predictions from BNNs in contrast to deterministic ANNs. On the other hand, many of the approximation steps that lead to a BNN are not well understood theoretically, and one can demonstrate empirically that they often lead to posterior approximations that are not accurate, e.g. (Foong et al. 2019). Some of those failures seem to be due to systematic simplifications in the approximating family (Yao et al. 2019). This phenomenon gets more severe, while at the same time harder to spot, when the neural networks are large, i.e. when the parameter vector is very high-dimensional. An accepted opinion seems to be that whenever BNNs do not work well, then it is not the Bayesian paradigm that is to blame, but rather the inability to approximate it well (Gal/Smith 2018). At the same time, however, there are works such as (Farquhar/Smith/Gal 2020) that claim that for certain neural network architectures simplified approximation structures get better the bigger (and in particular the deeper) the model is.

4.2 Challenges and prospects for Bayesian Neural Networks

The previous section sought to argue that there is great potential in using BNNs in practice; however, many questions, both from a theoretical and practical point of view, are still open. A natural formulation of BNNs can be based on free energy as a loss function that has been discussed in connection with a formal account of curiosity and insight in terms of Bayesian inference (see Friston et al. 2017): while the expected loss or risk in deep learning can be thought of as an energy that describes the goodness-of-fit of a trained ANN to some given data (where minimum energy amounts to an optimal fit), the free energy contains an additional entropy term that accounts for the inherent parameter uncertainty and has the effect of smoothing the energy landscape. The result is a trade-off between an accurate fit, which bears the risk of overfitting, and reduced model complexity (i.e. Occam's razor). From the perspective of statistical inference, e.g. (Jose/Simeone 2021), the free energy has the property that its unique minimizer in the space of probability measures is the sought Bayesian posterior (Hartmann et al. 2017). Selecting a BNN by free energy minimization therefore generates a model that, *on average*, provides the best explanation for the data at hand, and thus it can be thought of as making an inference to the best explanation in the sense of Harman (1965); cf. also (McAuliffe 2015).

Evidently, the biggest challenge seems to be a computational one: how can we approximate posterior distributions of large neural networks both well and efficiently? But even if the minimizer or the Bayesian posterior can be approximated, the evaluation of posterior accuracy (e.g. from the shape of the free energy in the neighborhood of the minimizer) is still difficult and one usually does not have clear guarantees. Furthermore, neural networks keep getting larger and more efficient methods that can cope with ever higher dimensionality are needed. Regarding the benefits of BNNs, there is an open debate on how much performance gains they actually bring in practice; cf. (Wenzel et al. 2020). Uncertainty quantification, on the other hand, is valuable enough to continue the Bayesian endeavor, eventually allowing for safety-critical applications or potentially improving active and continual learning.

5. Concluding remarks

The recent progress in artificial intelligence is undeniable and the related improvements in various applications are impressive. This article, however, provides only a snapshot of the current state of deep learning, and we have demonstrated that many phenomena that are intimately connected are still not well understood from a theoretical point of view. We have further argued that this lack of understanding not only slows down further systematic developments of practical algorithms, but also bears risks that become in particular apparent in safety-critical applications. While inspecting deep learning from the mathematical angle, we have highlighted five perspectives that allow for a more systematic treatment, offering already some novel explanations of striking observations and bringing up valuable questions for future research (cf. Section 1.2).

We have in particular emphasized the influence of the numerical methods on the performance of a trained neural network and touched upon the aspect of numerical stability, motivated by the observation that neural networks are often not robust (e.g. with respect to unexpected input data or adversarial attacks) and do not hold any reliable measure for uncertainty quantification. As a principled framework that might tackle those issues, we have presented the Bayesian paradigm and in particular Bayesian neural networks, which provide a natural way of quantifying epistemic uncertainties. In theory, BNNs promise to overcome certain robustness issues and many empirical observations are in line with this hope; however, they also bring additional computational challenges, connected mainly to the sampling of high dimensional probability distributions. The existing methods addressing this issue are neither sufficiently understood theoretically nor produce good enough (scalable) results in practice such that a persistent usage in applications is often infeasible. We believe that the theoretical properties of BNNs (or ANNs in general) cannot be fully understood without understanding the numerical algorithms used for training and optimisation. Future research should therefore aim at improving these numerical methods in connection with rigorous approximation guarantees.

Moreover, this article argued that many of the engineering-style improvements and anecdotes related to deep learning need systematic mathematical analyses in order foster a solid basis for artificial intelligence[10]. Rigorous mathematical inspection has already led to notable achievements in recent years, and in addition to an ever enhancing handcrafting of neural

---

10 This view addresses the skeptical challenge of Ali Rahimi who gave a presentation at NIPS Conference in 2017 with the title "Machine learning has become alchemy". According to Rahimi, machine learning and alchemy both work to a certain degree, but the lack of theoretical understanding and interpretability of machine learning models is major cause for concern.

network architectures, the continuation of this theoretical research will be the basis for further substantial progress in machine learning. We therefore conclude with a quote from Vladimir Vapnik (1999: X), one of the founding fathers of modern machine learning: "I heard reiteration of the following claim: Complex theories do not work, simple algorithms do. [...] I would like to demonstrate that in this area of science a good old principle is valid: Nothing is more practical than a good theory."

References

Ali, Alnur, Edgar Dobriban, and Ryan Tibshirani (2020). "The implicit regularization of stochastic gradient flow for least squares". In: *International Conference on Machine Learning*. Ed. by Hal Daumé III, and Aarti Singh. Vol. 119. Cambridge MA: JMLR, pp. 233–244.

Barrett, David G. T., and Benoit Dherin (2020). "Implicit gradient regularization". In: *ArXiv preprint arXiv:2009.11162*.

Barron, Andrew R. (1993). "Universal approximation bounds for superpositions of a sigmoidal function". In: *IEEE Transactions on Information Theory* 39.3, pp. 930–945.

Bartlett, Peter L. et al. (2020). "Benign overfitting in linear regression". In: *Proceedings of the National Academy of Sciences* 117.48, pp. 30063–30070.

Belkin, Mikhail et al. (2019). "Reconciling modern machine-learning practice and the classical bias–variance trade-off". In: *Proceedings of the National Academy of Sciences* 116.32, pp. 15849–15854.

Berner, Julius et al. (2021). "The modern mathematics of deep learning". In: *ArXiv preprint arXiv:2105.04026*.

Blundell, Charles et al. (2015). "Weight uncertainty in neural network". In: *International Conference on Machine Learning*. Ed. by Francis Bach, and David Blei. Vol. 37. Cambridge MA: JMLR, pp. 1613–1622.

Bottou, Léon, Frank E. Curtis, and Jorge Nocedal (2018). "Optimization methods for large-scale machine learning". In: *SIAM Review* 60.2, pp. 223–311.

Brown, Tom B. et al. (2017). "Adversarial patch". In: *ArXiv preprint*. URL: https://arxiv.org/abs/1712.09665.

Bubba, Tatiana A. et al. (2019). "Learning the invisible: A hybrid deep learning-shearlet framework for limited angle computed tomography". In: *Inverse Problems* 35.6, p. 064002.

Carbone, Ginevra et al. (2020). "Robustness of Bayesian neural networks to gradient-based attacks". In: *Advances in Neural Information Processing Systems* 33, pp. 15602–15613.

Carlini, Nicholas, Anish Athalye, et al. (2019). "On evaluating adversarial robustness". In: *ArXiv preprint arXiv:1902.06705*.

Carlini, Nicholas, and David Wagner (2017). "Towards evaluating the robustness of neural networks". In: *2017 IEEE Symposium on Security and Privacy*. Los Alamitos, CA: IEEE, pp. 39–57.

Chen, Lin et al. (2021). "Multiple Descent: Design Your Own Generalization Curve". In: *Advances in Neural Information Processing Systems* 34, pp. 8898–8912. URL: https://proceedings.neurips.cc/paper/2021/file/4ae67a7dd7e491f8fb6f9ea0cf25dfdb-Paper.pdf.

Cybenko, George (1989). "Approximation by superpositions of a sigmoidal function". In: *Mathematics of Control, Signals, and Systems* 2.4, pp. 303–314.

DeVore, Ronald, Boris Hanin, and Guergana Petrova (2021). "Neural network approximation". In: *Acta Numerica* 30, pp. 327–444.

Dinh, Laurent et al. (2017). "Sharp minima can generalize for deep nets". In: *International Conference on Machine Learning*. Ed. by Doina Precup, and Yee Whye Teh. Vol. 70. Cambridge MA: JMLR, pp. 1019–1028.

Du, Mengnan, Ninghao Liu, and Xia Hu (2019). "Techniques for Interpretable Machine Learning". In: *Communications of the ACM* 63.1, pp. 68–77.

E, Weinan, Jiequn Han, and Arnulf Jentzen (2017). "Deep learning-based numerical methods for high-dimensional parabolic partial differential equations and backward stochastic differential equations". In: *Communications in Mathematics and Statistics* 5.4, pp. 349–380.

Elbrächter, Dennis Maximilian, Julius Berner, and Philipp Grohs (2019). "How degenerate is the parametrization of neural networks with the ReLU activation function?" In: *Advances in Neural Information Processing Systems* 32, pp. 7790–7801.

Faber, Felix A. et al. (2017). "Prediction errors of molecular machine learning models lower than hybrid DFT error". In: *Journal of Chemical Theory and Computation* 13.11, pp. 5255–5264.

Farquhar, Sebastian, Lewis Smith, and Yarin Gal (2020). "Liberty or depth: Deep Bayesian neural nets do not need complex weight posterior approximations". In: *ArXiv preprint arXiv:2002.03704*.

Feinman, Reuben et al. (2017). "Detecting adversarial samples from artifacts". In: *ArXiv preprint arXiv:1703.00410*.

Foong, Andrew Y. K. et al. (2019). "On the expressiveness of approximate inference in Bayesian neural networks". In: *ArXiv preprint arXiv:1909.00719*.

Fraassen, Bas C. van (1980). *The Scientific Image*. New York: Oxford University Press.

Friston, Karl J. et al. (2017). "Active Inference, Curiosity and Insight". In: *Neural Computation* 29.10, pp. 2633–2683.

Gal, Yarin, and Zoubin Ghahramani (2016). "Dropout as a Bayesian approximation: Representing model uncertainty in deep learning". In: *International Conference on Machine Learning*. Ed. by Maria F. Balcan, and Kilian Q. Weinberger. Vol. 48. Cambridge MA: JMLR, pp. 1050–1059.

Gal, Yarin, and Lewis Smith (2018). "Sufficient conditions for idealised models to have no adversarial examples: a theoretical and empirical study with Bayesian neural networks". In: *ArXiv preprint arXiv:1806.00667*.

Geirhos, Robert et al. (2018). "Generalisation in Humans and Deep Neural Networks". In: *Advanced in Neural Information Processing Systems* 31, pp. 7549–7561.

Germain, Maximilien, Huyên Pham, and Xavier Warin (2021). "Neural networks-based algorithms for stochastic control and PDEs in finance". In: *ArXiv preprint arXiv:2101.08068*.

Géron, Aurélien (2017). *Hands-On Machine Learning with Scikit-Learn and TensorFlow: Concepts, Tools, and Techniques to Build Intelligent Systems*. 1st. Sebastopol: O'Reilly Media.

Goodfellow, Ian J., Jonathon Shlens, and Christian Szegedy (2014). "Explaining and harnessing adversarial examples". In: *ArXiv preprint arXiv:1412.6572*.

Hanna, Joseph F. (1983). "Empirical Adequacy". In: *Philosophy of Science* 50.1, pp. 1–34.

Harman, Gilbert H. (1965). "The Inference to the Best Explanation". In: *The Philosophical Review* 74.1, pp. 88–95. URL: http://www.jstor.org/stable/2183532.

Hartmann, Carsten et al. (2017). "Variational Characterization of Free Energy: Theory and Algorithms". In: *Entropy* 19.11, p. 626.

Hermann, Jan, Zeno Schätzle, and Frank Noé (2020). "Deep-neural-network solution of the electronic Schrödinger equation". In: *Nature Chemistry* 12.10, pp. 891–897.

Higham, Catherine F., and Desmond J. Higham (2019). "Deep Learning: An Introduction for Applied Mathematicians". In: *SIAM Review* 61.4, pp. 860–891.

Hochreiter, Sepp, and Jürgen Schmidhuber (1997). "Flat Minima". In: *Neural Computation* 9.1, pp. 1–42.

Ilyas, Andrew et al. (2019). "Adversarial examples are not bugs, they are features". In: *ArXiv preprint arXiv:1905.02175*.

Izmailov, Pavel et al. (2021). "What Are Bayesian Neural Network Posteriors Really Like?" In: *International Conference on Machine Learning*. Ed. by Marina Meila, and Tong Zhang. Vol. 139. Cambridge MA: JMLR, pp. 4629–4640. URL: https://proceedings.mlr.press/v139/izmailov21a.html.

Jose, Sharu Theresa, and Osvaldo Simeone (2021). "Free Energy Minimization: A Unified Framework for Modeling, Inference, Learning, and Optimization". In: *IEEE Signal Processing Magazine* 38.2, pp. 120–125.

Keskar, Nitish Shirish et al. (2016). "On large-batch training for deep learning: Generalization gap and sharp minima". In: *ArXiv preprint arXiv:1609.04836*.

Kurakin, Alexey, Ian J. Goodfellow, and Samy Bengio (2018). "Adversarial examples in the physical world". In: *Artificial intelligence safety and security*. Ed. by Roman V. Yampolskiy. New York: Chapman and Hall/CRC, pp. 99–112.

Kushner, Harold J., and G. George Yin (2003). *Stochastic Approximation and Recursive Algorithms and Applications*. New York: Springer.

LeCun, Yann (1998). *The MNIST database of handwritten digits.* (http://yann.lecun.com/exdb/mnist/).

Li, Qianxiao, Cheng Tai, and Weinan E (Aug. 2017). "Stochastic Modified Equations and Adaptive Stochastic Gradient Algorithms". In: *International Conference on Machine Learning*. Ed. by Doina Precup, and Yee Whye Teh. Vol. 70. Cambridge MA: JMLR, pp. 2101–2110.

Li, Qianxiao, Cheng Tai, and Weinan E (2019). "Stochastic Modified Equations and Dynamics of Stochastic Gradient Algorithms I: Mathematical Foundations". In: *Journal of Machine Learning Research* 20.40, pp. 1–47.

Liang, Tengyuan, Alexander Rakhlin, and Xiyu Zhai (2020). "On the multiple descent of minimum-norm interpolants and restricted lower isometry of kernels". In: *Conference on Learning Theory*. Ed. by Jacob Abernethy, and Shivani Agarwal. Vol. 125. Cambridge MA: JMLR, pp. 2683–2711.

Liu, Xuanqing et al. (2018). "Adv-BNN: Improved adversarial defense through robust Bayesian neural network". In: *ArXiv preprint arXiv:1810.01279*.

Ma, Junshui et al. (2015). "Deep neural nets as a method for quantitative structure–activity relationships". In: *Journal of Chemical Information and Modeling* 55.2, pp. 263–274.

Madry, Aleksander et al. (2018). "Towards Deep Learning Models Resistant to Adversarial Attacks". In: *International Conference on Learning Representations*. URL: https://openreview.net/forum?id=rJzIBfZAb.

Mandt, Stephan, Matthew D. Hoffman, and David M. Blei (2015). "Continuous-time limit of stochastic gradient descent revisited". In: *Neural Information Processing Systems (NIPS)*.

McAuliffe, William H. B. (2015). "How did Abduction Get Confused with Inference to the Best Explanation?" In: *Transactions of the Charles S. Peirce Society: A Quarterly Journal in American Philosophy* 51, pp. 300–319.

Mei, Song, and Andrea Montanari (2021). "The Generalization Error of Random Features Regression: Precise Asymptotics and the Double Descent Curve". In: *Communications on Pure and Applied Mathematics* 75.4, pp. 667–766.

Neal, Radford M. (1995). *Bayesian learning for neural networks*. PhD thesis, University of Toronto.

Neal, Radford M. (2011). "MCMC using Hamiltonian dynamics". In: *Handbook of Markov chain Monte Carlo* 2.11, p. 2.

Noé, Frank et al. (2019). "Boltzmann generators: Sampling equilibrium states of many-body systems with deep learning". In: *Science* 365.6457.

Nüsken, Nikolas, and Lorenz Richter (2021). "Solving high-dimensional Hamilton–Jacobi–Bellman PDEs using neural networks: perspectives from the theory of controlled diffusions and measures on path space". In: *Partial Differential Equations and Applications* 2.4, pp. 1–48.

Opper, Manfred et al. (1990). "On the ability of the optimal perceptron to generalise". In: *Journal of Physics A: Mathematical and General* 23.11, p. L581.

Popper, Karl R. (1984). "Duldsamkeit und intellektuelle Verantwortlichkeit". In: *Auf der Suche nach einer besseren Welt: Vorträge und Aufsätze aus dreißig Jahren*. München: Piper, pp. 303–328.

Quine, Willard Van (1953). "Two dogmas of empiricism". In: *From a logical point of view: Nine logico-philosophical essays*. Vol. 566. Cambridge, MA: Harvard University Press, pp. 20–46.

Rawat, Ambrish, Martin Wistuba, and Maria-Irina Nicolae (2017). "Adversarial phenomenon in the eyes of Bayesian deep learning". In: *ArXiv preprint arXiv:1711.08244*.

Reichenbach, Hans (1949). *The Theory of Probability: An Inquiry Into the Logical and Mathematical Foundations of the Calculus of Probability*. Berkeley: University of California Press.

Rice, Leslie, Eric Wong, and Zico Kolter (2020). "Overfitting in adversarially robust deep learning". In: *International Conference on Machine Learning*. Ed. by Hal Daumé III, and Aarti Singh. Vol. 119. Cambridge MA: JMLR, pp. 8093–8104.

Richter, Julius, Guillaume Carbajal, and Timo Gerkmann (2020). "Speech Enhancement with Stochastic Temporal Convolutional Networks." In: *Interspeech*, pp. 4516–4520.

Richter, Lorenz, Ayman Boustati et al. (2020). "VarGrad: A Low-Variance Gradient Estimator for Variational Inference". In: *Advances in Neural Information Processing Systems* 33, pp. 13481–13492.

Roberts, Daniel A. (2021). "SGD implicitly regularizes generalization error". In: *ArXiv preprint arXiv:2104.04874*.

Ronneberger, Olaf, Philipp Fischer, and Thomas Brox (2015). "U-Net: Convolutional networks for biomedical image segmentation". In: *International Conference on Medical image computing and computer-assisted intervention*. Ed. by Nassir Navab et al. Cham: Springer, pp. 234–241.

Roth, Kevin, Yannic Kilcher, and Thomas Hofmann (2020). "Adversarial Training is a Form of Data-dependent Operator Norm Regularization". In: *Advances in Neural Information Processing Systems* 33, pp. 14973–14985. URL: https://proceedings.neurips.cc/paper/2020/file/ab7314887865c4265e896c6e209d1cd6-Paper.pdf.

Rußwurm, Marc, and Marco Körner (2018). "Multi-temporal land cover classification with sequential recurrent encoders". In: *ISPRS International Journal of Geo-Information* 7.4, p. 129.

Sarker, Iqbal H. (2021). "Deep Learning: A Comprehensive Overview on Techniques, Taxonomy, Applications and Research Directions". In: *SN Computer Science* 2, p. 420.

Shalev-Shwartz, Shai, and Shai Ben-David (2014). *Understanding machine learning: From theory to algorithms*. New York: Cambridge University Press.

Smith, Samuel L. et al. (2021). "On the origin of implicit regularization in stochastic gradient descent". In: *ArXiv preprint arXiv:2101.12176*.

Soudry, Daniel et al. (2018). "The implicit bias of gradient descent on separable data". In: *The Journal of Machine Learning Research* 19.1, pp. 2822–2878.

Sterkenburg, Tom F. (2019). "Putnam's Diagonal Argument and the Impossibility of a Universal Learning Machine". In: *Erkenntnis* 84, pp. 633–656.

Sterkenburg, Tom F., and Peter D. Grünwald (2021). "The No-Free-Lunch Theorems of Supervised Learning". In: *Synthese* 17.4, pp. 519–541.

Szegedy, Christian, Vincent Vanhoucke, et al. (2016). "Rethinking the inception architecture for computer vision". In: *Proceedings of the IEEE conference on computer vision and pattern recognition*, pp. 2818–2826.

Szegedy, Christian, Wojciech Zaremba, et al. (2014). "Intriguing properties of neural networks". In: *ArXiv preprint arXiv:1312.6199*.

Tibshirani, Robert (1996). "Regression Shrinkage and Selection Via the Lasso". In: *Journal of the Royal Statistical Society: Series B (Methodological)* 58.1, pp. 267–288.

Vapnik, Vladimir (1999). *The nature of statistical learning theory*. New York: Springer.

Wang, Yisen et al. (2019). "On the Convergence and Robustness of Adversarial Training". In: *International Conference on Machine Learning*. Ed. by Kamalika Chaudhuri, and Ruslan Salakhutdinov. Vol. 97. Cambridge MA: JMLR, pp. 6586–6595.

Welling, Max, and Yee W. Teh (2011). "Bayesian learning via stochastic gradient Langevin dynamics". In: *International Conference on Machine Learning*. Ed. by Lise Getoor, and Tobias Scheffer. Cambridge MA: JMLR, pp. 681–688.

Wenzel, Florian et al. (2020). "How Good is the Bayes Posterior in Deep Neural Networks Really?" In: *International Conference on Machine Learning*. Ed. by Hal Daumé III, and Aarti Singh. Vol. 119. Cambridge MA: JMLR, pp. 10248–10259.

Wheeler, Gregory (2016). "Machine Epistemology and Big Data". In: *Routledge Companion to Philosophy of Social Science*. Ed. by Lee McIntyre, and Alex Rosenburg. London: Taylor & Francis.

Wolpert, David H. (1996). "The Lack of A Priori Distinctions Between Learning Algorithms". In: *Neural Computation* 8.7, pp. 1341–1390.

Yang, Hongkang, and Weinan E (Aug. 2022). "Generalization and Memorization: The Bias Potential Model". In: *Proceedings of the 2nd Mathematical and Scientific Machine Learning Conference*. Ed. by Joan Bruna, Jan Hesthaven, and Lenka Zdeborova. Vol. 145. Cambridge MA: JMLR, pp. 1013–1043. URL: https://proceedings.mlr.press/v145/yang22a.html.

Yao, Jiayu et al. (2019). "Quality of uncertainty quantification for Bayesian neural network inference". In: *ArXiv preprint arXiv:1906.09686*.

Zhang, Chiyuan, Samy Bengio, et al. (2021). "Understanding deep learning (still) requires rethinking generalization". In: *Communications of the ACM* 64.3, pp. 107–115.

Zhang, Ruqi, A. Feder Cooper, and Christopher De Sa (2020). "AMAGOLD: Amortized Metropolis Adjustment for Efficient Stochastic Gradient MCMC". In: *International Conference on Artificial Intelligence and Statistics*. Ed. by Silvia Chiappa, and Roberto Calandra. Vol. 108. Cambridge MA: JMLR, pp. 2142–2152.

Zhu, Xiao Xiang et al. (2017). "Deep learning in remote sensing: A comprehensive review and list of resources". In: *IEEE Geoscience and Remote Sensing Magazine* 5.4, pp. 8–36.

Zimmermann, Roland S. (2019). "Comment on 'Adv-BNN: Improved Adversarial Defense through Robust Bayesian Neural Network'". In: *ArXiv preprint arXiv:1907.00895*.

Appendix

A. Training of artificial neural networks

Let $\mathcal{F}$ be the set of neural networks $f_\theta = \Phi_\sigma$ of a certain predefined topology (i.e. with a given number of concatenated activation functions, interconnection patterns, etc.) that we want to train. Suppose we have N data points $(x_1, y_1), \ldots, (x_N, y_N)$ where, for simplicity, we assume that $y_n = f(x_n)$ is deterministic. For example, we may think of every x_n having a unique label $y_n = \pm 1$. Training an ANN amounts to solving the regression problem

$$f_\theta(x_n) \approx y_n$$

for all $n = 1, \ldots, N$. Specifically, we seek $\theta \in \Theta$ that minimizes the empirical risk (also: loss landscape)

$$J_N(\theta) = \frac{1}{N} \sum_{n=1}^{N} \ell(f_\theta(x_n), y_n)$$

over some potentially high-dimensional parameter set Θ.[11] There are few cases in which the risk minimization problem has an explicit and unique solution if the number of independent data points is large enough. One such case in which an explicit solution is available is when $f_\theta(x) = \theta^\top x$ is linear

---

11   Recall that we call the empirical risk J_N when considered as a function of parameters θ and $\mathcal{L}_N$ when considered as a function of functions.

and $l(z,y) = |z-y|^2$ is quadratic. This is the classical linear regression problem.

For ANNs, an explicit solution is neither available nor unique, and an approximation to $\widehat{f}_N \approx f^*$ must be computed by an suitable iterative numerical method. One such numerical method is called gradient descent

$$\theta_{k+1} = \theta_k - \eta_k \nabla J_N(\theta_k), \quad k = 0,1,2,3,\ldots,$$

where η_0, η_1, η_2 is a sequence of step sizes, called *learning rate*, that tends to zero asymptotically. For a typical ANN and a typical loss function, the derivative (i.e. the gradient)

$$\nabla J_N(\theta) = \frac{1}{N} \sum_{n=1}^{N} \nabla_\theta \ell(f_\theta(x_n), y_n)$$

with respect to the parameter θ can be computed by what is called *backpropagation*, essentially relying on the chain rule of differential calculus; see, e.g. (Higham/Higham 2019). Since the number of training points, N, is typically very large, evaluating the gradient that is a sum of N terms is computationally demanding, therefore the sum over the training data is replaced by a sum over a random, usually small subsample of the training data. This means that, for fixed θ, the derivative $\nabla J_N(\theta)$ is replaced by an approximation $\nabla \widehat{J}_N(\theta)$ that is random; the approximation has no systematic error, i.e. it equals the true derivative on average, but it deviates from the true derivative by a random amount (that may not even be small, but that is zero on average). As a consequence, we can rewrite our gradient descent as follows:

$$\theta_{k+1} = \theta_k - \eta_k \nabla \widehat{J}_N(\theta_k) + \zeta_k, \quad k = 0,1,2,3,\ldots, \tag{14}$$

where ζ_k is the random error invoked by substituting $\nabla J_N(\theta)$ with $\widehat{J}_N(\theta)$. Since ζ_k is unknown as it depends on the true derivative $\nabla J_N(\theta_k)$ at stage k that cannot be easily computed, the noise term in (14) is ignored in the training procedure, which leads to what is called *stochastic gradient descent* (SGD):

$$\theta_{k+1} = \theta_k - \eta_k \nabla \widehat{J}_N(\theta_k), \quad k = 0,1,2,3,\ldots. \tag{15}$$

Since the right hand side in (15) is random by virtue of the randomly chosen subsample that is used to approximate the true gradient, the outcome of the SGD algorithm after, say, t iterations will always be random.

As a consequence, training an ANN for given data and for a fixed number of training steps, t, multiple times will never produce the same regression function f_θ, but instead a random collection of regression functions. This justifies the idea of a trained neural as a probability distribution $Q(f(t)) = Q(f_{\theta(t)})$ rather than unique function $f(t) = f_{\theta(t)}$ that represents its random state after t training steps.

We should stress that typically, SGD does not converge to the optimal solution (if it converges at all), but rather finds a suboptimal local optimum (if any). From the perspective of mathematical optimization, it is one of the big mysteries of deep learning that despite being only a random and suboptimal solution, the predictions made by the resulting trained network are often suprisingly good Berner et al. 2021: Sec. 1.3. In trying to reveal the origin of this phenomenon, SGD has been analyzed using asymptotic arguments, e.g. (Li/Tai/E 2017, 2019; Mandt/Hoffman/Blei 2015). These methods rely on limit theorems, e.g. (Kushner/Yin 2003), to approximate the random noise term in (14), and they are suitable to understand the performance in the large data setting. However, they are unable to adress the case of finite, not to mention sparse training data. Recently, the finite data situation has been analyzed using backward error analysis, and there is empirical evidence that SGD incorporates an implicit regularization which favors shallow minimization paths that leads to broader minima and (hence) to more robust ANNs (Barrett/Dherin 2020; Smith et al. 2021; Soudry et al. 2018).

B. Optimal prediction and Bayes classifier

For prediction tasks, when the ANN is supposed to predict a quantity $y \in \mathbb{R}$ based on an input $x \in \mathbb{R}^d$, the generalization error is typically measured in the sense of the mean square error (MSE), with the quadratic loss

$$\ell(f(x), y) = (f(x) - y)^2.$$

Let

$$\operatorname{sgn}(z) = \begin{cases} 1, & z > 0 \\ 0, & z = 0 \\ -1, & z < 0 \end{cases}$$

be the sign function. Then, for the binary classification tasks, with $y \in \{-1, 1\}$ and a classifier $f(x) = \operatorname{sgn}(h(x))$ for some function $h \colon \mathbb{R}^d \to \mathbb{R}$

the quadratic loss reduces to what is called the 0-1 loss (up to a multiplicative constant):

$$\frac{1}{4}\ell(f(x), y) = \mathbf{1}_{(-\infty, 0]}(yh(x)) = \begin{cases} 0, & f(x) = y \\ 1, & \text{else}. \end{cases}$$

In this case $\mathcal{L}(f) = \mathbb{P}(Y \neq f(X))$ is simply the probability of misclassification. We define the *regression function*

$$g(x) = \mathbb{E}[Y|X = x]$$

to be the conditional expectation of Y given the observation $X = x$. Then, using the properties of the conditional expectation, the MSE can be decomposed in a Pythagorean type fashion as

$$\begin{aligned}\mathbb{E}[(f(X) - Y)^2] &= \mathbb{E}[(f(X) - g(X) + g(X) - Y)^2] \\ &= \mathbb{E}[(f(X) - g(X))^2] + 2\,\mathbb{E}[(f(X) - g(X))(g(X) - Y)] \\ &\quad + \mathbb{E}[(g(X) - Y)^2] \\ &= \mathbb{E}[(f(X) - g(X))^2] + \mathbb{E}[(g(X) - Y)^2]. \end{aligned}$$

The cross-term disappears since, by the tower property of the conditional expectation,

$$\begin{aligned}\mathbb{E}[(f(X) - g(X))(g(X) - Y)] &= \mathbb{E}[\mathbb{E}[(f(X) - g(X))(g(X) - Y)|X]] \\ &= \mathbb{E}[\mathbb{E}[(f(X) - g(X))g(X)|X]] \\ &\quad - \mathbb{E}[\mathbb{E}[(f(X) - g(X))Y|X]] \\ &= \mathbb{E}[(f(X) - g(X))g(X)] \\ &\quad - \mathbb{E}[(f(X) - g(X))\,\mathbb{E}[Y|X]] \\ &= 0. \end{aligned}$$

As a consequence, we have for all functions f:

$$\mathcal{L}(f) = \mathbb{E}[(f(X) - g(X))^2] + \mathbb{E}[(g(X) - Y)^2] \geq \mathbb{E}[(g(X) - Y)^2]$$

where equality is attained if and only if $f = g$. The findings can be summarized in the following two statements that hold with probability one:[12]

---

[12] If a statement is said to hold *with probability one* or *almost surely*, this means that it is true upon ignoring events of probability zero.

(1) The regression function is the minimizer of the MSE, i.e. we have $g = f^B$, with unique

$$f^B(x) \in \underset{f \in \mathcal{M}(\mathcal{X}, \mathcal{Y})}{\arg\min} \; \mathbb{E}[(f(X) - Y)^2].$$

(2) The MSE can be decomposed as

$$\mathcal{L}(f) = \mathbb{E}[(f(X) - \mathbb{E}[Y|X])^2] + \mathcal{L}^*,$$

where the *Bayes risk* $\mathcal{L}^* = \mathcal{L}(f^B)$ measures the variance of Y for given $X = x$ around its *optimal prediction*

$$f^B(x) = \mathbb{E}[Y|X = x].$$

The reasoning carries over to the classification task with $Y \in \{-1, 1\}$, in which case

$$g(x) = \mathbb{P}(Y = 1|X = x) - \mathbb{P}(Y = -1|X = x)$$

and the *optimal classifier* or *Bayes classifier* can be shown to be

$$f^B(x) = \operatorname{sgn}(g(x)) = \begin{cases} 1, & \mathbb{P}(Y = 1|X = x) > \mathbb{P}(Y = -1|X = x) \\ -1, & \mathbb{P}(Y = 1|X = x) < \mathbb{P}(Y = -1|X = x). \end{cases}$$

Limits and Prospects of Ethics in the Context of Law and Society by the Example of Accident Algorithms of Autonomous Driving

Peter Klimczak

1. Autonomous Driving

At the beginning of 2014, the Society of Automotive Engineers (SAE) published the SAE J3016 standard, which classifies road vehicles, i.e. automobiles, in terms of their automatic functions. SAE J3016 specifies six levels, which – despite a number of alternative classifications, e.g. by ADAC or the German Federal Highway Research Institute ("Autonomes Fahren" 2021) – have since become established even in Germany ("Autonomous Driving" 2018):

- *Level 0: No Automation* – Zero autonomy; the driver performs all the driving, but the vehicle can aid with blind spot detection, forward collision warnings and lane departure warnings.
- *Level 1: Driver Assistance* – The vehicle may have some active driving assist features, but the driver is still in charge. Such assist features available in today's vehicles include adaptive cruise control, automatic emergency braking and lane keeping.
- *Level 2: Partial Automation* – The driver still must be alert and monitor the environment at all times, but driving assist features that control acceleration, braking and steering may work together in unison so the driver does not need to provide any input in certain situations. Such automated functions available today include self-parking and traffic jam assist (stop-and-go traffic driving).
- *Level 3: Conditional Automation* – The vehicle can itself perform all aspects of the driving task under some circumstances, but the human driver must

always be ready to take control at all times within a specified notice period. In all other circumstances, the human performs the driving.
- *Level 4: High Automation* – This is a self-driving vehicle. But it still has a driver's seat and all the regular controls. Though the vehicle can drive and "see" all on its own, circumstances such as geographic area, road conditions or local laws might require the person in the driver's seat to take over.
- *Level 5: Full Automation* – The vehicle is capable of performing all driving functions under all environmental conditions and can operate without humans inside. The human occupants are passengers and need never be involved in driving. A steering wheel is optional in this vehicle.

Until five years ago, there was real euphoria around the development of autonomous cars, but since then developers, established car manufacturers and, even more so, IT companies, above all Google, have become disillusioned. John Krafcik, the CEO of Waymo and, as such, of the subsidiary of Google or rather Alphabet, to which Google outsourced its efforts in the field of self-driving cars in 2017, recently stated that the implementation of autonomous driving is "an extraordinary grind [and] a bigger challenge than launching a rocket and putting it in orbit around the earth" ("Rolling out" 2021).

In fact, we are still at most at level 3 of the SAE standard. The vehicles above this level are still being developed or tested as prototypes and are ready for use only to a very limited extent (on the current state of the art of autonomous vehicles, cf. Kleinschmidt/Wagner 2020: 7). The reasons for the relatively slow progress are of a technical nature: while driving on highways can be machine-sensed and processed sufficiently thanks to artificial intelligence, mixed traffic (cars, cyclists, pedestrians) on rural roads and in residential areas (especially cities) poses a problem that will remain difficult to solve in the future due to the multimodal, polysemous and culturally differentiated communication of the various road users (Färber 2015: 127). While technicians in particular, and linguists and semioticians more marginally, are concerned with these problems, ethicists and lawyers focus on other interrelated problems that are emerging.

The problems being discussed in the areas of ethics and jurisprudence have not yet become acute for manufacturers due to the fact that, currently, neither highly nor fully automated vehicles regularly participate in traffic. However, these ethical and legal questions eventually will arise and will have to be answered by the vehicle manufacturers and third-party providers of hardware and software for autonomous driving – such as Waymo, which ultimately wants to transfer the Android business model from the smartphone sector to the automotive sector[1] –, if the manufacturers do not want to make their product unattractive for customers and thus also investors due to moral sensitivities or real safety interests, or if they want to protect themselves or their own developers from civil and especially criminal prosecution.

Although technical development can continue in isolation from such questions, any failure to answer these ethical and legal questions will inhibit operation and sales and – since technical innovation[2] essentially involves, not least, the offering and selling of a new, innovative product – will prove inhibiting to technical innovation.[3] In this respect, ethics and law should, can and must be regarded as determinants of technical innovation.

---

[1] The business model, namely, of not producing the device, i.e. the smartphone or the car, but 'merely' offering the smartphone operating system or the hardware and software components for autonomous driving and thus achieving market dominance independent of the respective manufacturer.

[2] In my opinion, a successful definition of innovation has been proposed by Hoffmann-Riem, for whom innovations are – to put it simply – "significant, namely practically consequential improvements" that "can be socially desirable or undesirable," whereby the former is the case "if the innovation – for instance in the form of new products, processes or institutions – can contribute to overcoming a problem that is seen as in need of a solution" (Hoffmann-Riem 2016: 12).

[3] In the legal context, these are then legally uncertain conditions. Legal uncertainty – according to a central tenet of political economics – prevents the growth and stability of an economy, since the actors cannot assess the negative legal consequences of their actions (Wagner 1997: 228ff.). That this causal relationship can be transferred from macroeconomics to microeconomics, especially with regard to the realization of innovative technologies, is shown case-specifically in two contributions to the recent volume "Recht als Infrastruktur für Innovationen" (Datta 2019; Servatius 2019). Two older, yet still topical contributions appear in the anthology "Innovationsfördernde Regulierung"; of these, one implicitly (Kühling 2009: 62) and the other explicitly (Roßnagel 2009: 336) addresses said causality. Interestingly – or regrettably – the established introductions and handbooks to technology and innovation management do not address this relationship. See, for example, Abele 2019; Möhrle/Isenmann 2017; Wördenweber et al. 2020; Albers/Gassmann 2005.

2. Accident Algorithms – Law and Ethics in Their (Respective) Discourses

Ethical and legal questions and challenges with regard to autonomous driving are discussed in particular in the context of so-called accident algorithms and these, in turn and taken to the extreme, in the context of so-called trolley problems. Feldle, whose thesis on "Unfallalgorithmen. Dilemmata im automatisierten Straßenverkehr" is comprehensively dedicated to the topic, writes:

> In an unforeseen situation, where a human would only reflexively jerk the wheel around, a technical system can make pragmatic decisions. But even sophisticated "algorithm-driven collision avoidance systems" will not render all accidents avoidable. In extreme scenarios, if multiple interests are threatened, a technical system could in the future determine which legal protected interest is sacrificed for the good of another. Fatal accidents will also be part of this assessment. (Feldle 2018: 22)[4]

The latter in particular, Feldle goes on in the words of Schuster, is "one of the last largely unresolved legal problems of automated road traffic" (Schuster 2017: 13) and he refers to Hörnle's and Wohler's programmatic statement: "We are still only at the beginning of the necessary normative discussion" (Hörnle/Wohlers 2018: 12f.).

Legal treatises deal with ethical issues only marginally and mostly only in the context of noting that ethics has raised the aforementioned trolley problem.[5] A positive exception in this respect is the thesis cited above by Feldle from 2018, which, for example, deals with the position or rather proposals of the two ethicists Helvelke and Nida-Rümelin and subjects them to a legal examination (Feldle 2018: 189ff.). However, even Feldle does not provide an in-depth discussion of the ethical concepts. Conversely, ethical treatises on the trolley problem hardly address the connection between ethics and law. The two monographs by Zoglauer (1997 and 2017) are a welcome exception in this regard. The discussion presented in the following, however,

---

4 Quotations from German sources are translations.
5 Which – as will be seen later – is only half true, since such scenarios, as far as can be reconstructed, were first developed in jurisprudence and then popularized by ethics, with the result that they have found their way back into legal discourse.

differs from Zoglauer's in that, on the one hand, it explicitly deals with autonomous driving and, on the other hand, it does not regard the problems of legal derogation and judicial or supreme court deliberation, which Zoglauer has clearly identified, as a problem, but as a solution – namely as a solution for technical innovations.

It must be clearly stated that I assume that contradictory regulations have a negative effect on technical innovation,[6] which is why risks, and not opportunities, are always in the foreground. If one wishes to and shares the premises and arguments of the following remarks, the more implicit, less explicit call to create regulations can be seen as an opportunity, since, on the one hand, these create (legal) security for technical innovation and, on the other hand, corrections or, formulated more cautiously, changes will continue to be possible at any time thanks to the discursive character of ethics and law. By contrast, non-regulations offer neither security nor, by their very nature, the possibility of correction, since the latter would first require something that could be corrected.

One can of course take the position that non-regulations and absolute freedoms would be conducive, even indispensable, for technical innovation.[7] However, I would counter that in the case of accident algorithms, and especially in the case of accident algorithms in the context of the inevitable endangerment of human life, an extremely sensitive area, both ethically and legally, is involved and undesirable developments or an "anything goes" approach in such sensitive areas leads to a dramatic reduction in the trust and acceptance of society and consumers for a technical innovation (Klimczak et al. 2019: 44f.). Moreover, we are no longer in the initial stages of this technical development, in which prohibitions on thinking can indeed have a negative impact on technical innovation (Hoffmann-Riem 2016: 262ff.), but rather on the threshold of realizing the technology at issue.

---

6   If a contradiction cannot be resolved (see below, in particular with regard to the derogation principles), the situation would again be one of legal uncertainty. On legal uncertainty, see the remarks in the footnotes above.
7   This view was especially true in the 1980s and 1990s. Cf. Hoffmann-Riem 2016: 26f.

3. Human and Machine Decisions about Life and Death

For (almost) all of the following reflections on autonomous driving, a situation is assumed – as already mentioned – in which an accident with fatal personal injury has become unavoidable. One possible variation on such a scenario would be that an autonomously driving vehicle is driving on a country road. Two other vehicles are coming towards it, due, for example, to an unsuccessful overtaking maneuver. In the car that is in the same lane as the autonomously driving car, i.e. in the passing car, there are three occupants, while there is only one person in the other lane, i.e. in the car being overtaken. The only choices the vehicle AI has with regard to steering (i.e. longitudinal movement) are to keep to its lane, i.e. to make no changes, or to change lanes, i.e. to behave actively. In the first case (lane keeping), three people are killed, in the second case (lane changing), one person is killed.[8]

Examples like these are adaptations of a popular thought experiment in ethics that was introduced by Karl Engisch from a criminal law perspective[9] in his habilitation thesis in Law in 1930, and which Philippa Foot reformulated in 1967,[10] this time in English and in a moral philosophical context (as a comparative case for the abortion issue that was her actual focus); this experiment subsequently became extremely well-known (with active participation by Foot) as the trolley problem. Owing to the chronology, the thought experiments of Engisch, Foot and others do not in any way involve autonomous vehicles, and so the central difference between these classical case descriptions and those adapted for autonomous driving is between the different deciding agents. Therefore, the question that should be pursued by means of the original thought experiments is as to which premises, which presup-

---

8   For similar scenarios in the context of autonomous driving, see the list of common types in Schäffner 2020: 29f.
9   Cf. Engisch 1930: 288. Verbatim (in translation): "It may be that a switchman, in order to prevent an imminent collision which will in all probability cost a large number of human lives, directs the train in such a way that human lives are also put at risk, but very much less so than if he were to let things take their course."
10 Verbatim: "To make the parallel as close as possible it may rather be supposed that he is the driver of a runaway streetcar which he can only steer from one narrow track on to another; five men are working on one track and one man on the other; anyone on the track he enters is bound to be killed" (Foot 1967: 8).

positions form the basis when people make moral decisions:[11] as a driver, do I steer into the car in the oncoming lane because I see only one occupant there and spare the three people in the car that is in my lane? Or would I rather collide with the three occupants, i.e. accept more deaths, because in this case I do not have to actively intervene in the steering and the choice is therefore made by omission?

Such questions – and this is the unintended point of the original thought experiment – are of a completely counterfactual nature (Hevelke/ Nida-Rümelin 2015: 8): In a real-case scenario, the driver would not make a considered moral decision, but an instinctive one (Dilich et al. 2002: 238).[12] The rationality of human decision-making is limited even in such situations that do not take place under emotional and temporal pressure, because people have access to only limited information in decision-making situations and their capacities to process it as well as to consider the consequences of different options are limited (Klimczak et al. 2019: 41): people, therefore, fundamentally decide all too often on the basis of intuition and emotions without careful analysis, which is why human decisions are always susceptible to different types of cognitive distortions.

In contrast to human decision-making, machine decision-making is necessarily based on a calculation and thus an assessment.[13] However, this calculation is determined in advance: fundamental decisions must already be made during the development of the AI in question. This applies not only in the case of 'classical' AI programming due to the algorithms that need to be written, but also in the case of so-called machine learning procedures. For the latter, the selection and processing of training data is also added as a further decision. The machine decision is then the result of a calculation and only of a calculation. Thus, an automated decision process is free of cognitive distortions, but in general, and in the case of machine learning in particular, not free of 'biases' (Klimczak et al. 2019: 41): for example,

---

11 Accordingly, Foot immediately follows on from the quote above: "The question is why we should say, without hesitation, that the driver should steer for the less occupied track, while most of us would be appalled at the idea that the innocent man could be framed" (1967: 8).
12 The fact that people normally have no difficulty in explaining their decisions a posteriori/ex post does not change the fact that this decision did not actually come about in this way. It is a constructed, verbal rationality, not a factual one. Cf. Klimczak et al. 2019: 39.
13 Cf. here and in the following: Berkemer/Grottke 2023.

a character recognizer (OCR) expects to recognize the letter E much more readily than the letter X, which is justified rationally by the much higher frequency of the former, the so-called a priori probability, in the written German language. However, precisely this justified bias can lead to wrong decisions in individual cases. For this reason, the fact that migrants are underrepresented in management positions also leads to the fact that an algorithm based on a corresponding data set will hire fewer migrants.[14]

Since such objectively wrong decisions are grounded in the data set, AI applications based on machine learning principles nevertheless make exclusively rational decisions in the sense of both practical rationality – oriented to the relationship between ends and means – and formal rationality – i.e. based on universal rules.[15] For Artificial Intelligence, there is no room for spontaneity, no possibility of deviation from the calculations. This is true, even if popular and press opinion say otherwise, with regard to every AI procedure, hence also with regard to the currently fashionable machine learning, e.g. by means of neuronal networks. The difference between the former and the latter methods is not that the processes of neural networks are not completely computable (they absolutely are), but that they are neither formal-semantically nor intuitively interpretable, since the immense number of neuron connections is utterly incomprehensible for humans, which is why the former method is also counted among the white box methods, the latter among the black box methods (which also include hidden Markov models) (Klimczak et al. 2019: 40f.).

This means, on the one hand, that humans explicitly and implicitly (the latter through the provision of training data in the case of machine learning procedures) define criteria according to which decisions are then made by the AI in specific cases. On the other hand, this means that the purely counterfactual question in the original thought experiment about the basis of each moral decision and thus about the ethical legitimacy or justifiability of this decision basis now actually becomes relevant and virulent.

---

14 Pattern recognition, which inherently underlies machine learning, thus develops a performative effect that not only reproduces but also naturalizes detected similarities and differences. Cf. Chun 2018.

15 On these and other types of rationality following Max Weber, see Kalberg 1980.

4. Utilitarianism or Consequentialism

An oft-discussed approach in the technology discourse to answering the question of which of the two oncoming cars the autonomous driving vehicle should collide with is so-called utilitarianism. The goal of the utilitarian approach is the mathematical optimization of the benefit and harm consequences of an action (Zoglauer 1997: 161). Since it can be operationalized by machines, such an approach seems not only technically feasible,[16] but, at first glance, also rational, precisely because it can be operationalized by machines. While the former, i.e. technical feasibility, seems to be promising for the development of AI algorithms and thus technical innovations, the latter, i.e. rationality, seems to justify the utilitarian approach from the very outset in a society in which rationality is one (if not the most important) legitimation criterion: 'modern' societies are, after all, characterized not least by the fact that they are permeated by expectations of rationality. Accordingly, rule-governed decisions made on the basis of algorithms are evidence of the highest rationality (Meyer/Jepperson 2000; Lemke 2000).[17]

The problems in the concrete application or operationalization of utilitarian approaches, however, start with what shall be considered harm and what shall be considered benefit and how both are to be quantified. Let us first turn to the simpler question: the consequences of harm. In the context of the above example, it was assumed that the killing of all occupants of the respective vehicle is inevitable. A differentiation can only be made with regard to the number of fatalities. In this respect, a calculation as the comparison of the sums would be a simple and conceivable criterion.[18]

It would be more difficult if the crash did not lead to the death of all occupants but to injuries of varying severity. This would fall outside the actual scope of our deliberations, namely, the endangerment of at least two human lives and thus the question of the sparing and simultaneous sacrifice

---

16   Cf. Goodall 2014 or, more recently, Gerdes/Thornton 2015.
17   In this context, the myth of the computer as the embodiment of the ideal of rationality should not be underestimated. Cf.Kuhlmann 1985.
18   The questioning of a summation of deaths is quite justified; however, it is the result of a view that the death (or, in milder terms, the injury) of a person is accepted in order to spare others this death and is thus only a means to an end, in this case the rescue of other persons. This view, however, is one that arises from or corresponds to deontological ethics.

of one or the other human life, since it would then only be about (differing) non-fatal personal injury or about the contrast between fatal and non-fatal injury. However, just such a scenario shows the fundamental problems of utilitarianism most clearly, since questions like the following would now arise: how are the injuries to be weighted? Are they to be summed up in the case of several injured persons? How many non-lethal injuries outweigh one dead person? Can a death be weighed against other things at all? Such scoring may seem odd, but the valuation of injuries and even death is common in the insurance industry (Daniel/Ignatieva/Sherris 2019; Cristea/Mitu 2008). The difference, however, is that here, on the basis of such scoring, concrete decisions are made about for whom an injury or even death should be brought about, and not just whether or not an insurance policy should be effected. The relatively simple operationalization in utilitarianism is thus preceded by serious moral decisions.

The situation becomes even more difficult if not only the consequences of damage are included in the calculation (which then would also point in the direction of risk ethics – but more on this later), but if these are set off against the benefit, as is common in utilitarian approaches in the tradition of Bentham and Mill (Bentham 2013; Mill 2009). While in the case of harm, this could, in the context of personal injury as seen above, be relatively easily calculated from the probability, severity and duration of an injury (up to and including death), and only the scoring poses moral problems, in the case of benefit, the very determination of what is to be considered a benefit is problematic. What is benefit in the context of personal injury anyway? The most obvious, simplest, but perhaps also most trivial answer would be: the absence of harm. But this would define benefit as complementary to harm and vice versa. This is precisely not the case in utilitarianism (Zoglauer 1997: 160ff.). Moreover: a determination of benefit independent of harm would become inevitable at the very latest if the harm were to be the same in the case of both decisions, which would have to be assumed a priori in the scenario of the alternative death of at least one person.

The question of utility in the context of – not only fatal, but especially fatal – personal injury comes down to the question of the individual and thus differential value of people or groups of people. This insight is not only the result of howsoever informed, yet introspective considerations in the sense of monological ethics, but is also substantiated on a broad empirical basis. In particular, the specific studies and surveys of Rahwan et al. have shown that people make valuations about people even, or indeed especially, in the context of the trolley problem and thus in the case of (fatal) personal injury (Rahwan et al. 2018): for example, people socialized in Western cultures decide against elderly occupants, thus allowing the autonomous vehicle to collide with the vehicle in which elderly people are seated. In the eastern, i.e. Asian, cultural sphere, on the other hand, people decide against younger occupants. Seniority is apparently attributed a higher value there. Should age therefore to be taken into account in the AI's decision? And what about gender? Profession? Or with regard to China: social reputation, determined within the framework of the Social Credit System? Is such culturally dependent scoring justifiable?[19] Or is it, on the contrary, a necessity?[20]

So as not to be misunderstood: the questions raised above regarding the definition of benefit as well as the respective quantification of benefit and harm are not only difficult to answer morally (from a non-utilitarian point of view), but also pragmatically (from a utilitarian point of view). However, once they have been answered or the relevant valuations have been made, the decision can be effected mathematically and mechanically.

For utilitarianism, a decision on the physical integrity of persons – even and especially up to and including a decision on their death – on the basis of a harm-benefit calculation – is completely unproblematic, i.e. legitimate, from a moral point of view (Singer 2013: 207). Accordingly, utilitarianism could, on the one hand, provide the development of accident algorithms with the legitimacy for a machine decision about life and death, while, on the other hand, it generates from the considerations gained through thought experiments a whole scope of criteria to be considered. Whether with the current state of the art it is technically possible to account for every criterion is initially irrelevant: on the one hand, because following an old legal principle[21] what is not possible is not obligatory. Its non-consideration is therefore not a problem in itself. On the other hand, because what is not

---

19 For a critique of cultural relativism, see Zoglauer 2017: 253ff. and Zoglauer 2021.
20 The problem of whether harm and benefit of an action can be set off against each other at all (Zoglauer 1997: 163f.) will be left aside for the time being (and the reader is referred to the section on risk ethics below), since we are not concerned here with moral problems of utilitarianism but rather, in keeping with the topic, with procedural difficulties, i.e. those concerning operationalization/calculation.
21 This idea appeared in Roman law in various expressions, the variety of which also reflects its significance: "Ultra posse nemo obligatur", "Impossibilium nulla obligatio", "Impotentia excusat legem", "Nemo dat quod non habet", "Nemo potest ad impossibile obligari". Cf. Depenheuer 2014: para. 4.

possible today will be possible tomorrow and the criterion that cannot yet be technically implemented, by the fact that it has been thought of, shows the way for development.[22]

5. Deontological or Duty Based Ethics

While in the utilitarian paradigm a valuation of people and the setting off of their respective worth is no problem, both contradict the deontological prohibition of setting off or instrumentalizing humans in the spirit of Kant. Kant formulates the 'practical imperative' in his 1785 work "Grundlegung der Metaphysik der Sitten" as follows: "Act in such a way that you treat humanity, whether in your person or in the person of any other, never merely as a means, but at all times also as an end" (Kant AA IV: 429/Terence 2009: 45). Twelve years later, this was stated in greater detail in "Metaphysics of Morals":

> But a human being considered as a person, i.e., as a subject of a morally practical reason, is above all price. For as such (homo noumenon) he is not to be valued merely as a means to the ends of other people, or even to his own ends, but as an end in himself. This is to say, he possesses a dignity (an absolute inner worth), by which he exacts respect for himself from all other rational beings in the world, can measure himself against each member of his species, and can value himself on a footing of equality with them. (Kant AA VI: 434f.)

Two facts are decisive in this context: first, a human being (as a person) is "an ends in himself" and must never be misused "merely as a means." What is meant by this is that people may not be instrumentalized to achieve ends other than as ends in themselves, which would be the case in the scenario of sacrificing or harming a human life for the purpose of saving other human lives, even if it be several. The decisive factor is action, the human being as agent, so that, as will become even clearer in the following, the difference between action, or active action, and non-action, or omission,

---

22 At this stage, or perhaps already at a point beyond it, is probably where the metaverse that Mark Zuckerberg is currently massively advancing with his company Meta (formerly: Facebook) finds itself, in which even Goldman Sachs sees the future ("Goldman Sachs" 2022).

gains the highest relevance in practice. The vehicle AI in our AI thought experiment would, in any case, have to change lanes in order to spare the three occupants, thereby, through the death or injury of one human as a consequence of this action, misusing one human as a means to the end of saving the other three. However, offsets and instrumentalizations of humans are prohibited in the deontological paradigm.

The second important fact that arises from the passage quoted above from "Metaphysics of Morals" is the justification or derivation of the self-purpose of humans: a human is "above all price." This implies, on the one hand, the impossibility of determining the worth of a human being in relation to a commodity or a currency and, on the other hand, or rather as a consequence thereof, that no human being is worth more or less than another (Zoglauer 2017: 62). Thus, the attribution or determination and, consequently, calculation of any kind of benefit of a non-harming of human beings is not permissible. The equality of human beings that goes hand in hand with this absolute human dignity also prohibits the preferential treatment or disadvantaging of human beings, which, as will be seen below, is turned around and used as an argument in risk ethics for a harm-minimizing approach. First, however, let us consider in greater detail the consequences for a decision based on duty-based ethics of the dilemma discussed here.

Kant's prohibition of instrumentalization ultimately boils down to a non-harm principle that Zoglauer describes as follows: "Let nature take its course and do not actively intervene in events if it is foreseeable that innocent people will die as a result of the intervention" (Zoglauer 1997: 73). In the context of accident algorithms, one must not be led astray by the adjective "innocent". Even if the driver of the passing car in our scenario had proceeded to pass despite overtaking being prohibited, he would not be a "guilty" person. The term "innocent" in the aforementioned quote derives from thought experiments previously discussed by Zoglauer, including the scenario of a hijacked airplane with hostages to be used as a terrorist weapon, leading to the question of shooting down or not shooting down the plane, which would not only involve the death of the "guilty" hijackers/terrorists[23], but also of the "innocent" hostages. In our scenario, however, there can be no question of a comparable differentiation. It can be assumed that in the case of road traffic, "innocent" people are always involved. In the case of a dilemma with

---

23   On the thoroughly problematic concept of terrorist, see Klimczak/Petersen 2015.

necessary (fatal) personal injury, as discussed here for accident algorithms, this would mean that the AI would always be forced to non-action, to passivity. Specifically, the vehicle AI in our example would not be allowed to and would not change lanes, so would have to keep to its lane, resulting in the killing of three persons and not 'only' one person. While in utilitarianism the difference between action and non-action or omission of an action is morally irrelevant – hence action and non-action/omission are completely equal (Wolf 1993: 393) – duty-based ethics, as already touched upon above, rests on a rigorous differentiation, which would always lead to the AI not acting.

This non-action is not to be confused with the AI delegating the decision back to the human driver, which would be tantamount to freeing up the decision. The decision of an AI programmed on the basis of duty-based ethics would already have been made with the decision for non-action. The decision for non-action on the part of the AI is thus accompanied by the impossibility of action on the part of the human, which is much more far-reaching than an analogous decision for a human decision-maker: for a human decision-maker, the instrumentalization prohibition and the non-harm principle merely add up to precisely that: a prohibition or a principle, which can be violated or broken. An 'ought' does not necessarily entail an 'is'; human decision-makers can (and persistently do) disregard prohibitions and can, as such, decide otherwise. For an AI machine, however, an 'ought' goes hand in hand with an 'is'.[24]

This is a complete deprivation of the human being of the right of decision in an existential situation, namely one of life and death. Even if this may seem absurd, this disenfranchisement is actually inherent in the concept of autonomous driving, namely as a positive goal and as the highest achievable level 5 of the previously cited SAE standard for autonomous driving. The reader may remember:

> Level 5: Full Automation – The vehicle is capable of performing all driving functions under all environmental conditions and can operate without humans inside. The human occupants are passengers and need never be involved in driving. A steering wheel is optional in this vehicle. ("Autonomous Driving" 2018)

---

24   Cf. also and especially from a formal logic perspective Klimczak et al. 2014: 89.

While the SAE does not rule out a steering wheel or other control devices, but also does not regard them to be necessary anymore, this is generally seen as the main feature of Level 5: "Level 5 vehicles do not require human attention – the 'dynamic driving task' is eliminated. Level 5 cars won't even have steering wheels or acceleration/braking pedals" ("The 6 Levels" 2022).

Against the background of a conception of humanity based on autonomy, such a state of affairs may seem untenable, but delegating the decision to the person in the car would not help in such a situation, since, on the one hand, autonomous cars at level 5 should be able to carry out empty journeys, i.e. journeys without human occupants, as well as journeys with persons who do not have the capacity to drive a car, be they children, disabled persons or simply persons without a driving license. On the other hand, as various studies have shown (Merat et al. 2014; Lin 2015: 71f.), even the presence of a person who would be qualified to control the car would not help because, unless they had sufficiently monitored the driving process in advance, they would not be able to survey the situation quickly enough to make a decision that is at least to some extent conscious (albeit intuitive or instinctive). The 'decision' of the human driver, who would be thrown into a life-and-death situation, would thus ultimately amount to a random decision.[25]

Nevertheless, or for this very reason, such non-action of the AI, such necessary non-action, even if it could be easily programmed or executed as a non-action as an accident algorithm, hardly seems acceptable. While in the context of AI decisions or machine decisions the non-acceptability of a rigorous, invariable non-action becomes particularly apparent, because in this way the 'ought' of duty-based ethics becomes a realized 'is', even in the case of the discussion of non-action in the context of human decision-making, invariable non-action has been regarded as unsatisfactory.[26]

6. Hazard Diversion or Hazard Prevention

Accordingly, positions have been taken and proposals made in ethics as to the conditions under which, in the case of harmful non-action, harmful ac-

---

25 On chance, particularly in the context of machine-produced chance, see below.
26 This discomfort or dissatisfaction is most evident in that alternative proposals are being seriously discussed or suggested in the discourse as solutions, at least some of which will be outlined in the next section.

tion would be permitted as an alternative. The irony is that the decision for harmful action or harmful non-action is ultimately based on utilitarian criteria. For instance, Foot had already argued in her trolley example for acting and thus killing one person while saving the five people who would have been killed in the case of non-action, because more lives can be saved in this way (Foot 1997: 193). The fact that such a damaging, but precisely damage-minimizing, action is permitted is justified by her with the imperative of hazard prevention: it is – in Zoglauer's words – "merely diverting a danger not caused by oneself from a large crowd (five people) to a smaller crowd (one person)" (Zoglauer 2017: 242). Harmful action, if it redirects danger for the purpose of averting danger, is permitted. Anything that is not a mere diversion, on the other hand, would not be permissible:

> So we could not start a flood to stop a fire, even when the fire would kill more than the flood, but we could divert a flood to an area in which fewer people would be drowned. (Foot 1980: 159f.)

In respect to our example and the context accident algorithms, this would mean that a literal 'steering' of the vehicle and the ensuing collision with the one-passenger vehicle in the oncoming lane would be allowed because a hazard, the inevitable collision with one of the two cars, is imminent and the action, the change of lanes, would involve damage minimization.

What, however, would in our context or rather example be the analogous case for the flood that Foot considers not to be covered by the imperative of hazard prevention, namely the one triggered in a damage-minimizing manner in order to contain a fire? In the context of the trolley problem, it is worth referring to the so-called Fat Man thought experiment. This trolley variation, introduced by Thomson, assumes that the five people on the track could be saved by pushing a fat man off a bridge, since he would bring the streetcar to a halt with his corpulence, while, however, dying in the process (1976: 204). In this case, it is scarcely possible to speak of a diversion of danger and thus of hazard prevention: the trolley car, which no longer can be braked, could not otherwise possibly have run over the fat man and thus killed him – this would be different in the case of a flying object hazard. The fat man is a person completely uninvolved in and unrelated to the event.

Although in the context of this thought experiment it is sometimes pointed out that his being pushed off the bridge and thus his death can be seen as a means to the end of saving the five people (e.g. Zoglauer 2017: 78, 80) – which is also true –, this argument also applies to the change of lanes of the trolley car and the subsequent killing of the one person on the siding. The twist of the imperative of hazard prevention or hazard diversion lies precisely in the fact that it can indeed be used to justify a damaging action that results in a (quantitative) minimization of damage, but in the realization of this the injured party or parties was or were nevertheless turned into a means to an end, namely that minimization of damage. The exclusion of uninvolved or unrelated persons from the requirement to avert danger thus represents a restriction of the permission to act in a harmful manner for the purpose of utilitarian harm minimization.

With regard to the case of accident algorithms being considered here, however, an analogous case can hardly be described: after all, this scenario is literally about steering away from danger. The car with the three occupants approaching in the wrong lane is a participant in road traffic, thus it is not uninvolved.[27] This might also be true in an extended thought experiment for a pedestrian whose damage-minimizing crossing might offer itself as an alternative or third decision option: pedestrians are also road users. And even if the pedestrian were not a road user but were walking on the grass with an appropriate distance to the roadway, it would in this case still be the diverted danger, namely the car, that would run him over and prevent the deaths of the three occupants in the other car. Whether the scenario can still be considered realistic or not is irrelevant: the notion that the fat man could bring a streetcar to a halt with his corpulence is also highly improbable. The point is merely to show that all those potentially injured by an AI's driving decisions are involved or affected when it comes to danger prevention.

If we focus on the difference between participation and non-participation in the Fat Man thought experiment, no restriction on the prohibition of danger prevention and thus also no restriction on the permission to act in a harmful way can be deduced for the original trolley scenario. However, the Fat Man thought experiment presents another difference to the classical trolley case: it is not the trolley driver who performs the action, but a third party outside the object of danger, in this case outside the trolley. Thus, one could say that not only the injured party is a bystander, but also the injuring

---

27 Unless one defines bystanders by the fact that they do not come to harm in the case of the choice of omission, which would be an extremely trivial definition and would also lead to one never being able carry out a diversion of danger, which would make no sense in the context of the discussion of exceptions of danger diversions or would render them obsolete because no danger diversion would be permitted at all.

party. The injurer in the Fat Man case is not directly part of the danger, but nevertheless decides. Against this backdrop, the question of the status of the decision-making AI in the autonomous vehicle is almost unavoidable. Can an entity that is not a living being as a machine and can therefore suffer material damage but not personal injury still be said to be involved or affected? [28]

If the (direct) involvement of the injuring party in a hazard were to be regarded as a necessary prerequisite for the hazard prevention imperative and if the AI in the autonomous vehicle could not be assumed to be a direct participant, then the concept of hazard prevention and thus the permission to actively inflict harm for a harm-minimizing purpose would be ruled out for accident algorithms. What is at question is whether the involvement of the injuring party is actually a prerequisite: Foot's flood example, after all, assumes a person diverting the flood whose participation or affectedness is not further specified. And regardless of how exactly participation or affectedness of the damaging party is defined, the definitions will always be those for human decision-makers and not for machine decision-makers, whose being involved or affected is of an essential, i.e. metaphysical or ontological nature. In other words: either the imperative of hazard prevention leads to the fact that AI, being AI, will have to decide for non-action, as in the case of strict duty-based ethics, or to the fact that decisions will be made according to a harm-minimizing approach.[29]

---

28   In addition, it can be assumed that an AI in an autonomous vehicle will not be a local AI, but a decentralized cloud AI that is not on site at all, which means that participation is also not spatially given.

29   Regardless of whether the actual utilitarian approach is rejected due to the impossibility of offsetting benefits and harms or the problem of quantifying and defining benefits (see above) since this necessarily presupposes an individual-specific valuation of people, a harm-minimizing approach with risk ethics seems to be gaining ground, especially in the context of autonomous driving. The circle around Julian Nida-Rümelin (Hevelke/Nida-Rümelin 2015) does not, at any rate, see this as a violation of Kant's prohibition of instrumentalization. Other modifying concepts such as that of voluntariness, which have been designed and discussed for medical scenarios (Zoglauer 2017: 108ff.), do not need to be discussed here, since either no one in road traffic would explicitly accept consequences of harm voluntarily, or everyone in road traffic would have to accept consequences of harm voluntarily by implication of their participation in road traffic.

7. The Non-binding Nature of Ethics

Recapitulating what has been presented so far, it can be said: a utilitarian benefit-harm calculation is not justifiable on the basis of deontological ethics; the non-harm principle of deontological ethics, in turn, violates the utilitarian approach of thinking about a decision from the point of view of consequences. Thus, both ethical paradigms contradict each other – and not only that: both utilitarianism and duty-based ethics reach moral limits when viewed unbiasedly. Since ethics is not a natural science in which, due to the object area, a correspondence-theoretical approach between scientific statements and reality[30] is at least to some extent given, there is also in principle no reason in case of contradictory models of thought to ascribe a higher quality to the one than to the other.[31] And even models of truth and validity based on consensus and coherence (Zoglauer 2007: 250ff.) do not lead to success with regard to deciding in favor of one or the other ethics model.

To put it more succinctly: there is no compelling, necessary reason why the deontological notion of a prohibition of instrumentalization should be accepted without reservation. And the presented concepts of hazard prevention or diversion or those of risk ethics have shown (in an exemplary way) that possibilities for a restriction or a combination of deontological and utilitarian approaches are at least being sought or seriously entertained and thought through in the deontological paradigm. Regardless of whether a rigorous utilitarianism, a rigorous duty-based ethics, or a combination of both approaches is considered valid and thus action-guiding for specific decision-making and, in this context, for technical development and innovation, these are decisions, positings, none of which are obligatory.

Against the background of discursive theories of truth and decision, there have always been proposals for a procedural model in ethics – e.g. Rawls' (1951) "competent moral judges" who should make binding moral judgments or decisions – but it has never advanced as far as an institutionalization of ethical authorities. This is hardly surprising, since ethics is

---

30   Even if one were to accept the statistically recorded and calculated moral perception of society as just that very empirical basis, this is, as touched on in the text and footnotes above, at least in part culturally relative, both synchronously between cultures and diachronically within a culture.
31   On this and the following aspect, see Zoglauer 1997: 229–274.

a science, and even though certain schools of thought dominate in every science and their dominance is not only rationally justified but also strongly dependent on social factors (Kuhn 1962), science sees itself as free and open, which runs counter to explicit institutionalization.

8. Interdependencies between Ethics, Law and Society I

The lack of institutionalization in ethics and an associated procedural model for moral decisions/judgments is, however, also logical for another reason: with law, specifically law-making and jurisprudence, institutions already exist which, on the one hand, make judgments or decisions concerning morality and, on the other hand, are most closely intermingled or linked with ethical paradigms and discourses in ethics. Legislation – at least in functioning democracies – is based either directly or indirectly, at best ex ante, but at the least ex post, on a societal consensus as part of a societal discourse (Kunz/Mona 2015: 6ff.). Admittedly, this discourse might only in the rarest cases obey the rules of an ideal discourse as developed by Habermas (1981a, 1981b, 1984), Alexy (1994, 1995, 2004) et al. in the context of discourse ethics, precisely because in pluralistic industrial and post-industrial representative democracies not all discourse participants can – neither qualitatively nor quantitatively – have their say equally, be heard equally, have equal opportunity to access information and also actually participate in the discourse.[32] Moreover, topics and opinions that are considered taboo are virtually precluded from discourse, and opinions and views in general are even viewed with prejudice from the outset. Although, therefore, even in democracies there are no discourses free of domination in the sense of Habermas, in democratic systems with a reasonably functioning interplay of executive and legislative decision-making on the basis of the determination by voters of the majority composition of the legislature,[33] the will of society is reflected in legislation, i.e. in lawmaking.

This linkage is, therefore, of essential significance, since otherwise, due to the largely alternative-free, legally positivist functioning of legislation, it

---

32   On real discourses or practical discourses as distinct from ideal discourses (especially in the context of law), cf. Alexy 1995: 123ff.
33   Which can be provided for to a certain extent, in purely functional terms, by a sufficient alternation of government and opposition.

would be disconnected from the societal discourse. Extensive, positivistic lawmaking is, at least practically, without alternative because otherwise, on the one hand, legal decisions in the absence of legislation would be arbitrary, since they would depend on the individual sense of justice of the decision-maker (Kriele 1991: 135) and, on the other hand, legislation according to natural law would be constantly susceptible to the danger of the naturalistic fallacy (Zoglauer 1997: 204), i.e. the deduction of 'ought' from 'is'. Thus, however – i.e. due to the linkage of essentially positivist lawmaking to the societal discourse in democratic systems – the expert discourse on ethics can find its way into legislation, on the one hand, because it is itself connected to the broad societal discourse in a complex, diffuse interplay, and, on the other hand, because in the case of an indirect democracy it can indirectly influence lawmaking in the form of expert commissions and the advisory systems of political decision-makers.[34] Therefore, even if no ethical paradigm has any more claim to validity than another, one paradigm can and will dominate the ethical discourse and then most likely prevail in the societal discourse, thus ultimately forming the basis of institutionalized lawmaking.[35/36]

However, it is not only lawmaking that is institutionalized and standardized, but also a second, quite inseparable component, namely case law: statutory law, i.e. laws, not only can but also do necessarily contradict each other; this is, on the one hand, because different dominant ethical paradigms that existed at different times over the course of perpetual lawmaking formed the basis of the legislation, and, on the other hand, because the contradictory nature of the laws is even intended, since, by virtue of institutionalized case law, there is the possibility to weigh up and decide on a case-specific basis. The fundamental rights addressed in the case of accident algorithms, in particular, contradict or clash with each other to the greatest possible extent.

---

34   In the context of autonomous driving, see in particular the ethics committees of the German Federal Ministry of Transport, which, however, will not be considered in detail here, since their statements are not only non-binding but in the main also very vague; this must almost inevitably be the case, not only because the ethical discourse is pluralistic, but also, as described above, no school of thought can lay claim to (absolute) truth and will, therefore, in the normal case, i.e. with a heterogeneous composition of committee members, not be able to establish itself.
35   This will become clear in the next section when we look at legal issues.
36   In this respect, I disagree with the positivist understanding of law and morality as two independent norm spheres (cf. Kelsen 1979: 102 and, as overview, Zoglauer 1997: 133).

Regardless of the legal discourse on whether laws actually contradict each other in formal/formal-logical terms, only seem to contradict each other or do not contradict each other at all,[37] law has developed a number of derogation principles, such as the lex superior derogat legi inferiori rule, according to which a higher level rule abrogates a lower one, the lex specialis derogat legi generali rule, according to which a special rule takes precedence over a general one, or the lex posterior derogat legi priori, according to which newer rules override older ones.[38]

However, these derogation principles do not apply or help in cases where the conflicting rules have the same level of relevance or generality or were enacted at the same time. All this is not only the case with the aforementioned fundamental rights, but as prima facie norms they are even designed to be so: they are characterized precisely by the fact that their validity is systemically limited by other norms with which they compete, i.e. which contradict them (Alexy 1994: 87ff.). If the facts of a case indicate the application of two competing prima facie norms resulting in a conflict of principles, judicial balancing must come into play. A court must decide which norm takes precedence in the case in question. Kelsen allows this primacy of judicial decision to apply not only in the case of prima facie norms, but also when a judge's decision runs counter to established derogation principles (Kelsen 1979: 175ff.). The problem of a possible arbitrariness of judicial decisions associated with this is mitigated, at least to some extent, by the existence of several judicial instances and the possibility of taking legal action against judicial decisions.

Even if the judgment of the respective highest court must be accepted, regardless of whether it is seen to be just or unjust, and this judgment, moreover, will have, as a decision of the highest court, model character for future judgments at a lower level and thus become law itself, so to speak,[39] one cannot go so far as to claim that the whole of law "depends solely on the volition of judicial organs" (Zoglauer 1997: 136). At least in the medium and long term, in the event that a supreme court decision violates society's sense of justice, this sense of justice will assert itself through the influence

---

37   For a detailed sketch of this discourse from the perspective of the formal logician, see Zoglauer 1997: 125–146.
38   On derogation in detail, cf. Wiederin 2011: 104ff.
39   See Schick 2011 for a detailed discussion of the topics of interpretation and further development of the law.

of societal discourse[40] on the composition and decisions of the legislative branch as well as the filling of vacancies in the respective highest court or will at least find expression in some other milder form.[41]

9. The Judgment on the Aviation Security Act

As far as is apparent, there is no treatise dealing with the trolley problem in the context of autonomous driving that does not also extensively refer to or at least mention the ruling of the German Federal Constitutional Court (BVerfG) of February 15, 2006 on the Aviation Security Act (LuftSiG). The background to the LuftSiG was the attacks of September 11, 2001, in the United States and the debate that began in Germany in the aftermath as to how preventive action could be taken in a similar scenario (Feldle 2018: 146): in the event that terrorists take control of an airplane with uninvolved passengers and want to using it as a weapon by crashing it into a built-up area, would it be legal to shoot down the plane and thus sacrifice not only the lives of the terrorists but also those of the innocent passengers in order to save other human lives? This is, in any case, what the legislature wanted to create the legal basis for with the LuftSiG.

The fact that the scenario with the hijacked, presumably unrescuable passengers that is behind the Aviation Security Act is nevertheless applicable to the trolley problems of autonomous driving is thanks to the argumentation of the BVerfG. The court explicitly does not share the view that the lives of the passengers in the hijacked aircraft are already forfeited and speaks in this regard of the "uncertainties as regards the factual situation"[42]: either the passengers could take control of the aircraft and render the hijackers harmless, or the hijackers themselves could change their minds. Though unlikely, neither of these is out of the question. In the opinion of the BVerfG, there can be no question of "these people's lives being 'lost anyway already'".[43] This means, however, that the chances of rescue are no longer absolute, but only

---

40   Cf. again Kunz/Mona 2015: 6ff.
41   On the multifaceted interdependencies between the Federal Constitutional Court and the political system of the Federal Republic, cf. the numerous articles in the comprehensive handbook Van Ooyen/Möllers 2015.
42   BVerfG, judgment of February 15, 2006 – 1 BvR 357/05, para. 133.
43   BVerfG, judgment of February 15, 2006 – 1 BvR 357/05, para. 133.

gradually asymmetrical in relation to the probability of a rescue occurring. The airplane scenario is thus similar to the trolley scenario in that here a group of people is no longer irretrievably lost, so it is not merely a matter of saving or not saving people, in this case another group of people (since the highjacked people are lost anyway), but of sacrificing people in favor of saving other people. That these two scenarios are not identical but merely approximate each other is due to the fact that, if one takes the argumentation of the BVerfG to its logical end, no one has to come to any harm in the airplane scenario, so there could also be no fatalities at all and it is therefore precisely not a dilemma – quite in contrast to the trolley dilemma of autonomous driving.

This difference, which continues to exist but is not discussed in the literature, does not seem to be a problem because the court also deals with the scenario in which the lives of the aircraft passengers are already forfeited, which is ultimately only hypothetical for the court but is foundational for the legislature. The BVerfG argues with regard to "the assessment that the persons who are on board a plane that is intended to be used against other people's lives within the meaning of § 14.3 of the Aviation Security Act are doomed anyway"[44] that these people would also enjoy the "same constitutional protection". This would exist "regardless of the duration of the physical existence of the individual human being."[45] A diverging opinion of the state, according to the court, would render these people as mere objects, not only in the service of the kidnappers, but precisely in service of the state:

> By their killing being used as a means to save others, they are treated as objects and at the same time deprived of their rights; with their lives being disposed of unilaterally by the state, the persons on board the aircraft, who, as victims, are themselves in need of protection, are denied the value which is due to a human being for his or her own sake.[46]

Even the motive of saving other people by sacrificing the hijacked passengers does not change this: "Finally, § 14.3 of the Aviation Security Act also cannot be justified by invoking the state's duty to protect those against whose lives the aircraft that is abused as a weapon for a crime within the meaning of §

---

44   BVerfG, judgment of February 15, 2006 – 1 BvR 357/05, para. 132.
45   BVerfG, judgment of February 15, 2006 – 1 BvR 357/05, para. 132.
46   BVerfG, judgment of February 15, 2006 – 1 BvR 357/05, para. 124.

14.3 of the Aviation Security Act is intended to be used."[47] Or: "The fact that this procedure is intended to serve to protect and preserve other people's lives does not alter this."[48]

This reasoning of the BVerfG is interpreted such that in the case of "irretrievably lost life [...] the person concerned is left with the least possible remaining time" and if "even the sacrifice of this miniscule remainder of life cannot be justified, [...] then this applies a fortiori to the life of an old person whose exact date of death is impossible to predetermine" (Feldle 2018: 150f.). And since the qualitative differentiation of the choice of victim according to age can only be about the remaining time of life (Feldle 2018: 150f.), all qualitative valuations of human beings are thus prohibited (Feldle 2018: 152).

In its ruling, however, the Federal Constitutional Court not only opposed qualitative offsetting, but also, if only implicitly, quantitative offsetting, since it explicitly reproduces the Bundestag's view that "having a relatively smaller number of people killed by the armed forces in order to avoid an even higher number of deaths"[49] does not violate Article 2 (2) sentence 1 of the Basic Law and then the Court goes on to describe in detail[50] that the Aviation Security Act violates the Basic Law precisely because of Article 2 (2) sentence 1 of the Basic Law. The statements that it is 'only' about the prevention of "the occurrence of especially grave accidents within the meaning of Article 35.2 sentences 2 and 3 of the Basic Law"[51] and not "protecting the legally constituted body politic from attacks which are aimed at its breakdown and destruction"[52] can also be read along these same lines: the decisive factor would be a particular quality of consequence of the act, in this case the breakdown and destruction of the body politic, and not a quantity of consequence of some kind, measured in terms of human lives.[53]

In all conceivable cases, the BVerfG thus – as can be seen from the passages already quoted – explicitly cites Kant's prohibition of instrumentalization, on the one hand, and cites fundamental rights on the other:

---

47 BVerfG, judgment of February 15, 2006 – 1 BvR 357/05, para. 137.
48 BVerfG, judgment of February 15, 2006 – 1 BvR 357/05, para. 139.
49 BVerfG, judgment of February 15, 2006 – 1 BvR 357/05, para. 48.
50 BVerfG, Judgment of February 15, 2006 – 1 BvR 357/05, para. 75ff.
51 BVerfG, judgment of February 15, 2006 – 1 BvR 357/05, para. 136.
52 BVerfG, judgment of February 15, 2006 – 1 BvR 357/05, para. 135.
53 Even though this view is less justified than posited, cf. Feldle 2018: 153.

specifically, it states right at the beginning of the reasoning for the judgment[54] and repeatedly in what follows that a shooting down of the aircraft is incompatible with the right to life guaranteed in Art. 2 Abs. 2 S. 1 GG ("Everyone has the right to life and physical integrity.") in connection with the guarantee of human dignity from Article 1 paragraph 1 GG ("Human dignity shall be inviolable. To respect and protect it shall be the duty of all state authority."). Accordingly, the BVerfG ruled that Section 14 (3) of the LuftSiG was "The regulation is completely unconstitutional and consequently, it is void pursuant to § 95.3 sentence 1 of the Federal Constitutional Court Act"[55].

10. Interdependencies between Ethics, Law and Society II

The argumentation as well as the outcome of the judgment was partly met in the jurisprudential discourse with plain and strident criticism (Gropp 2006; Hillgruber 2007; Sinn 2004), not least also from a pragmatic point of view, because the state is thus forced to take no action and, in this respect, the concept of strict duty-based ethics has thereby prevailed. Nevertheless, the fact that the relevant part of the Aviation Security Act was declared unconstitutional and thus null and void and that the legislature enacted a new version of §14 LuftSiG that no longer allows for the preventive shooting down of a passenger plane, would suggest that the whole process contradicts the remarks above on the societal influence on jurisprudence or its interplay with societal discourse: not only do decisions of the highest courts have to be accepted as case law or de facto law – decisions of the Constitutional Court, in this case the Federal Constitutional Court, can even nullify laws that have been formally correctly passed by the legislature. Since the basis of the judgment was formed by Article 1 and Article 2 of the Basic Law, i.e. those very articles that are unchangeable under Article 79 (3) of the Basic Law, no constitutional amendment on the part of the legislature could have swayed the Federal Constitutional Court to change the basis of the judgment. To avoid any misunderstanding: my point is not that this would be desirable, but rather that jurisdiction in this regard is removed from the legislature and thus from that instance to which society, in the form of the electorate, has the most direct access.

---

54 BVerfG, judgment of February 15, 2006 – 1 BvR 357/05, para. 81.
55 BVerfG, judgment of February 15, 2006 – 1 BvR 357/05, para. 155.

Nevertheless, it must be pointed out that even if the judgments of the Federal Constitutional Court are less dependent on the will of the people or, in the terminology used here, more decoupled from the respective societal discourse, the judges nevertheless argued with Kant and thus with a philosopher who can be considered the most influential in Germany's ethical discourse. In other legal systems this is precisely not the case. In Anglo-Saxon legal systems, for example, the utilitarian view is certainly advocated in decisions about life and death (LaFave 2010: 557; Ormerod 2011: 371), which shows that decisions to this effect are certainly influenced by ethical and thus indeed elitist, but nonetheless societal, discourses.

Moreover, not only supreme court opinions but also those of the Federal Constitutional Court with regard to fundamental rights can change, as can be clearly seen in the *quantitative* offsetting of human lives. Even if the view that human lives must not be weighed against each other is virtually unquestioned in German legal opinion today and is based on the fundamental rights of the Basic Law, it only became established in the 1950s as part of the negotiations surrounding the euthanasia murders by the Nazi regime (Feldle 2018: 155), hence at a time when the Basic Law already existed. This, in turn, shows that an interpretation of fundamental rights as standing in contradiction to quantitative offsetting is not compelling. Lastly, but not least importantly, although fundamental rights are protected from amendment by virtue of the aforementioned 'eternity clause,' i.e. Article 79(3) of the Basic Law, this 'eternity' is tied to the legal force of the Basic Law. According to Article 146 of the Basic Law, the German people may still freely decide on a (new) constitution.[56]

In summary, even in the area of fundamental rights, the influence of societal discourse can be detected, albeit very directly and only in the long term, such that although legislation and case law are of primary importance for the development of technology, societal discourse in general and ethical discourse in particular open up the space for thought and possibility and

---

56 Interestingly, after German reunification, the path via Article 146 of the Basic Law was not chosen because, among other things (!), a weakening of fundamental rights was feared at the time.

provide stimuli, which are then reflected in legislation and case law in the medium and long term.[57]

References

Abele, Thomas (ed.) (2019). *Case Studies in Technology & Innovation Management*, Wiesbaden.

Albers, Sönke, and Oliver Gassmann (eds.) (2005). *Handbuch Technologie- und Innovationsmanagement*, Wiesbaden.

Alexy, Robert (1994). *Theorie der Grundrechte*, Frankfurt/Main.

Alexy, Robert (1995) *Recht, Vernunft, Diskurs. Studien zur Rechtsphilosophie*, Frankfurt/Main.

Alexy, Robert (2004). *Theorie der juristischen Argumentation*, Frankfurt/Main.

"Autonomous Driving – Hands on the Wheel or No Wheel at All." April 11, 2018. URL: https://newsroom.intel.com/news/autonomous-driving-hands-wheel-no-wheel-all/#gs.vctpcs.

"Autonomes Fahren: Das bedeuten Level 0 bis 5." June 15, 2021. URL: https://t3n.de/news/autonomes-fahren-assistenz-fahrautomatisierung-level-stufe-1332889/.

Bentham, Jeremy (2013). *An Introduction to the Principles of Morality and Legislation*, Saldenberg.

Berkemer, Rainer, and Markus Grottke (2023). "Learning Algorithms – what is artificial intelligence really capable of?" In: *Artificial Intelligence – Limits and Prospects*. Ed. by Peter Klimczak and Christer Petersen, Bielefeld 2023.

Chun, Wendy Hui Kyong (2018). "Queerying Homophily. Patterns of Network Analysis." In: *Journal of Media Studies* 18, pp. 131–148.

Cristea, Mirela, and Narcis Eduard Mitu (2008). "Experience Studies on Determining Life Premium Insurance Ratings: Practical Approaches." In: *Eurasian Journal of Business and Economics* 1.1, pp. 61–82.

Daniel, Alai, Katja Ignatieva, and Michael Sherris (2019). "The Investigation of a Forward-Rate Mortality Framework." In: *Risks* 7.2, (https://doi.org/10.3390/risks7020061).

---

57 Conversely, it can, therefore, be said that trends in societal and ethical discourse on the part of technical development should certainly be perceived, because this allows us to anticipate what future regulations might look like.

Datta, Amit (2019). "Die Haftung bei Verträgen über digitale Inhalte." In: *Recht als Infrastruktur für Innovation*. Ed. by Lena Maute and Mark-Oliver Mackenrodt (eds.), Baden-Baden, pp. 155–178.

Depenheuer, Otto (2014). "§ 269 Vorbehalt des Möglichen." In: *Handbuch des Staatsrechts der Bundesrepublik Deutschland, vol. XII: Normativität und Schutz der Verfassung*. Ed. by Josef Isensee and Paul Kirchhof, pp. 557–590.

Dilich, Michael A., Dror Kopernik, and John Goebelbecker (2002). "Evaluating Driver Response to a Sudden Emergency: Issues of Expectancy, Emotional Arousal and Uncertainty." In: *SAE Transactions* 111, pp. 238–248.

Engisch, Karl (1930). *Untersuchungen über Vorsatz und Fahrlässigkeit im Strafrecht*, Berlin.

Färber, Berthold (2015). Communication Problems between Autonomous Vehicles and Human Drivers. In: *Autonomes Fahren. Technische, rechtliche und gesellschaftliche Aspekte*. Ed. by Markus Maurer et al., Wiesbaden, pp. 127–150.

Feldle, Jochen (2018). *Notstandsalgorithmen. Dilemmata im automatisierten Straßenverkehr*. Baden-Baden.

Foot, Philippa (1980). "Killing, Letting Die, and Euthanasia: A Reply to Holly Smith Goldman." In: *Analysis* 41.3, pp. 159–160.

Foot, Philippa (1967). "The Problem of Abortion and the Doctrine of the Double Effect." In: *Oxford Review* 5, pp. 5–15.

Gerdes, J. Christian, and Sarah M. Thornton (2015). "Implementable Ethics for Autonomous Vehicles." In: *Autonomes Fahren. Technische, rechtliche und gesellschaftliche Aspekte*. Ed. by Markus Maurer et al., Wiesbaden, pp. 88–102.

"Goldman Sachs sieht Zukunft im Metaversum und Web3." March 29, 2022. URL: https://cvj.ch/invest/goldman-sachs-sieht-zukunft-im-metaversum-und-web3/.

Goodall, Noah J. (2014). "Ethical decision making during automated vehicle crashes." In: *Journal of the Transportation Research Board* 2424, pp. 58–65.

Gropp, Walter (2006). "The Radar Technician Case – A Defensive Emergency Triggered by Humans? Ein Nachruf auf § 14 III Luftsicherheitsgesetz." In: *GA [= Goltdammer's Archiv für Strafrecht]* 153.5, pp. 284–288.

Habermas, Jürgen (1981a). *Theorie des kommunikativen Handelns I: Handlungsrationalität und gesellschaftliche Rationalisierung*, Frankfurt/Main.

Habermas, Jürgen (1981b). *Theorie des kommunikativen Handelns II: Zur Kritik der funktionalistischen Vernunft*, Frankfurt/Main.

Habermas, Jürgen (1984). *Vorstudien und Ergänzungen zur Theorie des kommunikativen Handelns*, Frankfurt/Main.

Hevelke, Alexander, and Julian Nida-Rümelin (2015). "Self-driving cars and trolley problems: On Offsetting Human Lives in the Case of Inevitable Accidents." In: *Yearbook of Science and Ethics* 19, pp. 5–23.

Hillgruber, Christian (2007). "Der Staat des Grundgesetzes – nur 'bedingt abwehrbereit'? Plädoyer für eine wehrhafte Verfassungsinterpretation." In: *JZ – JuristenZeitung* 62.5, pp. 209–218.

Hoffmann-Riem, Wolfgang (2016). *Innovation und Recht – Recht und Innovation. Recht im Ensemble seiner Kontexte*, Tübingen.

Hörnle, Tatjana, and Wolfgang Wohlers (2018). "The Trolley Problem Reloaded, How are autonomous vehicles to be programmed for life-versus-life dilemmas?" In: *GA [=Goltdammer's Archive for Criminal Law]* 165.1, pp. 12–34.

Kalberg, Stephen (1980). "Max Weber's Types of Rationality: Cornerstones for the Analysis of Rationalization Processes in History." In: *American Journal of Sociology* 85.5, pp. 1145–1179.

Kant, Immanuel (1900ff). *Gesammelte Schriften*. Ed. by the Prussian Academy of Sciences. Berlin. URL: https://korpora.zim.uni-duisburg-essen.de/kant/verzeichnisse-gesamt.html

Kelsen, Hans (1979). *Allgemeine Theorie der Normen*, Vienna.

Kleinschmidt, Sebastian, and Bernardo Wagner (2020). "Technik autonomer Fahrzeuge." In: *Autonomes Fahren. Rechtsprobleme, Rechtsfolgen, technische Grundlagen*. Ed. by Bernd Opperman and Jutta Stender-Vorwachs, Munich, pp. 7–38.

Klimczak, Peter, Isabel Kusche, Constanze Tschöpe, and Matthias Wolff (2019). "Menschliche und maschinelle Entscheidungsrationalität – Zur Kontrolle und Akzeptanz Künstlicher Intelligenz." In: *Journal of Media Studies* 21, pp. 39–45.

Klimczak, Peter, and Christer Petersen (2015). "Amok. Framing Discourses on Political Violence by the Means of Symbolic Logic." In: *Framing Excessive Violence*. Ed. by Marco Gester, Steffen Krämer, and Daniel Ziegler, Basingstoke, pp. 160–175.

Kriele, Martin (1991). "Recht und Macht." In: *Einführung in das Recht*. Ed. by Dieter Grimm, Heidelberg, pp. 129–171.

Kühling, Jürgen (2009). "Innovationsschützende Zugangsregulierung in der Informationswirtschaft." In: *Innovationsfördernde Regulierung*. Ed. by Martin Eifert and Wolfgang Hoffmann-Riem, Berlin, pp. 47–70.

Kuhlmann, Stefan (1985). "Computer als Mythos." In: *Technology and Society* 3, pp. 91–106.

Kuhn, Thomas S. (1962). *The Structure of Scientific Revolutions*, Chicago.

Kunz, Karl-Ludwig, and Martino Mona (2015). *Rechtsphilosophie, Rechtstheorie, Rechtssoziologie. Eine Einführung in die theoretischen Grundlagen der Rechtswissenschaft*, Bern.

LaFave, Wayne (2010). *Criminal Law*, St. Paul.

Lemke, Thomas (2000). "Neoliberalism, State and Self-Technologies. A Critical Overview of 'Governmentality Studies.'" In: *Politische Vierteljahresschrift* 41.1, pp. 31–47.

Lin, Patrick (2015). "Why Ethics Matters for Autonomous Cars." In: *Autonomes Fahren. Technische, rechtliche und gesellschaftliche Aspekte*. Ed. by Markus Maurer et al., Wiesbaden, pp. 69–85.

Merat, Natasha, Hamish Jamson, Frank Lai, and Oliver Carsten (2014). "Human Factors of Highly Automated Driving: Results from the EASY and CityMobil Projects." In: *Road Vehicle Automation*. Ed. by Gereon Meyer and Sven Beiker, Cham, pp. 113–125.

Meyer, John W., and Ronald L. Jepperson (2000). "The 'Actors' of Modern Society. The Cultural Construction of Social Agency." In: *Sociological Theory* 18.1, pp. 100–120.

Mill, John Stuart (2009). *Utilitarianism*, Hamburg.

Möhrle, Martin G., and Ralf Isenmann (eds.) (2017). *Technologie-Roadmapping. Future Strategies for Technology Companies*, Wiesbaden.

Ormerod, David (ed.) (2011). *Smith and Hogan's Criminal Law*, New York.

Rahwan, Iyad et al. (2018). "The Moral Machine experiment." In: *Nature* 563, pp. 59–64.

Rawls, John (1951). "Outline of a Decision Procedure for Ethics." In: *The Philosophical Review* 60, pp. 177–197.

"Rolling out driverless cars is 'extraordinary grind', says Waymo boss." January 4, 2021. URL: https://www.ft.com/content/6b1b11ea-b50b-4dd5-802 d-475c9731e89a.

Roßnagel, Alexander (2009). "'Technikneutrale' Regulierung: Möglichkeiten und Grenzen." In: *Innovationsfördernde Regulierung*. Ed. by Martin Eifert and Wolfgang Hofmann-Riem, Berlin, pp. 323–338.

Schäffner, Vanessa (2020). "When ethics becomes a program: A Risk Ethical Analysis of Moral Dilemmas of Autonomous Driving." In: *Journal of Ethics and Moral Philosophy* 3, pp. 27–49.

Schick, Robert (2011). "Auslegung und Rechtsfortbildung." In: *Rechtstheorie. Rechtsbegriff – Dynamik – Auslegung*. Ed. by Stefan Griller and Heinz Peter Rill, Vienna, pp. 209–222.

Schuster, Frank Peter (2017). "Notstandsalgorithmen beim autonomen Fahren." In: *RAW [=Recht Automobil Wirtschaft]*, pp. 13–18.

Servatius, Michael (2019). "Das Verhältnis von Urheber und Verlag – Wohin steuert die Verlagsbeteiligung?" In: *Recht als Infrastruktur für Innovation*. Ed. by Lena Mauta and Mark-Oliver Mackenrodt, Baden-Banden, pp. 201–221.

Singer, Peter (2013). *Praktische Ethik*, Stuttgart.

Sinn, Arndt (2004). "Tötung Unschuldiger auf Grund § 14 III Luftsicherheitsgesetz – rechtmäßig?" In: *Neue Zeitschrift für Strafrecht* 24.11, pp. 585–593.

"The 6 Levels of Vehicle Autonomy Explained". URL: https://www.synopsys.com/automotive/autonomous-driving-levels.html.

Thomson, Judith Jarvis (1976). "Killing, Letting Die, and the Trolley Problem." In: *The Monist* 59, pp. 204–217.

Van Ooyen, Robert, and Martin Möllers (2015). *Handbuch Bundesverfassungsgericht im politischen System*, Wiesbaden.

Wagner, Helmut (1997). "Rechtsunsicherheit und Wirtschaftswachstum." In: *Ordnungskonforme Wirtschaftspolitik in der Marktwirtschaft*. Ed. by Sylke Behrends, Berlin, pp. 227–254.

Wiederin, Ewald (2011). "Die Stufenbaulehre Adolf Julius Merkls." In: *Rechtstheorie. Rechtsbegriff – Dynamik – Auslegung*. Ed. by Stefan Griller and Heinz Peter Rill. , Vienna, pp. 81–134.

Wolf, Jean-Claude (1993). "Active and Passive Euthanasia." In: *Archiv für Rechts- und Sozialphilosophie* 79, pp. 393–415.

Wördenweber, Burkard, Marco Eggert, Größer, André, and Wiro Wickord (2020). *Technologie- und Innovationsmanagement im Unternehmen*, Wiesbaden.

Zoglauer, Thomas: *Normenkonflikte – zur Logik und Rationalität ethischen Argumentierens*. Stuttgart – Bad Cannstatt 1997.

Zoglauer, Thomas (2017). *Ethical Conflicts between Life and Death. On hijacked airplanes and self-driving cars*. Hannover.

Zoglauer, Thomas (2021). "Wahrheitsrelativismus, Wissenschaftsskeptizismus und die politischen Folgen." In: *Wahrheit und Fake im postfaktisch-digitalen Zeitalter. Distinctions in the Humanities and IT Sciences*. Ed. by Peter Klimczak and Thomas Zoglauer, Wiesbaden, pp. 21–26.

Limits and Prospects of Big Data and Small Data Approaches in AI Applications

Ivan Kraljevski, Constanze Tschöpe, Matthias Wolff

Introduction

The renaissance of artificial intelligence (AI) in the last decade can be credited to several factors, but chief among these is the ever-increasing availability and miniaturization of computational resources. This process has contributed to the rise of ubiquitous computing via popularizing smart devices and the Internet of Things in everyday life. In turn, this has resulted in the generation of increasingly enormous amounts of data.

The tech giants are harvesting and storing data on their clients' behavior and, at the same time, introducing concerns about data privacy and protection. Suddenly, such an abundance of data and computing power, which was unimaginable a few decades ago, has caused a revival of old and the invention of new machine learning paradigms, like Deep Learning.

Artificial intelligence has undergone a technological breakthrough in various fields, achieving better than human performance in many areas (such as vision, board games etc.). More complex tasks require more sophisticated algorithms that need more and more data. It has often been said that data is becoming a resource that is more valuable than oil; however, not all data is equally available and obtainable. Big data can be described by using the "four Vs"; data with immense velocity, volume, variety, and low veracity. In contrast, small data do not possess any of those qualities; they are limited in size and nature and are observed or produced in a controlled manner.

Big data, along with powerful computing and storage resources, allow "black box" AI algorithms for various problems previously deemed unsolvable. One could create AI applications even without the underlying expert knowledge, assuming there are enough data and the right tools available (e.g. end-to-end speech recognition and generation, image and object recognition). There are numerous fields in science, industry and everyday life where AI has vast potential. However, due to the lack of big data, application is not straightforward or even possible. A good example is AI in medicine, where an AI system is intended to assist physicians in diagnosing and treating rare or previously never observed conditions, and there is no or an insufficient amount of data for reliable AI deployment. Thus, both big and small data concepts have limitations and prospects for different fields of application. This paper[1] will try to identify and present them by giving real-world examples in various AI fields.

Although the concept of non-human intelligence is as old as early humanity and can be witnessed in thousands of gods and mythological creatures, the idea of a machine capable of acting and behaving like a human being originated as early as antiquity. Mythical beings and objects were imbued with the ability to have intelligence and wisdom, and to be emotional. Throughout history, we have witnessed many attempts to create mechanical (much later also electrical) machines (such as the "automaton" Talos, the brazen guardian of Crete in Greek mythology) relatively successful in imitating human abilities. From early attempts to formalize human-level intelligence, cognition, and reasoning, from early antique on through medieval philosophers and up to 17th-century scholars, the physical symbol system hypothesis (PSSH) (Russell/Norvig 2009) laid the foundation of modern AI. Later, in the 20th century, advances in mathematics, especially logic, proved that any form of mathematical reasoning could be automated despite its limits.

The birth of AI as a modern research discipline is considered to be in the 1950s, when scientists from different research fields started to articulate the idea of the artificial brain.Since then, progress in AI has been primarily determined by technological developments and varying public interests. Because of unrealistic expectations, the field survived two "AI Winters." However, recent advances in computer science, particularly in machine learning, fueled by ever-increasing computing and storage performance, has led to an astronomical increase in research studies and previously unimaginable achievements. Artificial intelligence is increasingly becoming part of people's everyday lives and is achieving, in some respects, superhuman abilities. This has sparked some old and some new fears about the ethics and dangers of artificial intelligence.

---

1   The article was finished in March 2021.

To define artificial intelligence, we should first explain human intelligence. Finding a simple definition of human intelligence is seemingly impossible. In Legg et al. (2007), the authors succeeded in compiling 70 informal definitions, which is, as far as we know, the most extensive and most referenced collection thus far. The definitions could be nuanced into a more straightforward and a more general one: "Intelligence is a very general mental capability that, among other things, involves the ability to reason, plan, solve problems, think abstractly, comprehend complex ideas, learn quickly and learn from experience." (Gottfredson 1997)

Artificial intelligence could be categorized as one strictly demonstrated by machines (Artificial General Intelligence), such as that implemented in Unmanned Aerial Vehicles (UAV), autonomous driving systems or remote surgery. The second one imitates bio-inspired natural intelligence (Artificial Biological Intelligence) as in humans (humanoid robots) and animals (evolutionary algorithms, artificial neural networks, immune systems, biorobotics and swarm intelligence).

For a long time, the central paradigm to solve general artificial intelligence problems was the symbolic approach, known as "good old-fashioned AI." It was mainly based on the idea that intelligence can be emulated by manipulating symbols. The principal methodologies were based on formal logic or pure statistics (neat) and anti-logic (scruffy). The most prominent example of the latter is ELIZA, the first natural language processing (NLP) program. Without any formal knowledge, ad-hoc rules and scripts were optimized by humans until human-machine-like conversational behavior was achieved.

With the emergence of larger and more affordable computing memory necessary to store knowledge, AI scientists started building knowledge-based expert systems in the form of production rules, e.g. a sequence of "if-then" statements. Symbolic AI failed to fulfill expectations, primarily due to the combinatorial explosion, scalability and the fact it was only successful in solving very simple rather than real domain problems. It slowly faded into the first AI winter triggered by the Lighthill report (McCarthy 1974), which lasted until the 1980s. Approaches based on cybernetics and brain simulation experienced a similar fate, having been abandoned even earlier in the 1960s.

Consequently, in that period, other approaches appeared that were not based on symbolic reasoning and specific knowledge representations. Embodied intelligence in robotics (from control theory) promotes the idea that body aspects, such as perception and movement, are required for higher intelligence. Furthermore, soft computing approaches (such as fuzzy systems and evolutionary algorithms) provide approximate solutions for problems that are deemed unsolvable from the point of view of logical certainty.

Statistical AI employs sophisticated mathematical apparatuses, including information and decision theory (Bayesian), hidden Markov models (HMM) and artificial neural networks (ANN), achieving better performance in many practical problems without the need for semantic understanding of the data. The shift from symbolic to statistical-based AI was a consequence of its limitations, and it is considered to be diverting away from explainable AI.

It is worth mentioning that the advances also influenced the appearance and disappearance of different information technology paradigms. Larger and more affordable computer memory enabled knowledge-based expert systems. The development of digital electronic components such as metal-oxide-semiconductors (MOS) and very-large-scale integration (VLSI) provided even more computational power, which led to a revival in artificial intelligence neural networks.

Artificial Neural Networks

The computational model for artificial neural networks appeared in the 1940s and was a biologically inspired attempt to replicate how the human brain works. The basic units are the artificial neurons which can be organized and interconnected in various ways and topologies. The artificial neuron represents a simple mathematical function where multiple inputs are separately weighted, summed and passed through a threshold to activate one or more other neurons. In this sense, an artificial neural network represents a directed weighted graph (Guresen/Kayakutlu 2011).

There are many ways that ANNs could be organized using different types of neurons and various connectivity patterns of neuron groups (layers). Commonly, ANNs have zero or few (shallow) or more hidden layers (deep) between the input and the output layer, where extremes like a single (e.g. perceptron) and unlayered networks are also possible. An artificial neural network is known as "feed-forward" when each neuron in a layer connects to all of (fully connected) or a group of neurons (pooling) from the previous layer. Other connectivity patterns are also possible, such as fully recurrent neural networks, Hopfield networks, Boltzmann machines and self-organizing maps (SOM).

The network parameters, such as connection weights, bias and activation thresholds, are estimated in a learning or training process. Sample observations in the form of input data with the corresponding desired outputs are necessary for supervised learning. The network's parameters are adapted to minimize the difference between the expected and the predicted outcomes. The difference is quantified with a loss or cost function and backpropagated to compute the gradient of the weights. The procedure is repeated, either with stochastic (each input produces weight change) or batch (accumulated error in a batch of inputs produces the weight change) learning mode until the desired accuracy is reached, or there is no more improvement observed in the loss function (Goodfellow et al. 2016).

Deep Learning

ANNs have had a complicated history since the very first emergence of the concept. The hype cycle for this technology is atypical, with many ups and downs. The initial excitement about the perceptron (1957) disappeared quickly because only linear separability was possible; this was mitigated with the multilayer perceptron (1969), which again raised expectations. However, this lasted only until the appearance of support vector machines (1998), which provided better performance than ANNs while also boasting better theoretical background and understandability.

Things changed again in 2006 after overcoming crucial numerical issues, like the problem of "vanishing" or "exploding" gradients. Due to the availability of more powerful computers, it was suddenly feasible to use architectures with increased numbers and sizes of hidden layers (deep neural networks), capable of outperforming the support vector machines (SVMs) in many different classification tasks (Temam 2010). Deep neural networks (DNN) are architectures with many hidden layers made of different cell types that can be combined and provide better data representation (Schmidhuber 2015). For instance, convolutional layers could accept external multidimensional data (e.g. images), learn the distinctive features and pass their output to the recurrent layers to capture spatial or time dependencies, which will serve the output to a fully connected layer to classify the image into one of the expected categories (e.g., cats or dogs).

The size of such architectures quickly increased from thousands to billions of trainable parameters, making the training quite challenging (Rajbhandari et al. 2019) while providing a significant increase in classification performance. Just to mention a few notable examples in the field of NLP, there are the Bit-M (Kolesnikov et al. 2019) with 928M, Megatron-LM from NVIDIA (Shoeybi et al. 2019) with 8.3B, Turing-NLG from Microsoft (Rasley et al. 2020) with 17B and GPT-3 from OpenAI (Brown et al. 2020) with 175B parameters. The latter, which is considered the largest artificial language model, was dwarfed by the Google Brain team model, which has a staggering 1.6 trillion parameters (Fedus et al. 2021).

The training and optimizations of large and performant models have many implications. First, there is the financial costs to train such a model. The costs can range from a couple of thousand to several million dollars (e.g. for the 350GB large Open AI GPT-3 model, the costs are around $12M). Second, there is an issue with the availability of proper computing infrastructure. Supercomputers with multiple instances of specialized hardware (GPUs and TPUs) are not affordable or accessible to most AI communities (researchers, startups and casual enthusiasts). Third, one must consider the levels of energy and power consumption. Strubell et al. (2019) showed that the yearly power consumption of the tech giants equals that of the entire United States, whereas on a global level, 3-7% of electrical energy is consumed by computing devices (Joseph et al. 2014). About 50% of the electrical energy consumption in data centers is used only for cooling (Meijer 2010). In turn, energy and power consumption directly influence the carbon dioxide footprint. For instance, the carbon emissions (CO_2 emission in lbs.) to train one model on a GPU with tuning and experimentation (78,468) surpasses the average annual emissions of two cars (36,156 per car) (Strubell et al. 2019).

Finally, we come to the data that is collected, processed and stored in data centers, data that are in a reinforcing loop with deep learning. Deep learning requires an abundance of data for the training of large models. On the other hand, the tremendous growth of generated data allows applying even more complex algorithms and creating even larger models, which, when used in consumer devices or similar appliances, in turn generates even more data.

The Data

The "digital transformation" and the advances in computing and communication technology are the driving factors for data creation and consumption growth. Only in the last two years, more data was created than in the previous entirety of human history. The most recent Global DataSphere forecast published by IDC predicts more than 59 zettabytes of data creation and consumption in a year, doubling the amount of two years before and surpassing that of the previous 30 years together (Völske et al. 2021).

In so-called "Surveillance capitalism" (Zuboff 2015), consumer devices' users voluntarily provide sensitive data to the tech giants in return for free applications and services, not fully aware that their behavioral data is transformed into a commodity. The data security and data protection aspects are regulated in most countries, like the General Data Protection Regulation (EU) law in European Union. Despite that, in recent years, there have been numerous breaches committed by the tech corporations, where personal data was used for social media analytics in business intelligence or political marketing (notable cases involve AOL, Facebook and Cambridge Analytica).

The value of data and the ability to govern data in an organization is considered an essential asset. Nowadays, almost no business decision could be made without valuable knowledge extracted from a waste amount of structured or unstructured data. On the other hand, there are still areas where the volume and data collection rate are the opposite of what we have described. Natural and technological processes that last long and have lower dynamics provide data at a much slower rate. Therefore, applying artificial intelligence in such cases requires substantially different approaches than those relying on an abundance of data.

Artificial Intelligence Applications

We would like to illustrate the recent advances in artificial intelligence with examples where AI achieved near-human and superhuman abilities. Those achievements are a direct result of having sophisticated machine learning algorithms, computational power, and of course, a vast amount of data. According to Haenlein and Kaplan (2019), there are three evolutionary stages of AI, namely artificial narrow intelligence – ANI, artificial general intelligence – AGI and artificial super intelligence – ASI and three different types of AI systems: analytical AI, human-inspired AI and humanized AI.

Although the big corporations (such as Google or Tesla) are revolutionizing the ways in which artificial intelligence interacts with humans and the environment, all the existing solutions could be described as "Weak AI" (artificial narrow intelligence). In distinction to general AI (AGI), weak AI strives to solve a specific task. In its essence, it is just a sophisticated algorithm responding to sensory inputs or user behavior. We usually see those in everyday life, in our smartphones, smart home devices, personal assistants. They are merely machine learning algorithms that adapted themselves and improved their skills according to user's feedback and behavior. Such systems are not getting smarter by themselves, and their usability and prediction performance always depend on the available data. For instance, a personal voice assistant can learn the speech and language specificities of its user. However, it cannot handle requests that are not foreseen or easily understand a new dialect or language. Although deep learning and big data contributed to ANI achieving impressive results in some application areas, closing in on or even surpassing human abilities, currently, we are still far from developing an AGI (Fjelland 2020).

When comparing artificial intelligence with human abilities, there were two events in recent human history in which AI competed against humans in zero-sum games, that have drawn the whole world's attention and focus on AI. The first event that gained broader public attention was the chess computer Deep Blue's (IBM) match against the reigning world champion in chess in 1997, Garry Kasparov. Playing chess better than humans was always considered one of the "Holy Grail" milestones in AI. Chess requires everything that makes up human intelligence: logic, planning and creativity. A computer beating a human would prove the supremacy of AI over human abilities. Using supercomputer power with custom-build hardware (Hsu et al. 1995) to allow evaluation of millions of possible moves in a second, the machine won only one game in the tournament. Although Deep Blue, being merely a fine-tuned algorithm that exhibits intelligence in a limited domain (Hsu 2002), was nothing like AI nowadays, it passed the chess Turing test, which was a historic moment.

Almost twenty years afterward, in 2017, a similar event took place. AlphaGo (DeepMind), a computer that plays the game Go, beat a human professional player on equal terms. Go is considered much more difficult for computers to play against humans because of the almost infinite combinations of board positions and moves. Traditional approaches, such as heuristics, tree search and traversal (Schraudolph et al. 1994), applied for chess were not applicable in this case. Neither would a pure deep learning approach be feasible due to the data requirements to train a network for all the possible outcomes. Instead, an algorithm that combines tree search techniques (Monte-Carlo) with machine learning was devised. Historical games (30 million moves from 160,000 games) were used for supervised training and computer self-play for reinforced learning of "value networks" for board position evaluations and "policy networks" for move selection (Silver et al. 2016).

Although trained to mimic human players, during the famous game 2 in the match against the professional Korean Go player Lee Sedol, AlphaGo made the famous move 37 (Metz 2016), considered by Go experts as a "unique" and "creative" move that no human player would play. That emerged from the algorithm's underlying objective to maximize the probability of winning, regardless of the margin, even losing some points, in contrast with human players. That showed that AlphaGo exhibited AI-analytical rather than human-inspired AI abilities. The original AlphaGo system went through several transformations. It was further developed into MuZero (Schrittwieser et al. 2020), an algorithm that can learn to play games without knowing the game rules and achieved superhuman performance in Atari Games, Go, Chess and Shogi.

Natural Language Processing

Natural Language Processing is another milestone in the advancements towards AGI. With the greater human dependency on computers to communicate and perform everyday tasks, it is gaining more attention and importance. NLP is one of the most prominent and widespread areas where ANI excels, and there are many examples of NLP in action in our everyday lives at home or work.

NLP allows machines to understand human language conveyed by spoken and written words or even gestures, which are tremendously diverse, ambiguous, and complex. It is quite problematic for the NLP to achieve near-human performance due to the nature of language itself, with many obstacles in the form of unstructured language data, less formal rules and a lack of a realistic context.

NLP solutions are employed to analyze a large amount of natural language data to perform numerous tasks in different applications: written text and speech recognition and generation; morphological, lexical and relational semantics; text summarization, dialogue management, natural language generation and understanding, machine translations, sentiment analysis, question answering and many, many others. Despite the recent advances, language processing is still presented with plenty of unsolved problems.

NLP shares a history timeline with AI in its progression from symbolic, statistical approaches to the recent neural and deep learning-based approaches (Goldberg 2016). The revival of neural networks in the form of deep learning, along with the ever-increasing availability of unstructured textual online content (big data), propelled research in NLP, introducing new algorithms and models (Young et al. 2018).

It is pretty challenging to build a state-of-the-art NLP model from scratch, particularly for a specific language domain or task, due to the lack of the required and appropriate data. Therefore, transfer learning by leveraging extensive and generalized pre-trained NLP models is the typical approach to solve a specific problem by fine-tuning a dataset of a couple of thousand examples which saves time and computational resources.

The pre-trained NLP models opened a new era, and we will mention some of the most recent state-of-the-art (SotA) models that can close the gap to human performance in many different NLP tasks. The Bidirectional Encoder Representations from Transformers or BERT (Devlin et al. 2018) developed at Google is an enormous transformer model (340M parameters) trained on a 3.3-billion-word corpus not requiring any fine-tuning to be applied to specific NLP tasks. The Facebook AI team introduced RoBERTa (Liu et al. 2019) as a replication study of BERT pretraining with more data, better hyperparameters and training data size optimizations. To anticipate the continuous growth of the models' size, the need for computational resources and to provide acceptable performance for downstream tasks (chatbots, sentiment analysis, document mining, and text classification), the A Lite BERT (ALBERT) architecture was introduced by Google (Lan et al. 2019). XLNet was developed by the researchers at Carnegie Mellon University, which has a generalized autoregressive pretraining method that outperforms BERT on tasks like question answering, natural language inference, sentiment analysis and document ranking (Yang et al. 2019). The OpenAI GPT-3 model (Brown et al. 2020) is an up-scaled language model surpassing in size the Turing-NLG (Rosset 2020), which aims to avoid fine-tuning (zero-shot) or at least to use a few-shot approach. It is an autoregressive language model with 175B parameters and trained on all-encompassing data that consist of hundreds of billions of words.

All the top-performing NLP models created by the tech giants have in common their data-hungry complex deep learning architectures, trained on supercomputing systems with thousands of CPUs and GPUs (TPUs), consequently creating colossal models. Despite breaking records in numerous benchmarks, they are still making trivial mistakes (e.g. in machine translation); therefore, SotA NLP models are yet to close the gap on the AGI.

Speech Technologies

NLP applications have been present for a long time, but the arrival of virtual personal assistants with AI technology brought the AI experience much closer to ordinary users. Smart personal assistant technology encompasses many AI-capable technologies, and its increasing adoption and popularity are due to the recent advances in speech technologies.

The first modern smart assistant is Siri (Apple), which appeared in 2011 on the smartphone as standard software. Google introduced its personal assistant Google Assistant (2016), a follower of Google Now, and recently Google Duplex, which can communicate in natural language and became famous for demonstrating robocalling to a hair salon (Leviathan/Matias 2018). A few years later, after the appearance of Siri, AI personal assistants went mainstream when Amazon introduced Alexa Echo, a smart loudspeaker. Alexa is capable of voice interaction, understanding questions and queries and providing answers, controlling smart home systems and many other skills whose number is steadily increasing thanks to the large developer community. Microsoft's voice assistant Cortana has also become a standard feature on their Windows operating systems. Recognizing and understanding human speech and interacting in a human voice are considered AI benchmarks to be mastered on the route towards AGI.

Automatic speech recognition (ASR) has a long history. Like NLP, its crucial milestones correspond with AI's general advances, but practical and widespread application has been possible only for the last two decades. The technology experienced breakthroughs, rapidly dropping the word error rates, capitalizing on deep learning and big data. Suddenly, a massive amount of speech data became available, as consumers using voice queries provided already quasi-transcribed speech in many different styles and environments.

For deep learning, the paradigm "There is no data like more data" (Bob Mercer at Arden House 1985) is the key to success. Now it is possible to train end-to-end speech recognition systems with raw speech signals as input and the transcriptions in the form of a sequence of words as outputs. During training on tens of thousands of hours of speech, the neural network model learns the optimal acoustic features, phono-tactic and linguistic rules, syntactic and semantic concepts. There is no need for algorithms, linguistics, statistics, error analysis, or anything else that requires human expertise (black-box approach) as long as there are enough data.

The current SotA speech recognition systems demonstrate impressive performance on standard recognition tasks (Librispeech, TIMIT). The most recent framework from the Facebook research team, the wav2vec 2.0 (Baevski et al. 2020) (trained on 960 hours of speech), achieved a word-error-rate (WER) of 1.8/3.3 percent on "test-clean/other" of Librispeech and phoneme-error-rate of 7.4/8.3 percent on "dev/test" on TIMIT. In Zhang et al. (2020), WERs of 1.4/2.6 percent on the LibriSpeech test/test-other sets are achieved. Such impressive results are achieved on standard speech corpora in restricted conditions, domain, and language, and cannot necessarily be directly translated to real-world situations. The study (Georgila et al. 2020) shows that the current SotA of off-the-shelf speech recognizers perform relatively poorly in domain-specific use cases under noisy conditions. In summary, it thus appears that despite the impressive achievements, speech recognition technology has yet to close the gap, and it is expected to pass the Turing test for speech conversation in 40 years (Huang et al. 2014). However, history has already proven that this could happen much sooner than expected.

Computer Vision

Computer vision (CV) is a field where, like no other, some of the AI challenges are considered to be completely solved. Improvements in the CV hardware in terms of computing power, capacity, optics and sensor resolutions paved the way for high-performance and cost-effective vision systems (cameras, sensors and lidar) to consumer devices. Coupled with sophisticated video-processing software and social networks, the smartphone becomes the ideal crowd-sourcing platform for generating image and video data. Traditional CV methods were replaced with end-to-end systems that, like speech recognition, avoided the need for expert analysis and fine-tuning while achieving greater accuracy in most of the tasks (O'Mahony et al. 2019).

The traditional CV task is image recognition, where the objective is to recognize, identify or detect objects, features and activities. The image recognition finds the 2D or 3D positions of an object and classifies it in some category. On the other hand, identifying an object also recognizes a particular instance (such as a person's face or a car license plate). Simultaneously, detection provides information on whether some object or condition is present or not in the observed scene (anomalies in manufacturing industries, medical conditions, obstacles detection), which could also be consistently recognized and identified. Other major CV tasks are motion analysis (same as image recognition but over time), scene reconstruction (extracting a 3D model from the observed scene) and image restoration (such as denoising, upscaling, colorization).

The SotA deep learning algorithms for image recognition use convolutional neural networks (CNNs), leveraging the increase in computing power and data available to train such networks (Krizhevsky et al. 2012). Since 2011 (Ciresan et al. 2011), CNNs have regularly achieved superhuman results in standard computer vision benchmarks (MNIST, CIFAR, ImageNet), which influence industry (such as health care, transport and many other areas). ImageNet (Deng et al. 2009) is the database commonly used for benchmarking in object classification (Russakovsky et al. 2015). It consists of millions of images and object classes. Currently, the new state-of-the-art top-1 accuracy of 90.2% on ImageNet (Pham et al. 2020) is achieved by the method of pseudo labels. A pre-trained teacher network generates pseudo labels on unlabeled data to teach a student network, and it is continuously adapted by the student's feedback, which generates better pseudo labels.

There are various CV applications, like image super-resolution (Grant-Jacob et al. 2019), face and image recognition in consumer devices, search engines and social networks. In healthcare, medical image analysis, such as MRI, CT scans and X-rays, allows physicians to understand and interpret images better by representing them as 3D interactive models. Autonomous vehicles, like UAV, submersibles, robots, cars and trucks, employ many of computer vision's general tasks. Many car producers already offer autonomous driving as a feature in their products despite it being far from perfect. Human pose and gesture recognition finds application in real-time sports and surveillance systems, augmented reality experience, gaming and improving the life of hearing and speech impaired people (sign language recognition). In agriculture, CV is used in farm management, animal and plant recognition, and in monitoring and predictive maintenance in the manufacturing industry, in the military for battle scene analysis, assisting law enforcement, education and many others. All in all, however, it must be noted that even if CV achieves human capabilities in pattern matching, it still cannot extract and represent the vast amount of human experience to understand the whole context and the hidden object dependencies.

Healthcare

There are so many AI applications in healthcare and medicine that it would be impossible to mention all of them in the space given. Advancements of AI in healthcare are among the most beneficial uses to humankind and recently gained more attention with focused research and development in combating the COVID19 pandemic.

AI in healthcare has a long history; it has been strongly influenced by the discoveries and advances in medicine and computing technology in the last fifty years. Deep learning enabled the replication of human perceptual processes by natural language processing and computer vision. Computing power resulted in faster and better data processing and storage, leading to an increase in electronic health record systems, which offer the required security and privacy level. In turn, this made the data necessary for machine learning and AI in healthcare affordable and available, a prerequisite for rapid advancement in this area.

AI can transform the healthcare industry and make it more personal, predictive and participatory. However, the greatest challenge for AI is ensuring its adoption in daily clinical practice. For now, its potential has primarily been demonstrated in carefully controlled experiments, and few of the AI-based tools (medical imaging) have been approved by regulators for use in real hospitals and doctors' offices (Davenport/Kalakota 2019).

Many AI-enabled technologies are applicable in healthcare. The core applications can be divided into: disease diagnostics and treatment, medical devices, robotic-assisted surgery, medical imaging and visualization, administrative tasks, telemedicine, precision medicine and drug discovery (Rong et al. 2020). However, the most promising area of application is clinical data management, which aims to provide better and faster health services. Some examples are: collection, storing and mining of medical records in the form of demographic data, medical notes, electronic records from medical devices, physical examinations, clinical laboratory and image data (Jiang et al. 2017). With NLP, it is possible to analyze a massive amount of unstructured medical data, even entire healthcare systems, and discover unknown and hidden patterns in medical condition diagnostics, therapies and drug treatments, creating insights for healthcare providers in making better clinical decisions.

Limits and Prospects of Big Data and Small Data

As already presented in the previous section on major AI applications, deep learning advances are the main driving force of AI technology. However, recently it has become apparent that deep learning has its limitations. The critical voices lately raised the concern that we face another AI winter, primarily due to AI scientists' and companies' unrealistic and ambitious promises. Besides that, since deep learning and AI have a significant influence on our lives and societies, the question of understanding the underlying principles and limitations becomes ever more critical. We need to understand how deep learning works and, when it fails, why it failed. For instance, some AI systems achieved the superhuman ability to recognize objects. However, even a slight divergence from the training data renders the predictions unusable. Deep learning models can recognize an image because they learned not the object, but other features, such as the background. In other applications, like face recognition, the results are strongly biased against minority groups and gender because they were not part of the training data, and so on.

The main issue is that given enough (big) data, the deep learning neural network always tries to find the simplest possible solution to the problem; no matter the task, it just might find a "shortcut" solution (Geirhos et al. 2020). One solution is to provide even more data that include adversarial examples. Another is to combine symbolic AI with deep learning by introducing hard-coded rules (hybrid systems), which are as good as the data or the expertise they are based on.

On the other hand, AI must learn from less data, as we humans do. In some cases, employing deep learning would be overkill, as the traditional machine learning techniques can often solve a problem much more efficiently. Therefore, it is essential to challenge the "black-box" approach in deep learning and understand the underlying principles, providing interpretable and explainable AI.

Big vs. Small Data

One of the drawbacks of using AI algorithms is the need and consumption of an enormous amount of data. In many real-world use-cases, employing data-driven AI methods is not feasible because of the limited amount of available data. The desired accuracy is not achievable due to various datasets' constraints, mainly when they are high-dimensional, complicated or expensive. An example would be time-consuming data collection where a specific industrial system does not produce enough data in a foreseeable period to train an AI system. Also, in personalized medicine (Hekler et al. 2019), big data approaches are impossible. All such cases are considered examples of "small" as a counterpart to "big" data. So far, we have shown that most state-of-the-art AI applications would not be possible at all if there were no big data.

To define small data (Kitchin/McArdle 2016), we shall first present definitions of big data (Boyd/Crawford 2012; Hilbert 2016) and try to give the complementary definitions of the big data attributes while keeping in mind that there will be substantial overlap without a clear distinction between them. Although there is no consensus in the interpretation of definitions of big data (Ward/Barker 2013; Favaretto et al. 2020) showed that most of their interviewees agreed on the following: "Big Data are vast amounts of digital data produced from technological devices that necessitate specific algorithmic or computational processes to answer relevant research questions."

Most small and medium enterprises deal with little and highly structured data. These could be in the form of transaction logs, invoices, customer support or business reports and email communications. The volume of such data is relatively small, mostly averaging a few GBs. To get business intelligence from such data by machine-learning requires smart approaches that are suitable for small data. Most of the definitions about data encompass big data's key properties, which are popularly described by the "Vs" attributes. It started with the 3 "Vs" and quickly escalated to more than a few dozen (McAfee et al. 2012; Patgiri/Ahmed 2016).

The "Vs"

The first definition of big data according to the 3 "Vs" appeared in 2001 (Laney et al. 2001), with Volume, Variety, Velocity, and later was expanded by IBM to include Veracity. Additional to these four fundamental "Vs", many others appeared over the years, further enhancing the definitions of big data properties. Here, we will mention only the most prominent ones and try to contrast them against small data traits:

- *Volume.* This attribute presents the sheer quantity of the data, where the volume contains various data types. Social networks, e-commerce, IoT

and other internet services or applications generate vast data that traditional database systems cannot handle. By contrast, in small data, the volume is much smaller, making it easily accessible and easy to understand. For instance, think of an Excel table containing production figures in a company that are easily readable and interpretable by the CEOs.
- *Velocity.* This represents data generation rate (such as from the Internet of Things, social media), analysis and processing to satisfy specific standards or expectations. The data flow is massive and continuous. As an illustration, the velocity of big data can be expressed by the velocity of the data produced by user searches in real time. For instance, Google processes more than "80,000 search queries every second",[2] and these figures have already become obsolete while you were reading this paragraph. On the other hand, the small data accumulation is relatively slow, and the data flow is steady and controlled.
- *Variety.* Big data comes as structured, semi-structured and unstructured data with any combination of these, such as in documents, emails, texts, audio and video files, graphics, log files, click data, machine and sensor data. In contrast, small data is structured and in a well-defined format collected or generated in a controlled manner (tables, databases, plots).
- *Veracity.* This attribute of big data refers to quality, reproducibility and trustworthiness. Reproducibility is essential for accurate analysis, and veracity refers to the provenance or reliability of the data source, its context, and the importance of the analysis based on it. Knowing the veracity of the data avoids risks in analysis and decisions based on the given data. The quality of big data cannot be guaranteed. It can be messy, noisy and contain uncertainty and errors, meaning that rigorous validation is required so that data can be used. Small data, on the other hand, is produced in a controlled manner. It is less noisy and possesses higher quality and better provenance.
- *Value.* The value of data is hard to define; usually, it denotes the added value after producing and storing the data, involving significant financial investments. The data is more valuable when various insights can be extracted and the data can be repurposed. It has a lower value when it has limited scope and cannot be reused for different purposes, which mostly corresponds with small data collected for a specific task.

---

2 www.worldometers.info

- *Validity.* This is another aspect of veracity. It is the guarantee for data quality, authenticity and credibility. It indicates how accurate and correct the data is for the intended use. Big data has quantity which almost always results in a lack of quality. In such cases, substantial effort is necessary to preprocess and clean the data before it can be used at all. Consistent data quality, standard definitions and metadata are small data qualities because they are defined before the collection process begins.
- *Variability.* This characteristic refers to the fact that the meaning of the data can continuously be shifting depending on the context in which they are generated, which is in contrast to inflexible generation, as is the case in small data.
- *Volatility.* Data durability determines how long data is considered valid and how long it should be stored before it is considered irrelevant, historical or no longer valuable. Due to the volume and the velocity, this attribute is getting more important because it is directly related to storage complexity and expenses. Because of that, small data is inheritably easier to handle and could be archived much longer.
- *Viability.* The data should reflect the reality of the target domain and the intended task. The entire system could be fully captured, or of just being sampled. Using relevant data will provide robust models that are capable of being deployed and active in production. As we already saw, there are many examples where AI applications fail due to the mismatch of the training data and actual real data. Big data originate from broad and diverse sources, and it is not always possible to filter out domain-specific information. For instance, an NLP system built on textual content arising from popular books will fail in tasks where medical records, which are difficult to collect due to patient privacy protection concerns, are supposed to be processed.
- *Vulnerability.* While any security breach in systems storing big data has enormous consequences (e.g. leaked credit card numbers, personal accounts information), the damage is relatively low and limited in the case of small data.
- *Visualization.* Because of the technical challenges in storage and computing resources, different approaches must make the big data's insights visible and understandable. Simple charts, graphs and plots suitable for small data are not feasible for exploratory analysis in big data because of the volume and the number of data points with complex relationships. It is necessary to decrease data size before actual graphical rendering,

feature extraction and geometric modeling can be implemented. It is possible to employ clustering, tag clouds and network diagrams for unstructured data, correlation matrices, heat maps, treemaps, histograms, box, whisker plots, etc. (Olshannikova et al. 2016).

- *Virality*. This describes how quickly the data is spread or broadcasted from a user and picked up and repeated by other users or events.
- *Viscosity*. This is a measure of how difficult it is to work with the data, and it could be described as the lag between the data occurrence and the following conversion from data to insights. It appears primarily due to different data sources, integration of data flows and the subsequent processing phase.
- *Versatility*. This describes the extensionality and scalability of the data, adding or changing new attributes easily and rapidly expanding in size, against the data which is difficult to administer and have limited extensionality and scalability.
- *Vagueness*. This concerns the interpretation issues with the results being returned. The meaning of the produced correlations is often very unclear and misinterpreted as causation. Regardless of how much data is available, better or more accurate results are not possible. Small data has the advantage that it is easier to interpret and comprehend by humans, making it less prone to misinterpretations.
- *Vocabulary*. This is the ontology or the language used to describe an analysis's desired outcome, specific definitions and relationships with other terms. Big data has complex and unknown relationships; consequently, the employed ontology to describe these intricacies is complex.
- *Venue*. This refers to different locations and arrangements where data is processed, like multiple platforms of various owners with different access and formatting requirements. It could be distributed in a cloud (data warehouses, data lakes) or locally at the customers' workstations.

We can summarize all the big data traits and provide a more straightforward definition of them as "Enormous amount of rapidly generated and unstructured data that is too complex for human comprehension." Whereas, in contrast, a popular explanation of small data has been given as "data that connects people with timely, meaningful insights (derived from big data and/or 'local' sources), organized and packaged – often visually – to be accessible, understandable, and actionable for everyday tasks." (Small Data Group 2013).

In the end, there are complex relationships between big and small data where no clear line could be drawn. Big data could simultaneously be small data and vice versa. Small data could always be extracted from big data, it could become big data by extending it, or it can exist independently (Huang/Huang 2015).

Approaches to Big and Small Data

As no clear line can be drawn between big and small data, the same applies to choosing the approaches for handling and processing the data. Which method should be selected depends strongly on the data properties (see the Vs), the specific objective, the intended application task or problem. Sometimes, having a good sample of small data and applying traditional machine learning paradigms provide better results than employing big and noisy data with deep learning. Some expert knowledge and expertise are still necessary to make the right choice. Also, defining simple guidelines that consider the common traits of small data could help provide answers. Here, AI will play a more critical role in discovering an appropriate machine learning approach (AutoML) for a given problem (He et al. 2021).

The data attributes, some of which are already known before the collection or acquisition, some of which are discovered in the exploratory analysis phase, implicitly define the appropriate methodology. Common issues with small data could be identified according to the above-mentioned "V"-attributes as unlabeled, insufficient data, missing data, rare events and imbalanced data.

Unlabeled data are, by some of their attributes (volume, velocity and veracity), closer to big than small data. On the other hand, they exhibit small data properties like limited scope, weak relationality and inflexible generation. Insights of unlabeled data are unknown; the data contain a variety of novel outputs. Processing and analyzing unlabeled data require substantial effort involving organizational, technical and human resources. That is even more pronounced in specific tasks because the data type and acquisition are restricted to the task.

Insufficient amount of data. This is the most common case in small data. The data volume is relatively small and limited due to expensive collection (Krizhevsky et al. 2009) or generation and the low velocity or creation rate. However, sometimes the data are abundant but with low veracity, where the data points are not capturing the domain sufficiently. With insufficient data, the features cannot be well discriminated and standard machine learning algorithms cannot provide proper modeling. The data are complete and fully labeled; however, due to the small number or to the low veracity of the data points, the boundaries between the target categories are less defined, and the ML algorithms will not generalize well for unseen data.

Missing data. Data can be missing due to technical issues during data collection (e.g. sensor failure) or human factors, e.g. flawed experimental or data collection procedure. It can also be interpreted as missing feature values or missing class samples. Preprocessing, consolidation or generation of missing samples or attributes is required to utilize such data.

Rare events. Rare or low probability events, known as outliers or anomalies, differ from the noise that arises from the random variance. They could result from natural variations, system behavior changes, faulty measurement equipment or foreign origin. Due to a large amount of "normal" data, detecting rare events or anomalies is usually relevant for big data and its property of veracity. However, very few and occasional observations contain valuable information of high interest for the intended task; hence, data with anomalies also fit the definition of small data.

Imbalanced data. Even when sufficient data exist, the data count with the desired features could be minimal because of uneven and non-uniform sampling of the domain. Therefore, the approaches usually applied in big data would be unacceptable and not provide the expected performance level. In many real-world applications, the minority class is more important because the information of interest belongs to this class, such as medical diagnostics, detection of banking fraud, network intrusion and oil spills.

Conclusions

We have tried to identify and present the limitations and prospects of big and small data by providing real-world examples and presenting SotA in different AI applications, which has led us to the following results: In the era of big data, small data is gaining more significance. Small data approaches promote AI's democratization, where small and medium enterprises can create tailored AI solutions without the need for massive data storage and computing infrastructure. Often, small data is a result of big data mining and analysis, transformed into smart data, which is more accessible, interpretable, actionable and provides the distilled insights of the big data.

The sheer volume of small data restricts many recent SotA approaches in machine and deep learning, indicating suitable algorithms for small data, combining expert knowledge with the black box approaches into hybrid AI systems. Looking forward, it seems clear that AI is developing towards a system able to learn and create an efficient AI system for the given data and tasks, which could open up machine learning and AI to non-experts.

References

Baevski, Alexei, Henry Zhou, Abdelrahman Mohamed, and Michael Auli (2020). "wav2vec 2.0: A framework for self-supervised learning of speech representations." In: *arXiv.org*. URL: https://arxiv.org/abs/2006.11477.

Boyd, Danah, and Kate Crawford (2012). "Critical questions for big data: Provocations for a cultural, technological, and scholarly phenomenon." In: *Information, communication & society* 15.5, pp. 662–679.

Brown, Tom B., Benjamin Mann, Nick Ryder, Melanie Subbiah, Jared Kaplan, Prafulla Dhariwal et al. (2020). "Language models are few-shot learners." In: *arXiv.org*. URL: https://arxiv.org/abs/2005.14165.

Ciresan, Dan Claudiu, Ueli Meier, Jonathan Masci, Luca Maria Gambardella, and Jürgen Schmidhuber (2011). "Flexible, high performance convolutional neural networks for image classification." In: *Twenty-second international joint conference on artificial intelligence*.

Davenport, Thomas, and Ravi Kalakota (2019). "The potential for artificial intelligence in healthcare." In: *Future healthcare journal* 6.2, p. 94.

Deng, Jia, Wei Dong, Richard Socher, Li-Jia Li, Kai Li, and Fei-Fei Li (2009). "Imagenet: A large-scale hierarchical image database." In: *2009 IEEE conference on computer vision and pattern recognition*. IEEE, pp. 248–255.

Devlin, Jacob, Ming-Wei Chang, Kenton Lee, and Kristina Toutanova (2018). "Bert: Pre-training of deep bidirectional transformers for language understanding." In: *arXiv.org*. URL: https://arxiv.org/abs/1810.04805.

Favaretto, Maddalena, Eva de Clercq, Christophe Olivier Schneble, and Bernice Simone Elger (2020). "What is your definition of Big Data? Researchers' understanding of the phenomenon of the decade." In: *PloS one* 15.2, e0228987.

Fedus, William, Barret Zoph, and Noam Shazeer (2021). "Switch Transformers: Scaling to Trillion Parameter Models with Simple and Efficient Sparsity." In: *arXiv.org*. URL: https://arxiv.org/abs/2101.03961.

Fjelland, Ragnar (2020). "Why general artificial intelligence will not be realized." In: *Humanities and Social Sciences Communications* 7.1, pp. 1–9.

Geirhos, Robert, Jörn-Henrik Jacobsen, Claudio Michaelis, Richard Zemel, Wieland Brendel, Matthias Bethge, and Felix A. Wichmann (2020). "Shortcut learning in deep neural networks." In: *Nature Machine Intelligence* 2.11, pp. 665–673.

Georgila, Kallirroi, Anton Leuski, Volodymyr Yanov, and David Traum (2020). "Evaluation of Off-the-shelf Speech Recognizers Across Diverse Dialogue Domains." In: *Proceedings of the 12th Language Resources and Evaluation Conference*, pp. 6469–6476.

Goldberg, Yoav (2016). "A primer on neural network models for natural language processing." In: *Journal of Artificial Intelligence Research* 57, pp. 345–420.

Goodfellow, Ian, Yoshua Bengio, and Aaron Courville (2016). "6.5 Back-propagation and other differentiation algorithms." In: *Deep Learning*, MIT Press, pp. 200–220.

Gottfredson, Linda S. (1997). "Mainstream science on intelligence: An editorial with 52 signatories, history, and bibliography." In: *Intelligence* 24.1, pp. 13–23.

Grant-Jacob, James A., Benita S. Mackay, James A.G. Baker, Yunhui Xie, Daniel J. Heath, Matthew Loxham et al. (2019). "A neural lens for super-resolution biological imaging." In: *Journal of Physics Communications* 3.6, p. 65004.

Guresen, Erkam, and Gulgun Kayakutlu (2011). "Definition of artificial neural networks with comparison to other networks." In: *Procedia Computer Science* 3, pp. 426–433.

Haenlein, Michael, and Andreas Kaplan (2019). "A brief history of artificial intelligence: On the past, present, and future of artificial intelligence." In: *California management review* 61.4, pp. 5–14.

He, Xin, Kaiyong Zhao, and Xiaowen Chu (2021). "AutoML: A Survey of the State-of-the-Art." In: *Knowledge-Based Systems* 212, p. 106622.

Hekler, Eric B., Predrag Klasnja, Guillaume Chevance, Natalie M. Golaszewski, Dana Lewis, and Ida Sim (2019). "Why we need a small data paradigm." In: *BMC medicine* 17.1, pp. 1–9.

Hilbert, Martin (2016). "Big data for development: A review of promises and challenges." In: *Development Policy Review* 34.1, pp. 135–174.

Hsu, Feng-hsiung (2002). *Behind Deep Blue: Building the computer that defeated the world chess champion*. Princeton University Press.

Hsu, Feng-hsiung, Murray S. Campbell, and A. Joseph Hoane Jr (1995). "Deep Blue system overview." In: *Proceedings of the 9th international conference on Supercomputing*, pp. 240–244.

Huang, Po-Chieh, and Po-Sen Huang (2015). "When big data gets small." In: *International Journal of Organizational Innovation (Online)* 8.2, p. 100.

Huang, Xuedong, James Baker, and Raj Reddy (2014). "A historical perspective of speech recognition." In: *Communications of the ACM* 57.1, pp. 94–103.

Jiang, Fei, Yong Jiang, Hui Zhi, Yi Dong, Hao Li, Sufeng Ma et al. (2017). "Artificial intelligence in healthcare: past, present and future." In: *Stroke and vascular neurology* 2.4.

Joseph, Siny, Vinod Namboodiri, and Vishnu C. Dev (2014). "A MarketDriven framework towards environmentally sustainable mobile computing." In: *ACM SIGMETRICS Performance Evaluation Review* 42.3, pp. 46–48.

Kitchin, Rob, and Gavin McArdle (2016). "What makes Big Data, Big Data? Exploring the ontological characteristics of 26 datasets." In: *Big Data & Society* 3.1. URL: https://doi.org/10.1177%2F2053951716631130.

Kolesnikov, Alexander, Lucas Beyer, Xiaohua Zhai, Joan Puigcerver, Jessica Yung, Sylvain Gelly, and Neil Houlsby (2019). "Big transfer (bit). General visual representation learning." In: *arXiv.org*. URL: https://arxiv.org/abs/1912.11370 p. 8.

Krizhevsky, Alex, and Geoffrey Hinton (2009). *Learning multiple layers of features from tiny images*. Technical Report. University of Toronto.

Krizhevsky, Alex, Ilya Sutskever, and Geoffrey E. Hinton (2012). "Imagenet classification with deep convolutional neural networks." In: *Advances in Neural Information Processing Systems* 25, pp. 1097–1105.

Lan, Zhenzhong, Mingda Chen, Sebastian Goodman, Kevin Gimpel, Piyush Sharma, and Radu Soricut (2019). "Albert: A lite bert for self-supervised learning of language representations." In: *arXiv.org*. URL: https://arxiv.org/abs/1909.11942.

Laney, Doug et al. (2001). "3D data management: Controlling data volume, velocity and variety." In: *META group research note* 6.70, p. 1.

Legg, Shane, Marcus Hutter et al. (2007). "A collection of definitions of intelligence." In: *Frontiers in Artificial Intelligence and applications* 157, p. 17.

Leviathan, Yaniv, and Yossi Matias(2018). "Google Duplex: an AI system for accomplishing real-world tasks over the phone.". URL: https://ai.googleblog.com/2018/05/duplex-ai-system-for-natural-conversation.html

Liu, Yinhan, Myle Ott, Naman Goyal, Jingfei Du, Mandar Joshi, Danqi Chen et al. (2019). "Roberta: A robustly optimized bert pretraining approach." In: *arXiv.org*. URL: https://arxiv.org/abs/1907.11692.

McAfee, Andrew, Erik Brynjolfsson, Thomas H. Davenport, D.J. Patil, and Dominic Barton (2012). "Big data: the management revolution." In: *Harvard business review* 90.10, pp. 60–68.

McCarthy, John (1974). "Professor Sir James Lighthill, FRS. Artificial Intelligence: A General Survey." In: *Artificial Intelligence* 5.3, pp. 317–322 (https://doi.org/10.1016/0004-3702(74)90016-2).

Meijer, Gerhard Ingmar (2010). "Cooling energy-hungry data centers." In: *Science* 328.5976, pp. 318–319.

Metz, Cade (2016). "In two moves, AlphaGo and Lee Sedol redefined the future." In: *Wired*, March 16 (Available online at http://www.wired.com, checked on 6/28/2021).

O'Mahony, Niall, Sean Campbell, Anderson Carvalho, Suman Harapanahalli, Gustavo Velasco Hernandez, Lenka Krpalkova, Lenka et al. (2019). "Deep learning vs. traditional computer vision." In: *Science and Information Conference*. Springer, pp. 128–144.

Olshannikova, Ekaterina, Aleksandr Ometov, Yevgeni Koucheryavy, and Thomas Olsson (2016). "Visualizing big data." In: *Big Data Technologies and Applications*. Ed. by Borko Furht and Flavio Villanustre, Cham: Springer, pp. 101–131.

Patgiri, Ripon, and Arif Ahmed (2016). "Big data: The v's of the game changer paradigm." In: *2016 IEEE 18th International Conference on High Performance Computing and Communications; IEEE 14th International Conference on Smart City; IEEE 2nd International Conference on Data Science and Systems (HPCC/SmartCity/DSS)*, pp. 17–24. URL: https://doi.org/10.1109/HPCC-SmartCity-DSS.2016.0014.

Pham, Hieu, Qizhe Xie, Zihang Dai, Quoc V. Le (2020). "Meta pseudo labels." In: *arXiv.org*. URL: https://arxiv.org/abs/2003.10580.

Rajbhandari, Samyam, Jeff Rasley, Olatunji Ruwase, and Yuxiong He (2019). "Zero: Memory optimization towards training a trillion parameter models." In: *arXiv.org*. URL: https://arxiv.org/abs/1910.02054.

Rasley, Jeff, Samyam Rajbhandari, Olatunji Ruwase, and Yuxiong He (2020). "Deepspeed: System optimizations enable training deep learning models with over 100 billion parameters." In: *Proceedings of the 26th ACM SIGKDD International Conference on Knowledge Discovery & Data Mining*, pp. 3505–3506.

Rong, Guoguang, Arnaldo Mendez, Elie Bou Assi, Bo Zhao, and Mohamad Sawan (2020). "Artificial intelligence in healthcare: review and prediction case studies." In: *Engineering* 6.3, pp. 291–301.

Rosset, Corby (2020). "Turing-nlg: A 17-billion-parameter language model by Microsoft." In: *Microsoft Research Blog* 2, p. 13.

Russakovsky, Olga, Jia Deng, Hao Su, Jonathan Krause, Sanjeev Satheesh, Sean Ma et al. (2015). "Imagenet large scale visual recognition challenge." In: *International journal of computer vision* 115.3, pp. 211–252.

Russell, Stuart, and Peter Norvig (2009). *Artificial Intelligence: A Modern Approach*, 3rd ed. Edition, USA: Prentice Hall Press.

Schmidhuber, Jürgen (2015). "Deep learning in neural networks: An overview." In: *Neural networks* 61, pp. 85–117.

Schraudolph, Nicol N., Peter Dayan, and Terrence J. Sejnowski (1994). "Temporal difference learning of position evaluation in the game of Go." In: *Advances in Neural Information Processing Systems*, p. 817.

Schrittwieser, Julian, Ioannis Antonoglou, Thomas Hubert, Karen Simonyan, Laurent Sifre, Simon Schmitt et al. (2020). "Mastering atari, go, chess and shogi by planning with a learned model." In: *Nature* 588.7839, pp. 604–609.

Shoeybi, Mohammad, Mostofa Patwary, Raul Puri, Patrick LeGresley, Jared Casper, and Bryan Catanzaro (2019). "Megatron-lm: Training multi-billion parameter language models using model parallelism." In: *arXiv.org*. URL: https://arxiv.org/abs/1909.08053.

Silver, David, Aja Huang, Chris J. Maddison, Arthur Guez, Laurent Sifre, George van den Driessche et al. (2016). "Mastering the game of Go with deep neural networks and tree search." In: *Nature* 529.7587, pp. 484–489.

Strubell, Emma, Ananya Ganesh, and Andrew McCallum (2019). "Energy and policy considerations for deep learning in NLP." In: *arXiv.org*. URL: https://arxiv.org/abs/1906.02243.

Temam, Olivier (2010). "The rebirth of neural networks." In: *SIGARCH Computer Architecture News* 38.3, p. 349. URL: https://doi.org/10.1145/1815961.1816008.

Völske, Michael, Janek Bevendorff, Johannes Kiesel, Benno Stein, Maik Fröbe, Matthias Hagen, and Martin Potthast (2021). "Web Archive Analytics." In: *INFORMATIK 2020: Gesellschaft für Informatik*. Ed. by Ralf H. Reussner, Anne Koziolek, and Robert Heinrich, Bonn, pp. 61–72.

Ward, Jonathan Stuart, and Adam Barker (2013). "Undefined by data: a survey of big data definitions." In: *arXiv.org* URL: https://arxiv.org/abs/1309.5821.

Yang, Zhilin, Zihang Dai, Yiming Yang, Jaime Carbonell, Ruslan Salakhutdinov, and Quoc V Le (2019). "Xlnet: Generalized autoregressive pretraining for language understanding." In: *arXiv.org*. URL: https://arxiv.org/abs/1906.08237.

Young, Tom, Devamanyu Hazarika, Soujanya Poria, and Erik Cambria (2018). "Recent trends in deep learning based natural language processing." In: *IEEE Computational Intelligence Magazine* 13.3, pp. 55–75.

Zhang, Yu, James Qin, Daniel S. Park, Wei Han, Chung-Cheng Chiu, Ruoming Pang et al. (2020). "Pushing the Limits of Semi-Supervised Learning for Automatic Speech Recognition." In: *arXiv.org*. URL: https://arxiv.org/abs/2010.10504.

Zuboff, Shoshana (2015). "Big other: surveillance capitalism and the prospects of an information civilization." In: *Journal of Information Technology* 30.1, pp. 75–89.

Artificial Intelligence and/as Risk

Isabel Kusche

Artificial Intelligence (AI) is a notion that has stimulated both the imagination and the engineering efforts of generations. Currently, however, AI predominantly refers to an ensemble of technologies and applications that digitally compute very large and heterogeneous data sets in a way that seems to mimic human intelligence, although it actually works very differently (Datenethikkommission 2019). This ensemble is a subset of technologies based on sophisticated algorithms, i.e. sets of instructions, given to and executed by computers (Buiten 2019: 49). Algorithms are associated with intelligence when they are complex enough to learn, i.e. to modify their own programming in reaction to data (Buiten 2019: 49–50; Datenethikkommission 2019: 273). Such machine-learning algorithms encompass a number of classes, among them artificial neural networks. Although the concept for this class of algorithms was inspired by the structure of neural networks in the brain, they do not actually model a brain or even a part of it. With regard to specific, clearly demarcated tasks related to the identification of patterns in large amounts of data, they perform much better than the human brain thanks to their implementation of advanced statistics to find patterns in data.

Artificial neural networks lend themselves to a great variety of applications, from natural-language processing to autonomous driving. Their utility is based on predictions that are derived from the patterns they find in large amounts of data. Consequently, artificial neural networks are expected to be superior instruments in predicting risks. In mid-August 2020, a search on Google Scholar for the combined keywords "risk prediction" and "machine learning" returned about 19,800 results. A scan of the first 150 results, sorted by relevance as determined by the Google algorithm, indicates a great variety of risks that machine learning algorithms are expected to predict better than previous methods. Various applications in medicine are especially prominent, ranging from the risk prediction of specific diseases to the risk of particularly severe progressions of a disease and mortality. Other risks addressed with machine learning algorithms include aviation incidents, city traffic accidents, delays in construction projects, problems with supply chains, urban flood risks, driving behavior, criminal behavior, bankruptcy and suicide attempts. Substituting "artificial intelligence" for "machine learning" in the search leads to fewer results (around 10,600) but similar applications.

Most of these applications seem completely benign and extremely useful. Moreover, they seem to carry forward existing practices of risk calculation to render an uncertain future more predictable. At the heart of risk calculation is a promise of tamed contingency. Statistical techniques deal with the occurrence of events. In this context, prediction is not necessarily focused on avoiding future events based on knowledge of past events, but on managing their consequences (Aradau/Blanke 2017: 375–78). Prediction does not focus on concrete situations deemed undesirable or even dangerous; rather, it is about identifying a complex of risk factors, each indicating an increased likelihood that an undesirable event might occur (Makropoulos 1990: 421). In the case of work accidents, for example, risk calculation is not about preventing any specific accident, but about managing the phenomenon of infrequent but regularly occurring accidents. This phenomenon becomes observable only through statistics. The key to managing it is insurance, which is based on predicting the frequency of accidents (O'Malley 2009: 32–33). The specific conditions of insurance may take a number of factors into account, such as employees' skill level, work-specific training or the quality and maintenance of technological equipment. Importantly, these risk factors are abstract and detached from any particular individual who might be in danger or endanger others (Castel 1991). Similarly, crime statistics render an uneven distribution of crime observable, in terms of both socio-demographics of perpetrators and victims and geographical distribution of crime scenes. The knowledge produced in this way then may inform specific interventions directed towards the collectives identified as being at risk.

Risk analysis has not been limited to the prediction of events for which statistical records exist or are feasible in principle. Risk models for extremely rare events such as nuclear power plant failures cannot draw on statistical data. They replace these with expert judgements, which assign probabilities to various events based on past research and experience. Since machine learning needs large amounts of training data, AI applications would seem less promising for the risk analysis of rare technological or natural hazards. Researchers still expect them to be better in terms of predictive accuracy and/or computational burden, provided they take into account the challenges related to the nature of available data (Guikema 2020). Yet the greatest impact of machine learning on the management of contingency is expected in fields of application where statistics have played a large role in the past.

From the point of view of computer science, machine-learning algorithms are, like statistical procedures, probabilistic. There are also social scientists who see AI applications mainly as a continuation and intensification of contingency management based on statistical knowledge. Yet others point out that the developments actually amount to a break with this governance tradition. Rouvroy and Berns (2013) stress the amassment of data that are processed in search of correlations, resulting in data profiles. Profiles resemble combinations of risk factors in that they constitute knowledge that abstracts from the individual and enables predictions about individuals based on this abstraction. However, de Laat (2019: 322) emphasizes that the combination of massive amounts of data and AI re-introduces a focus on the individual. Conceptually, it would imply the end of insurance, which manages the uncertainty of the individual case (accident yes/no, illness yes/no, joblessness yes/no) by transforming it into a risk that characterizes a collective. Statistics does not reveal individualized risks, but AI is supposed to be able to do just that (Barry/Charpentier 2020). Provided machine-learning algorithms have access to sufficient amounts of individual-level data, they promise to predict for the individual whether they will or will not have an accident, lose their job or commit a crime.

Such potential does not necessarily mean that the technology will actually be used in that way. Firstly, individual-level data are more readily available in some cases than in others. In the case of insurance, for example, it is easier to gather large amounts of individual-level data deemed pertinent to the risk of having a car accident than to the risk of developing cancer. Driving behavior is a clearly circumscribed activity, many aspects of which can be measured by telematics devices built into cars themselves. By contrast, health-related behavior is much more diverse and less easily captured, although people who opt to use health apps also provide a plethora of individual-level information.

Secondly, established organizational structures and practices may block or dilute the application of AI for individual risk assessment. Barry and

Charpentier (2020) demonstrate that car insurance products have (so far) changed much less than the availability of relevant behavioral data and machine learning might suggest. Although new variables based on such data are added to existing classifications of drivers, which become more refined as a result, classification itself is maintained. In other words, risks are not individualized. This is perhaps not surprising, considering that fully-individualized risk would amount to predicting individual accidents with high certainty, thus undermining the fundamental concept of insurance. At the very least it would lead to very high and thus unaffordable insurance rates for high-risk individuals and challenge the business model of insurance companies (ibid: 9).

Thirdly, however, potential applications may not be implemented due to profound concerns about their possible wider consequences. That means AI itself would be considered (too) risky. It is this perspective on AI applications as a possible risk that the following sections will discuss. Their aim is to explore how the prominence of thinking in terms of risks does not only feed into the promise of AI but also informs and delimits reflections about the (un-)desirability of AI applications.

Risky AI

The 2020 European Commission's White Paper on Artificial Intelligence states that AI "can also do harm. This harm might be both material (safety and health of individuals, including loss of life, damage to property) and immaterial (loss of privacy, limitations to the right of freedom of expression, human dignity, discrimination for instance in access to employment), and can relate to a wide variety of risks" (European Commission 2020: 10). In recent years, strands of research and public activism have converged towards highlighting ways in which machine-learning applications pose risks – to individuals, certain groups or even democratic society as we know it. At a time when advances in machine learning constantly seem to open up new possible applications, the uncertainty about its social implications has grown.

Anxieties and fears are not focused on safety with regard to possible technological disasters, like the 1984 chemical release at Bhopal or the 1986 Chernobyl nuclear catastrophe, or the possible normalcy of accidents (Perrow 1984). Nor do they concern unforeseen impacts on biological systems and the well-being of individuals or ecologies when new substances or modified organisms are released into the environment (Wynne 2001). This does not mean that there are no safety concerns when it comes to applications of AI. The possibility of malfunction is in fact an ongoing concern for engineers and computer scientists using AI applications. For example, the so-called deep learning of artificial neural networks is about identifying patterns in training data and then using the trained model to classify unfamiliar data. However, the way in which a model arrives at its classifications is completely different from human cognition and thus not (easily) interpretable. This opens up the possibility of misclassification in cases that a human would find self-evident. When such errors occur, engineers face particular difficulties in understanding and controlling them because they are the result of a type of data-processing that defies human logic. Moreover, small changes to input data that humans are unable to recognize may alter the output completely (Campolo/Crawford 2020). Malicious attackers could make use of such adversarial examples to deliberately cause malfunctions, for example in the computer vision and collision avoidance systems of autonomous cars, resulting in accidents and loss of lives (Garfinkel 2017).

Accordingly, the European Commission's White Paper on Artificial Intelligence demands clear safety provisions in connection with AI applications, which are deemed necessary to protect not only individuals from harm but also businesses from legal uncertainty about liability (European Commission 2020: 12). This poses particular challenges, not only because autonomous behavior is the promise and selling point of certain AI systems. Most AI systems also use at least some components and software code not created by the AI developers themselves but drawn instead from open-source software libraries. The complex interactions of different software and hardware components can render the detection of failures and malfunctions as well as their attribution to specific components and thus to producers or creators extremely difficult (Scherer 2015: 369–73).

Yet different from cases like nuclear energy or genetic engineering, there are concerns apart from health hazards and the survival of human beings or other living creatures. Wider societal implications of AI ensuing from applications that may operate perfectly in terms of reliability and safety take center stage. The European Commission's White Paper is explicit in this regard when it declares "AI based on European values and rules" (European Commission 2020: 3) as the goal of a common European approach to AI. That implies the technological feasibility of AI based on other, or possibly no, values. The explicit reference to values acknowledges that "AI is not merely another utility that needs to be regulated only once it is mature; it is a powerful force that is reshaping our lives, our interactions, and our environments" (Cath et al. 2018: 508).

The recognition that values are at stake when AI is designed and applied is reflected in the fact that the most prominent symptom of uncertainty about its societal consequences is the call for AI ethics and an abundance of science- or industry-led ethical guidelines (Hagendorff 2020). Calls for ethical, trustworthy, responsible or beneficial AI all appeal to ethical principles to delineate what AI applications should do and what they should not do (Jobin et al. 2019: 392–94). Comparing AI to other technologies perceived as risky, the ubiquitous recourse to ethics may come as a surprise. Critics see it as an attempt to avoid government regulation and as lacking any significant impact on the individuals and companies developing and applying AI (Greene et al. 2019; Hagendorff 2020). Yet it may also indicate that the risks of AI are seen as different from and as less well-defined than the risks posed by previous technologies.

Jobin et al. (2019) identify transparency, justice and fairness, responsibility and accountability as well as privacy as the most common ethical values and principles to which private companies, governments, academic and professional bodies and intergovernmental organizations refer in their documents on AI ethics. Non-maleficence, including the general call for safety and security, is also an ethical principle towards which many statements and guidelines on AI ethics converge (ibid: 394). However, this apparent convergence is contradicted by the many differences in how these principles are interpreted in the documents and which measures are proposed to realize them (ibid: 396). More precisely, questions of implementation and oversight are typically not even addressed. In another review of AI ethics guidelines, Hagendorff (2020) notes that technical solutions are increasingly available to satisfy certain interpretations of principles such as accountability, privacy and fairness. 'Explainable AI', 'differential privacy' and tools for bias mitigation are all technical approaches to render AI applications compatible with corresponding values. Yet other values, for example sustainability or the integrity of democratic political processes, are conspicuously absent from AI ethics guidelines, possibly because technological fixes seem out of reach (ibid: 104–5).

Greene et al. (2019) focus on seven high-profile statements on AI ethics and their common underlying assumptions that connect values, ethics and technologies. They highlight that these statements frame ethical design and oversight as matters for primarily technical, and secondarily legal, experts (ibid: 14). Although the statements recognize the role of values in designing AI applications, they never question the development of such applications in principle, thus implying a technological determinism that inevitably leads to more and more AI (ibid: 15–16). Uncertainty about particular consequences of AI thus contrasts with certainty about the necessity and inevitability of AI in general. The overall narrative regarding possible negative effects of AI that "[p]oor ethics lead to bad designs, which produce harmful outcomes" (ibid: 17) also suggests that ethics guidelines can reduce (or even eliminate) the uncertainty about consequences of AI.

The distinction between ethical and unethical AI is thus linked to the possibility of risks, but the exact nature of this link remains unclear. There are a number of "potential risks, such as opaque decision-making, gender-based or other kinds of discrimination, intrusion in our private lives or being used for criminal purposes" (European Commission 2020: 1) that AI entails. Obviously, unethical AI would ignore these risks and therefore likely lead to rights violations. It is less clear, however, whether ethical AI is expected to eliminate, minimize or just somewhat reduce these risks.

Again, the comparison to concerns about safety is instructive. Safety is itself a value that is somewhat more specified than non-maleficence as a guiding ethical principle. Yet there is no completely safe technology. Accidents happen, which was precisely the reason why the instrument of insurance, based on statistical calculation of risks, developed (O'Malley 2009). Without the possibility to calculate risks or rationally assess them in some other way (Collier 2008), the notion of risk is hardly more than an empty signifier for the many things that can go wrong.

In sum, expectations of ethics appear to be very high when it comes to dealing with the risks of AI. Disappointment seems almost inevitable. Ethics is presented as a soft version of legal regulation although it cannot ensure compliance and consequently is no functional equivalent to law (Rességuier/Rodrigues 2020). In line with the focus on ethical principles, the implied notion of AI risks is very broad. It denotes potential for the realization of unwanted, negative consequences (Tierney 1999: 217), which remain unspecified but whose negativity would derive from a violation of values.

Quantification and Standardization

Any attempt at a risk-based regulation of AI applications would require a level of concretization that at least renders risk estimates feasible. Considering the close link between the concept of risk, statistical thinking and thus quantification, it is perhaps no surprise that one approach to rendering ethical principles concrete and actionable is the search for quantifiable measures of how well AI systems perform in this regard. However, artificial neural networks already pose challenges to attempts to quantify the uncertainty with which they make their predictions (Begoli et al. 2019). There are uncertainties regarding the training data, i.e. how well they represent the phenomenon in question and how accurate the data have been labelled. There are further uncertainties about the chosen AI model, namely how well it fits the purpose, in terms of performance characteristics and model limitations. There are also uncertainties with regard to what appropriate tests of the trained model should look like (Begoli et al. 2019: 21; Buiten 2019: 51–53). While interpretability of models would minimize many of these epistemic uncertainties, there is a trade-off with performance in terms of predictive accuracy.

These difficulties notwithstanding, computer scientists have made various proposals to not only measure performance in the narrow sense, but also characteristics such as fairness, i.e. the extent to which models produce equal, non-discriminatory outcomes for different groups. The more technical of such proposals do not even address the huge gap between fairness as an ethical principle or abstract value and the proposed quantitative measure (e.g. Speicher et al. 2018). Others stress that judgements about fairness are always context-dependent trade-offs with other values and principles; they limit the possible benefit of fairness measurement to providing a baseline of quantitative evidence that may enter into the deliberation of courts about specific cases (Wachter et al. 2020). Normative questions are thereby delegated to the judiciary and the legal framework already in place.

However, if the notion of immaterial risks is taken seriously, such risks might extend beyond provisions within the existing legal framework, which implies that the judiciary might also be incapable of bridging the gap between normative principle and the minimization or mitigation of harm. In fact, it is the anticipation of this possibility that triggered the demand for ethical guidelines in the first place. A particularly ambitious attempt towards a concretization of such guidelines comes from the AI Ethics Impact Group (2020), led by the Bertelsmann Stiftung and VDE (Verband der Elektrotechnik Elektronik Informationstechnik). Their approach to an operationalization of AI ethics is two-pronged. On the one hand, they propose how to specify values and translate them into observables, resulting in a context-independent AI Ethics label for AI systems. On the other hand, they propose classifying the application context of AI systems in terms of a risk matrix, the idea being that riskier application contexts require higher ethical standards.

The proposal highlights both the rationale and the limits of addressing uncertainty about consequences of AI in terms of values and risks. The context-independent ethics rating is based on an incremental translation of abstract values into criteria, indicators and finally observables. It requires that values are first defined, then rendered measurable and balanceable. As the proposal emphasizes, it is "not possible to logically deduce criteria or indicators from values but to argue for these in deliberative processes" (AI Ethics Impact Group 2020: 17). The proposal abstains from specifying the participants in such deliberations but suggest that these "normative decisions should be made in a scientific and technically informed context" (ibid: 16). The deliberations are supposed to result in a clear picture of "an AI system's ethical characteristics" (ibid: 31).

For the complementary classification of application contexts, the proposal foresees regulators as the decision-makers (ibid: 39), at the same time calling for "the participation of stakeholders with a broad, interdisciplinary perspective" (ibid: 37). The authors propose a risk matrix that distinguishes classes of applications depending on how much potential harm an AI system could cause and how much those negatively affected depend on the AI system. As the proposal readily admits, the two dimensions are hardly separate since "correlations between the dimensions arise depending on the weight of individual aspects in the internal composition" (ibid: 37); furthermore, both dimensions demand value judgements and in particular the resolution of value conflicts. Moreover, there may be thresholds beyond which even very low-probability risks are deemed unacceptable (ibid: 37).

In sum, the notion of risk underlying this proposal has little to do with risk as a calculative technique. The repeated call for stakeholder involvement and the emphasis on deliberation and values indicate that the potential harm of AI applications cannot be predicted based on calculations. Yet the ambition is to arrive at a somewhat standardized assessment of AI that goes beyond case-by-case decisions about which applications are acceptable and which are not.

Lesson Learnt?

The emphasis on the role of values and the need for ethical principles amounts to a dream come true for many social scientists focusing on risk assessment and risk management. It seems that the approach to risks of AI has been greatly informed by analyses of the shortcomings that troubled and derailed earlier attempts to assess and manage technological risks. About 20 years ago, Wynne (2001: 446) was still showing evidence of a categorical distinction between risk concerns and ethical concerns in relation to genetically-modified organisms (GMOs). While scientific expertise was supposed to deal with the former, vaguely informed and more emotional lay publics were prone to focus on the latter, in keeping with institutionalized expectations about the separation of risk and ethics. Around the same time, Jasanoff (1999: 140–45) pointed out how formal risk assessment is a particular type of expert knowledge, with taken-for-granted yet contingent assumptions about causation, agency and uncertainty. According to her, it understands causation of harms as mechanistic, locates the sources of risk in inanimate objects and renders the cultural and political origins of uncertainty invisible by translating it into formal quantitative language. Jasanoff at least detected the emergence of a different conception of risk-based regulation that would conjoin scientific analysis with political deliberation, encourage feedbacks, recursion and revision based on experience, and acknowledge that the regulatory process is ultimately about decision-making and not science (ibid: 149–50).

At first sight, approaches to AI seem to address these concerns about risk management. The proliferation of ethics guidelines that are initiated and developed by computer scientists and supported by tech companies suggests that an emphasis on ethics is no longer disparaged as the emotional reaction of laypeople. The proposal of the AI Ethics Impact Group, for example, appears to be in line with an understanding of technological risks that recognizes the central role of ethics, values and political deliberation when it comes to the regulation of AI applications. Moreover, the German Data Ethics Commission points out that risks do not only originate from the technological design of an application but also from human decisions in using the technology (Datenethikkommission 2019: 167). It also notes that the effects of some AI applications may be unacceptable, necessitating a ban.

Yet awareness of the political and cultural context in which risk-based regulation inevitably takes place remains superficial. Firstly, the consideration of ethics is reframed as a task for experts and thus transformed into a question of finding the right experts for it. This is, for example, indicated by the call for "the participation of stakeholders with a broad, interdisciplinary perspective" (AI Ethics Impact Group 2020: 37), which suggests that it will be experts after all who bring different views about the operationalization and prioritization of values to the table. The consideration of ethics thus primarily manifests as the consultation of legal scholars, theologians, ethicists and experts in data protection, who collaborate with computer scientists and industry representatives, as, for example, in the German Data Ethics Commission (Bundesministerium des Innern, für Heimat und Bau 2019).

Secondly, the concession that risks are not only located in technological objects but can arise from human decisions in using the technology is of little consequence when the focus of possible regulation remains on "an AI system's ethical characteristics" (AI Ethics Impact Group 2020: 31). The idea of an ethics label in particular attempts to locate values context-independently in technical objects. It implies that it is possible to decontextualize and objectivize values. As well as the appeal to ethical expertise, this suggests that it is possible to get this kind of assessment 'right'. Appropriate ethical assessments are apparently those that include diverse but well-informed stakeholders who deliberate about the operationalization of values until they find one that all parties involved can agree with.

Thirdly, the political and cultural origins of risk and uncertainty are again blurred as a result. The decontextualized nature of expert ethical assessments inevitably ignores the possibility that values, and in particular their ordering in cases of conflicting values, may vary both spatially and temporally. Admittedly, the European Commission's White Paper calls for "AI based on European values and rules" (European Commission 2020: 3). Yet its overall focus is on working towards global championship and leadership in AI applications. This implies that both European values and solutions to value conflicts are (at least potentially) universal. By contrast, sociological analyses of values and their prioritization in situations of conflict stress that orderings of values are plural, temporal and adaptable to political exigencies (Luhmann 1962; Boltanski/Thévenot 2006; Kusche 2021). The trend towards attempting to quantify specific values veils the contextual nature of value judgements even more and suggests a distinction between ethics experts, whose function is to remind everyone of abstract principles, and technical experts, who propose and implement appropriate performance measures.

The attention paid to ethical concerns in relation to AI may thus be commendable compared to a risk regulation that focuses on possible future harms without acknowledging that values inevitably enter the equation. Yet it sidesteps the full implications that a thorough consideration of values would have, especially in view of the notion of immaterial risks.

Risk, Decision-making and Non-knowledge

Although AI ethics guidelines fail to regulate design and business decisions regarding AI applications, their proliferation indicates the recognition that risks and decisions are closely connected. Value conflicts do not just disappear; they demand decisions. Moreover, the concretization of values is a matter of making decisions in the first place, and talking about deliberation instead indicates primarily a preference for involving many decision-makers instead of only a few. In the absence of deducible criteria or indicators for specific values, any decision about such criteria is itself uncertain. Adhering to such criteria could ultimately lead to the violation of values and to corresponding negative consequences – it is, inevitably, itself a risk. If such criteria are quantified, the role that decisions played in arriving at the respective measures is rendered invisible; by contrast, an emphasis on deliberation is at least a reminder that decision-making is unavoidable. Yet the implications of the necessity of risky decisions when dealing with risks of AI only become clear once they are considered as only one instance of the constitutive character that risk has for modern society.

Risk does not denote an objectively measurable hazard, but is a way to deal with contingency, attributing uncertain negative events in the future to decisions, as opposed to misfortune, God's will, laws of nature or any other external cause. The probabilistic approach to risk, common to classical statistics and advanced machine-learning algorithms, is a symptom of how ubiquitous the attribution of future events to contingent decisions is. Yet for the same reason, as Luhmann (1991: 28–31) argues, the opposite of risk is not safety but danger, that is a possible future negative event attributed externally and not to one's own decision-making. By contrast, safety is something to strive for, be it in the face of risk or danger, but not in the sense of a specific goal that can be reached. It is a value (ibid: 28) that may orient decisions in the face of an unknown future, which always entails the possibility of events that one would prefer to avoid.

The distinction between risk and danger highlights the difference that it makes whether negative future events are attributed internally, that is to one's own decisions, or externally. Since the attribution to external causes includes the attribution to decisions others have made, the distinction risk/danger is closely connected to another distinction, namely that between decision-makers and those affected by decisions (ibid: 111–19). Risks run by decision-makers can turn into dangers for those who experience consequences without having been involved in the respective decisions. When dangers are deemed considerable and can be attributed to risks taken by others, a conflict between decision-makers and those affected becomes likely (Japp/Kusche 2008: 90–92). The latter may refuse to accept what they observe as danger and turn against those seen as responsible for it. Excluded from the decision-making, they can take recourse to protesting against the danger and against the decision-makers to whom it is attributed.

The introduction and spread of new technologies are, although not the only case, a very prominent case in which attributions to risk and danger have often fueled conflicts between decision-makers and those affected. Policy-makers, companies and business associations have become increasingly aware that broad popular resistance against technologies can pose both political and economic problems. Due to its capacity to make collectively binding decisions, the political system attracts a plethora of expectations. Resistance against technologies will almost inevitably turn into demands for regulation or even bans. Based on past experience, with the prolonged protests against nuclear power being probably the most impactful in Germany, political actors can anticipate the necessity to get involved and address the question of potential harms. Moreover, in the case of AI national governments and the European Commission even take explicit responsibility for the various effects that these applications may have when they actively promote their adoption and further development in the interest of competitive economies (European Commission 2020). This is politically risky in the sense that it would seem to create clear targets for blame in case AI applications turn out to have consequences deemed negative by significant numbers of voters. Similarly, businesses wishing to develop and sell or use a new technology can anticipate not only legal problems with liability in case of possible harms but also threats to revenues when the respective technology meets broad resistance from clients and consumers. As political consumers, the latter may choose to prioritize ethical concerns even when they are not directly affected by negative effects of a particular product or service (Brenton 2013).

Against this backdrop, both political actors and businesses can anticipate that they will be seen as decision-makers with regard to AI. A common way to deal with the political risks implied is to defer to specialized expertise and science-based decision-making (Jasanoff 1990). Scientific research routinely deals with non-knowledge, but typically in a way that specifies what is not yet known, thereby laying the foundation for new knowledge (Merton 1987: 7). Specified non-knowledge entails the expectation that it will be transformed into knowledge, given enough time, as a result of further research. This does not mean that scientific activity gradually decreases the amount of specific non-knowledge and increases the amount of knowledge. Rather, the specification of non-knowledge defines a soluble scientific problem, whose solution inevitably points to new non-knowledge to be specified by further scientific research (Merton 1987; Japp 2000). Yet when a soluble scientific problem is defined in congruence with a political decision-making problem, specified non-knowledge also suggests the possibility of informed decision-making in combination with certified experts that can be invoked to justify the decisions made.

That is why risk as a calculative technique appears to be attractive to decision-makers faced with uncertainty. It transforms specified non-knowledge into knowledge about likelihoods. This sort of knowledge is enticing in many policy fields, for example policing and crime. Whenever there is extensive data about past events, risk calculations are feasible. The availability of big data extends the reach of such calculations to new fields of application. A reliance on risk calculations, whether based on classical statistics or sophisticated deep-learning algorithms, transforms the political problem of crime into various problems of specified non-knowledge. A resulting prediction, for example about the neighborhoods in a particular city where break-ins will most likely occur within the next month, presents an actionable knowledge that can guide decisions about the deployment of limited police forces. Such knowledge is not expected to prevent all break-ins, but only more break-ins than if decisions were taken without such knowledge.

However, the problem of risky AI cannot be addressed in the same way. It is a problem that is potentially created by all the unspecified non-knowledge that is excluded in the course of specifying non-knowledge, to which the selection of training data, of a particular AI model and all the other steps involved in the creation and implementation of an AI application contribute. Accordingly, there is no empirical data on which to base a calculation that could deal with this non-knowledge; decisions can only rely on judgements of those deemed to be in possession of relevant experience. Yet whenever there is few or no empirical data, the idea that risks could be estimated benefits from a spillover effect (Tierney 1999: 219). Although the method of specifying non-knowledge is utterly different when there is no data to calculate likelihoods, the notion of risk analysis invokes a scientific specification of non-knowledge to legitimate its results. By contrast, if the term risk were dropped or clearly delineated as an everyday expression marking the possibility of negative consequences that decisions about using AI may have, the deeply political dimension of such decisions would become obvious.

Conclusion: Risk and Depoliticization

The plausibility of risk estimates for many technologies benefits from spillover effects. Yet this did not prevent public resistance, for example against nuclear energy or genetically modified organisms, in the past. Firstly, those opposed to a technology aligned themselves with experts who arrived at other conclusions (van den Daele 1996). Secondly, they rejected the notion of specified non-knowledge and observed unspecified non-knowledge instead (Japp 2000), interpreting the existence of different expert opinions as proof that the non-knowledge could not be specified. Unspecified non-knowledge implies non-quantifiable, catastrophic risk (ibid: 231), with people rejecting possible future harms completely, deeming them unacceptable on principle.

As of now, such a politicization of technology based on the distinction between decision-makers and those affected is not in sight in the case of AI. Although this may change in the future, which is, of course, unknown in this respect as in any other, there is reason to believe that it will not change as long as the notion of risk continues to frame the debate. One of its peculiarities is that the underlying technology of AI applications is itself based on probabilistic calculation and aimed at decision problems. Hence the depoliticization of problems that AI applications are supposed to tackle and the depoliticization of problems that AI applications potentially create are intertwined. Automating decisions about eligibility for welfare benefits, the allocation of police forces, or the deletion of social media posts means by definition that the attribution of responsibility and associated risks shifts. What used to be decisions of policy makers and administrators in relation to particular issues or cases turn into decisions about whether and how to deploy a corresponding AI system. They thus turn into a matter of the risks related to that system. To the extent to which these risks are framed as a matter of research specifying non-knowledge, the depoliticization by AI and the depoliticization of AI are likely to reinforce each other.

Concurrently, the incorporation of ethical principles into the discourse about risks of AI sidesteps the distinction between specifiable non-knowledge and unspecified non-knowledge that fueled resistance to technologies in the past. When the principles on which one might base a rejection of possible future harms categorically are drawn into the framework of risk, they are presented as negotiable, if not quantifiable, and as unpolitical at the same time. This is good news for those who prioritize the further development and spread of AI applications. It is rather bad news for those who fear irreversible societal consequences of some AI applications and believe that trade-offs between values or ethical principles are common and inevitable, but inherently political.

References

AI Ethics Impact Group (2020): "From Principles to Practice. An interdisciplinary framework to operationalise AI ethics." In: *Bertelsmann Stiftung*. URL: https://www.bertelsmann-stiftung.de/fileadmin/files/BSt/Publikationen/GrauePublikationen/WKIO_2020_final.pdf.

Aradau, Claudia, and Tobias Blanke (2017): "Politics of Prediction: Security and the Time/Space of Governmentality in the Age of Big Data." In: *European Journal of Social Theory* 20.3, pp. 373–391.

Barry, Laurence, and Arthur Charpentier (2020): "Personalization as a Promise: Can Big Data Change the Practice of Insurance?" In: *Big Data & Society* 7.1. URL: https://doi.org/10.1177/2053951720935143.

Begoli, Edmon, Tanmoy Bhattacharya, and Dimitri Kusnezov (2019): "The Need for Uncertainty Quantification in Machine-Assisted Medical Decision Making." In: *Nature Machine Intelligence* 1.1, pp. 20–23.

Boltanski, Luc, and Laurent Thévenot (2006): *On Justification: Economies of Worth. Princeton Studies in Cultural Sociology*. Princeton: Princeton University Press.

Brenton, Scott (2013): "The political motivations of ethical consumers." In: *International Journal of Consumer Studies* 37.5, pp. 490–497.

Buiten, Miriam C. (2019): "Towards Intelligent Regulation of Artificial Intelligence." In: *European Journal of Risk Regulation* 10.1, pp. 41–59.

Bundesministerium des Innern, für Heimat und Bau (2019): "Mitglieder der Datenethikkommission der Bundesregierung". URL: https://www.bmi.bund.de/DE/themen/it-und-digitalpolitik/datenethikkommission/mitglieder-der-dek/mitglieder-der-dek-node.html.

Campolo, Alexander, and Kate Crawford (2020): "Enchanted Determinism: Power without Responsibility in Artificial Intelligence." In: *Engaging Science, Technology, and Society* 6, pp. 1–19. URL: https://doi.org/10.17351/ests2020.277.

Castel, Robert (1991): "From Dangerousness to Risk." In: *The Foucault Effect. Studies in Governmentality*. Ed. by Graham Burchell, Colin Gordon, and Peter Miller, Chicago: Chicago University Press, pp. 281–298.

Cath, Corinne, Sandra Wachter, Brent Mittelstadt, Mariarosaria Taddeo, and Luciano Floridi (2018): "Artificial Intelligence and the 'Good Society': The US, EU, and UK Approach." In: *Science and Engineering Ethics* 24.2, pp. 505–528.

Collier, Stephen J. (2008): "Enacting catastrophe: preparedness, insurance, budgetary rationalization." In: *Economy and Society* 37.2, pp. 224–250.

Daele, Wolfgang van den (1996): "Objektives Wissen als politische Ressource: Experten und Gegenexperten im Diskurs." In: *Kommunikation und Entscheidung: Politische Funktion öffentlicher Meinungsbildung und diskursiver Verfahren, WZB-Jahrbuch 1996*. Ed. by Wolfgang van den Daele and Friedhelm Neidhardt, Berlin: Edition Sigma, pp. 297–326.

Datenethikkommission (2019): *Gutachten der Datenethikkommission*. URL: https://datenethikkommission.de/gutachten/.

European Commission (2020): *White Paper on Artificial Intelligence: A European Approach to Excellence and Trust*. URL: https://ec.europa.eu/info/publications/white-paper-artificial-intelligence-european-approach-excellence-and-trust_en.

Garfinkel, Simson (2017): "How angry truckers might sabotage self-driving cars." In: *MIT Technology Review* 120.6, p. 14.

Greene, Daniel, Anna Lauren Hoffmann, and Luke Stark (2019): "Better, Nicer, Clearer, Fairer: A Critical Assessment of the Movement for Ethical Artificial Intelligence and Machine Learning." Hawaii International Conference on System Sciences. URL: http://hdl.handle.net/10125/5965.

Guikema, Seth (2020): "Artificial Intelligence for Natural Hazards Risk Analysis: Potential, Challenges, and Research Needs." In: *Risk Analysis* 40.6, pp. 1117–1123.

Hagendorff, Thilo (2020): "The Ethics of AI Ethics: An Evaluation of Guidelines." In: *Minds and Machines* 30.1, pp. 99–120.

Japp, Klaus P. (2000): "Distinguishing Non-Knowledge." In: *Canadian Journal of Sociology* 25.2, pp. 225–238.

Japp, Klaus P., and Isabel Kusche (2008): "Systems Theory and Risk." In: *Social Theories of Risk and Uncertainty: An Introduction*. Ed. by Jens O. Zinn, Malden, MA: Blackwell, pp. 76–105.

Jasanoff, Sheila (1990): *The fifth branch: science advisers as policymakers*. Cambridge, Mass: Harvard University Press.

Jasanoff, Sheila (1999): "The Songlines of Risk." In: *Environmental Values* 8, pp. 135–152.

Jobin, Anna, Marcello Ienca, and Effy Vayena (2019): "The Global Landscape of AI Ethics Guidelines." In: *Nature Machine Intelligence* 1.9, pp. 389–399.

Kusche, Isabel (2021): "Systemtheorie und Ideologie. Eine Spurensuche." In: *Die Rückkehr der Ideologie*. Ed. by Heiko Beyer and Alexandra Schauer, Frankfurt: Campus, pp. 111–139.

Laat, Paul B. de (2019): "The Disciplinary Power of Predictive Algorithms: A Foucauldian Perspective." In: *Ethics and Information Technology* 21.4, pp. 319–329.

Luhmann, Niklas (1962): "Wahrheit und Ideologie: Vorschläge zur Wiederaufnahme der Diskussion." In: *Der Staat* 1.4, pp. 431–448.

Luhmann, Niklas (1991): *Soziologie des Risikos*. Berlin; New York: W. de Gruyter.

Makropoulos, Michael (1990): "Möglichkeitsbändigungen: Disziplin und Versicherung als Konzepte zur sozialen Steuerung von Kontingenz." In: *Soziale Welt* 41.4, pp. 407–423.

Merton, Robert K. (1987): "Three Fragments from a Sociologist's Notebooks: Establishing the Phenomenon, Specified Ignorance, and Strategic Research Materials." In: *Annual Review of Sociology* 13.1, pp. 1–29.

O'Malley, Pat (2009): "'Uncertainty makes us free'. Liberalism, risk and individual security." In: *Behemoth – A Journal on Civilisation* 2.3, pp. 24–38.

Perrow, Charles (1984): Normal accidents: living with high-risk technologies. New York: Basic Books.

Rességuier, Anaïs, and Rowena Rodrigues (2020): "AI Ethics Should Not Remain Toothless! A Call to Bring Back the Teeth of Ethics." In: *Big Data & Society* 7.2. URL: https://doi.org/10.1177/2053951720942541.

Rouvroy, Antoinette, and Thomas Berns (2013): "Gouvernementalité algorithmique et perspectives d'émancipation: Le disparate comme condition d'individuation par la relation?" In: *Réseaux* 177.1, pp. 163–196. URL: https://doi.org/10.3917/res.177.0163.

Scherer, Matthew U. (2015): "Regulating Artificial Intelligence Systems: Risks, Challenges, Competencies, and Strategies." In: *Harvard Journal of Law and Technology* 29.2, pp. 354–400.

Speicher, Till, Hoda Heidari, Nina Grgic-Hlaca, Krishna P Gummadi, Adish Singla, Adrian Weller, and Muhammad Bilal Zafar (2018): "A Unified Approach to Quantifying Algorithmic Unfairness: Measuring Individual &Group Unfairness via Inequality Indices." In: *Proceedings of the 24th ACM SIGKDD International Conference on Knowledge Discovery & Data Mining*, London/United Kingdom: ACM, pp. 2239–2248. URL: https://doi.org/10.1145/3219819.3220046.

Tierney, Kathleen J. (1999): "Toward a Critical Sociology of Risk." In: *Sociological Forum* 14.2, pp. 215–242.

Wachter, Sandra, Brent Mittelstadt, and Chris Russell (2021): "Why Fairness Cannot Be Automated: Bridging the Gap Between EU Non-Discrimination Law and AI." In: *Computer Law & Security Review* 41, July 2021, 105567. URL: https://doi.org/10.1016/j.clsr.2021.105567.

Wynne, Brian (2001) "Creating Public Alienation: Expert Cultures of Risk and Ethics on GMOs." In: *Science as Culture* 10.4, pp. 445–481.

When You Can't Have What You Want
Measuring Users' Ethical Concerns about Interacting with AI Assistants Using MEESTAR

Kati Nowack

As new AI technologies emerge, we need to assure these are in alignment with ethical values, standards and goals of individual users as well as society. Ethical implications associated with AI systems have been discussed extensively in the literature, where much theorizing *about* users has taken place but not enough empirical research *with* users has been conducted. In this explorative questionnaire study, I aimed at investigating the extent to which the MEESTAR model (e.g. Manzeschke et al. 2016) originally developed within the context of inclusive assistance systems for the elderly can be applied more generally to users' needs. To this end, sixty-four participants were presented with different AI scenarios in which the ethical values of *autonomy, safety, privacy, care, justice, participation* and *self-conception* were either violated or not. Ratings of concern in response to violations as well as ratings of the importance assigned to these aspects show that, firstly, *participation* and *care* generally need to be considered in the development of new AI systems whilst *privacy* was largely disregarded by participants. Secondly, the results indicate some mismatches between ratings of concern and importance: participants assigned importance to *safety, justice, autonomy* and *self-conception* but appeared less concerned with violations of these values. This supports the notion of a growing need to strengthen digital literacy by including more information about users' rights and about the consequences of violations in AI interaction. Finally, findings of any impact of gender, technical experience and time perspective on concern and importance ratings are discussed.

1. Introduction

Whenever new media and technologies emerge, they are met with scepticism and concerns by individuals and society. At the beginning of the silent film era, Münsterberg (1916) warned that the audiences could no longer follow realistic processes, since cuts and close-ups in the film would interrupt the natural narrative flow. When television arrived in living rooms, it was met with discussions about the harm it could cause physically or psychologically (Friedmann 1962; Heymann 1962; Rintelen 1962). Empirical evidence eliminated many fears: watching TV did not lead to epileptic seizures, X-ray damage or aggressive behaviour.

In the end, new media and technologies prevailed. No one could imagine living without movies, tv or the internet now! We rely on these media to meet our various needs. There is our need for information (e.g. seeking advice, curiosity), for personal identity (e.g. affirmation of our own identity, identification with others by means of social comparison), for a sense of belonging not only during COVID lockdowns as well as simple entertainment needs (e.g. distraction, escapism, relaxation; Rosengren et al. 1985; Zillmann 1988). Regarding people's core need for belonging or relatedness (Vansteenkiste et al. 2020), media serve to establish and maintain social contacts. They can even act as substitute for direct interpersonal contacts and relationships. Moreover, relatedness is important for our well-being according to Self-Determination Theory (SDT; Ryan/Deci 2000). Here, intelligent assistants such as emotional support robots developed for companionship can serve to meet those needs (Baecker et al. 2020). Humans generally try to avoid or reduce unpleasant states and to prolong pleasant states. Therefore, users prefer media offerings that allow them to be in pleasant states for as long and intensively as possible or that help to reduce (or eliminate) the intensity of unpleasant states (Zillman 1988). Accordingly, AI doesn't need to be a source of distrust, fear, and doom: who wouldn't appreciate a parking assistant when faced with a tight parking space?

However, to understand and successfully use new AI technologies, people need to develop digital literacy (e.g. Jones/Hafner, 2012). Even though different definitions of digital literacy exist, this concept usually entails different forms of literacy necessary to master interaction with technical devices: media literacy, computer literacy, internet literacy and information literacy (Leaning 2019). For instance, media literacy commonly refers to the ability to understand, evaluate and use media critically, independently and responsibly (cf. Potter 2010). Achievement of media literacy, however, is a life-long process (Baacke 1999).

A consistency motive is also discussed as important cofactor in the acceptance and use of new technologies such as smart home devices (Marikyan et al. 2020; Donsbach 1989, 1991). Humans strive for a balanced state of their worldview, beliefs, thoughts, goals and behaviour. In the event of contradictions between our thoughts, goals and convictions or between our thinking and our acting, we experience cognitive dissonance. This cognitive dissonance is perceived as unpleasant, thus motivating us to reduce this state of tension (e.g. Festinger 1957). In a recent study, cognitive dissonance was observed when the performance of AI such as smart home devices didn't match high user expectations, which led to feelings of anger, guilt and regret (Marikyan et al. 2020). However, cognitive dissonance and dissatisfaction may not only be induced by lacking performance of AI. People will also distrust AI if it violates important values, standards and goals.

1.1 Ethical Implications

To address such ethical implications, Manzeschke (2015, 2014) developed a model to ethically evaluate AI technologies (Weber 2019). Although the MEESTAR model (i.e. Modell zur ethischen Evaluation sozio-technischer Arrangements) has been primarily developed for the context of nursing and health care for the elderly (e.g. assistive technologies), these ethical dimensions or values emphasized should also be important for AI users in general: *autonomy, safety, privacy, care, justice, participation* and *self-conception* (Manzeschke et al. 2016). Table 1 gives an overview over how Manzeschke et. al. (2016) define these ethical values in the context of MEESTAR.

Developed for the evaluation of specific technical applications, the literature suggests that ethical standards are important for our well-being in a variety of contexts. For instance, *autonomy* has been defined as a core psychological need and its importance in designing AI systems has already been emphasized in the theoretical literature (Calvo et al. 2020; Ryan/Deci 2017; Vansteenkiste et al. 2020). From a psychological perspective, *self-conception* is influenced by various identity processes and factors such as social comparison processes aiming at positive distinctiveness, which also entails the need for experiences of competence and mastery. Like *autonomy*, competence has been identified as a core psychological need (Vansteenkiste et al. 2020), which should also influence user experiences with AI. For *privacy*, empirical evidence is mixed: whilst some studies emphasize user concerns linked to the violation of *privacy*, other findings suggest that users often neglect the implications that a violation of their own *privacy* may have (Acosta/Reinhardt 2020).

Table 1: Definitions of the seven ethical values by MEESTAR (Manzeschke et al., 2016)

Ethical Value	Definition
Autonomy	maximum freedom in own decisions or actions; includes acceptance and facilitation of autonomy of people with disabilities by their integration or inclusion
Safety	protection against serious harm (e.g. physically, mentally, financially) and against unethical practices
Privacy	extent to which people can protect their personal beliefs and actions from the public eye; entails the right to bypass observation and regulation; control over the information people are willing to share
Care	extent to which a person (or AI) can care for those partially or not at all able to care for themselves; entails questions about when technically assisted care may become ethically difficult because it opposes the personal beliefs and goals of the person being cared for (e.g. by creating unacceptable dependencies)
Justice	extent to which equal access to AI systems is provided to all humans in a non-discriminatory and unbiased way
Participation	degree to which of access, rights, and services necessary to be part of the community and society are granted to everyone
Self-conception	how we perceive ourselves; often influenced by the images and social narratives about what is a normal, healthy or successful self

For *justice* in terms of perceived fairness and equity as well as for *participation* in terms of inclusion in decision-making processes, impacts on psychological well-being have been demonstrated in the context of organizational processes: perceived procedural injustice in organizations negatively affects employees' psychological well-being, whilst organizational inclusion enhances employees' psychological well-being (Le et al. 2018; Qin et al. 2014). For *care*, the importance of caregivers enabling care receivers to remain in control of their care has been empirically demonstrated at least in the context of the elderly (Broese van Groenou 2020).

The literature above indicates that these seven ethical values can influence our well-being in a variety of contexts. In this study, I aimed at investigating the extent to which these values may be applied to the AI context. I was also interested in the extent to which individual difference variables will impact users' motivational needs, moral standards and considerations of ethical implications.

1.2 Individual Difference Variables Possibly Affecting Interaction with AI

Technical experience and age influence how people interact with technical devices: in touch interaction, younger participants interacted more intuitively with AI than older participants. Technically experienced participants interacted more intuitively with AI than those with less technical experience (Nowack 2018).

Age and gender have also been shown to influence psychological needs, ethical values, and risk perception (Beutel/Marini 1995). *Autonomy* seems to vary with age: Older participants pursue their goals with greater autonomy than younger participants (Mackenzie et al. 2018). Furthermore, women assign greater importance to the well-being of others (which relates to *care*) and less importance to being competitive (which relates to *self-conception*) compared to men (Beutel/Marini 1995). Women also demonstrated a greater awareness than men for a variety of risks including technological risks (e.g. Cyber Incidents). Here, women showed higher ratings of risk likelihood as well as higher impact ratings in the event of such an incident (Brown et al. 2021). Another individual difference variable linked to risk perception and willingness to engage in risky behaviour is an aspect of individual temporal orientation, namely time perspective (Zimbardo/Boyd 1999).

The construct of time perspective denotes a preference to rely on a particular temporal frame (i.e. past, present or future) for decision-making processes and behaviour. Individuals differ in the extent to which they emphasize one time perspective over the others (Zimbardo et al. 1997). For instance, present-oriented people tend to base their decisions and actions on the immediate rewards a present situation offers. Future-oriented people focus on expected consequences that a present behaviour may have for the future. Past-oriented people mainly base their present actions on previous outcomes and events they recall from their past. The concept of time perspective has not only been investigated within the context of psychological time such as relationships with other aspects of temporal orientation or temporal event knowledge (Nowack/van der Meer 2013; 2014; Nowack et al. 2013). Time perspective has also been linked to general well-being, consumer behaviour, environmental engagement as well as risk perception (Klicperová-Baker et al. 2015; Milfont et al. 2012; Mooney et al. 2017). Whilst future-oriented individuals show a greater anticipation of consequences that a present behaviour may have for the near and distant future (Strathman et al. 1994), present time perspective has been linked to a low consideration of future consequences, sensation seeking, aggression, impulsivity and risk-taking behaviour (Zimbardo/Boyd 1999). For instance, present-oriented people show more risky driving behaviours and more often report the use of alcohol, tobacco and drugs (Keough et al. 1999; Zimbardo et al. 1997). Recent research also links past negative as well as present fatalistic time perspectives to increased risky driving behaviours, and future time perspective to low risky driving behaviour (Măirean/Diaconu-Gherasim 2021). Here, future time perspective appeared to facilitate risk perception with a mediating effect on risky driving behavior. The extent to which time perspective may influence user concerns, risk perception and ethical standards in an AI context, however, has not been investigated yet.

Based on the MEESTAR model (Manzeschke et al. 2016) and the literature cited above, I tested the following three hypotheses:

1. In line with the MEESTAR model, I expected that people are concerned with violations of the ethical values of *autonomy*, *privacy*, *self-conception*, *care*, *participation*, *safety* and *justice*. I also expected participants to rate these ethical values as important when interacting with AI.
2. I expected an impact of individual difference variables on ratings of concern when AI violates ethical values: age, gender, technical experience and time perspective should influence the extent of concern and, thus, median and agreement rates with the MEESTAR model (i.e. MEESTAR strength).
3. I expected an impact of individual difference variables on the extent to which people assign importance to these ethical values: age, gender,

technical experience and time perspective should influence importance rates (i.e. median and MEESTAR strength).

2. Method

2.1 Participants

Sixty-four German adults (28 women, 36 men) aged between 19 and 72 years ($M = 36{,}7$ years; $SD = 14{,}9$ years) took part in this study. All were German native speakers. All procedures performed in the study were in accordance with the ethical principles stated in the 1964 Helsinki Declaration. Informed consent was obtained from all individual participants included in the study.

2.2 Materials and Procedure

2.2.1 Technical Experience

All participants were asked to indicate the frequency with which they used a variety of technical devices at home (e.g. *smartphone, laptop, tablet pc*) as well as in public (e.g. *ticketing machine, self-service banking*) on a short paper-and-pencil questionnaire. For a total of seventeen items, participants simply had to select one of the following response options: 0 – *I don't know this device*, 1 – *never*, 2 – *rarely*, 3 – *once per month*, 4 – *once a week*, 5 – *almost daily*, 6 – *once per day* and 7 – *more than once per day*. The mean of all responses was calculated for each participant with a higher score indicating greater technical experience.

2.2.2 Time Perspective

To measure individuals' time perspective, a German version of the Zimbardo Time Perspective Inventory (ZTPI; Zimbardo/Boyd 1999) was used. Characterized by high retest-reliability and validity (Milfont/Bieniok 2008; Zimbardo/Boyd 1999), the original ZTPI consists of 54 items measuring time-related attitudes and behaviours on a 5-point Likert scale ranging from 1 (very uncharacteristic of me) to 5 (very characteristic of me) to distinguish between five dimensions: Past Negative, Past Positive, Present Fatalistic, Present Hedonistic and Future. To overcome the difficulty of the time dimension being confounded with valence in some ZTPI-items, a simplified version that excludes highly emotional items consisting of thirteen items for each the past, present and future dimension was used. This shorter version of the ZTPI has previously been successfully applied in other studies (Nowack et al. 2013; Nowack/van der Meer 2013; 2014).

2.2.3 Ethical Aspects

To investigate the extent to which users may be concerned when ethical values are violated in interactions with intelligent home devices, two paper-and-pencil questionnaires (questionnaire A and questionnaire B) were developed. Each questionnaire consists of seven different scenarios with each scenario focusing on one of the seven ethical aspects of *justice, safety, participation, care, self-conception, privacy* and *autonomy* that are emphasized by the MEESTAR model. In questionnaire A, the ethical aspects of *justice, participation* and *care* were violated. In the remaining four scenarios, the ethical aspects *safety, self-conception, privacy* and *autonomy* were not violated. In questionnaire B, the ethical aspects of *safety, self-conception, privacy* and *autonomy* were violated. In the remaining three scenarios, the ethical aspects *justice, participation* and *care* were not violated. Please see table 2 for some examples as well as the Appendix for all the scenarios.

Table 2: Example scenarios for the ethical value of care: scenario without violation (left) and scenario with violation of this aspect (right)

care – No violation	care – violation
Marie has multiple sclerosis. Too much heat causes her illness to flare up again. It is therefore important that Marie avoids excessively high temperatures when showering. Since Marie, due to her illness (shaky hands; inability to perform fine motor movements), cannot operate her heating control via the keyboard or the display, her father visits her twice a week to adjust the water to a comfortable temperature for her before showering.	Marie has multiple sclerosis. Too much heat causes her illness to flare up again. It is therefore important that Marie avoids excessively high temperatures when showering. Since Marie, due to her illness (shaky hands; inability to perform fine motor movements), cannot operate her heating control via the keyboard or the display, she uses voice control to adjust the water to a temperature that is comfortable for her before she takes a shower.

After completing the questionnaires ascertaining their technical experience, time perspective and demographic data, participants were presented with either questionnaire A or questionnaire B depending on their participant number (i.e. uneven number – questionnaire A; even number – questionnaire B). After reading each scenario, participants were asked to indicate 1.) the extent to which they felt concerned about how ethical standards were fulfilled in that scenario and, 2.) the importance they generally ascribe to that ethical aspect. Participants rated their concern on a 5-point Likert scale ranging from 1 (*feeling not concerned at all*) to 5 (*feeling strongly concerned*). Likewise, the importance could be indicated on a 5-point Likert scale ranging from 1 (*completely unimportant*) to 5 (*very important*). The experiment was run in German; all items have been translated here into English.

2.3 Design

Age, technical experience and time perspective were considered as continuous independent between-subjects variables, gender as categorical independent between-subjects variable. For every participant, questionnaire responses (ratings of concern and importance) were recorded as dependent variables.

2.4 Data Selection, Cleaning and Reduction

Rates of concern as well as importance rates were calculated from the questionnaire responses and analyzed using the IBM SPSS Statistics Version 28. For Likert Scales, the most appropriate method as measures of central tendency are analyses of the median or mode (cf. Jamieson 2004). Whilst the median denotes the middle value in the list of all numbers, the mode is the value that occurs most often. Kruskal-Wallis-tests were conducted to examine influences of age, gender, technical experience and the violation of ethical aspects on participants rates of concern and on the rated importance of the seven ethical aspects. For a better differentiation, frequencies in per cent were also calculated for the different response options. After testing whether participants' responses significantly differed from random distribution[1], agreement rates (i.e. percentage of answers consistent with the MEESTAR model) were calculated, firstly, for the rates of concern when ethical aspects were violated, and, secondly, for importance rates that participants generally assigned to the seven ethical aspects. Neutral responses were coded as *not conforming* to the theory. An index of MEESTAR strength

---

1 Pearson's chi-square test showed that the five response options were not equally preferred (i.e. no random distribution).

based on Cohen's Kappa was then calculated whilst considering a probability of 40 per cent of responding in agreement with the MEESTAR model (i.e. only two of the five response options were in concordance; see also Nowack 2018; Hurtienne et al. 2010; Cohen 1960)[2].

Analyses of variance (ANOVA) as well as independent-samples t-tests were conducted to compare ratings of concern when ethical values are violated compared to when they are not. Repeated-measures analyses of variance (ANOVA) as well as paired-samples t-tests were conducted to compare ratings of concern as well as importance ratings of the seven ethical aspects after testing for normal distribution (Shapiro-Wilk test). Independent samples t-tests were also conducted to examine influences of age, gender, technical experience and the violation of ethical aspects on the frequencies (in per cent) of rates of concern and importance of the seven ethical aspects.

All effects are reported as significant at $p < .05$ (Bonferroni correction for multiple comparisons).

3. Results and Discussion

3.1 Hypothesis 1 – Agreement with The MEESTAR Model

To test the first hypothesis that people are concerned with violations of the ethical values of *autonomy, privacy, self-conception, care, participation, safety* and *justice*, I analysed whether participants reliably detected violations of the ethical values in the scenarios. As depicted in Figure 1, violations were detected and led to significantly higher ratings of concern compared to the scenarios in which ethical values were not violated.

---

[2] MEESTAR strength (MS) $= \frac{observed\, agreement - .40(i.e., probability\, of\, agreement)}{1 - .40(i.e., probability\, of\, agreement)}$

Figure 1: Median of concern expressed by participants for scenarios in which ethical aspects were violated compared to scenarios in which not violation took place

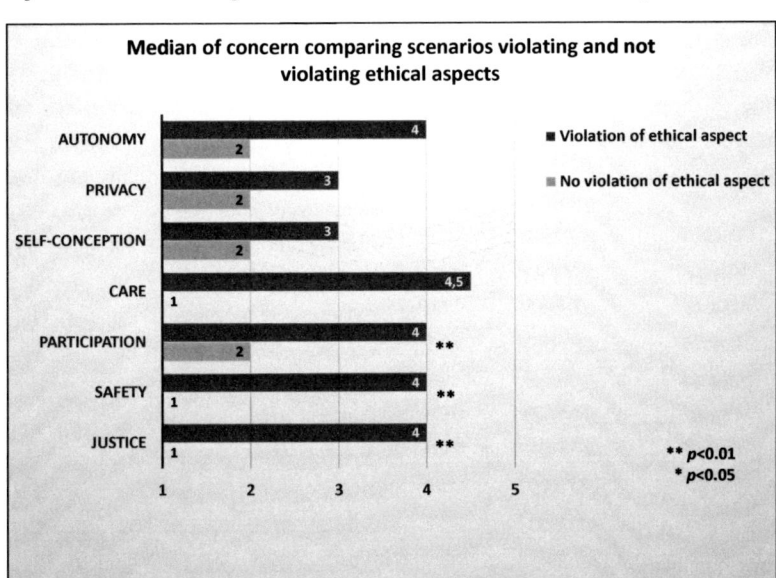

I then calculated the agreement rates with the MEESTAR model (i.e. MEESTAR strength) for the ratings of concern when an ethical value was violated in the scenarios. MEESTAR strength ranges from -1 to 1 with negative scores indicating disagreement and a score of 0 indicating selection by chance (Viera/Garrett 2005). MEESTAR strengths below .20 indicate only slight agreement, below .40 fair agreement, below .60 moderate agreement. MEESTAR strengths of at least .61 relate to substantial agreement whilst MEESTAR strengths of .81 and above indicate almost perfect agreement with the theory (cf. Viera/Garrett 2005).

In this study, the general agreement with the MEESTAR model for all ethical values is just reaching moderate agreement ($Mean = .40$; $SD = .56$). For design purposes, one should usually aim for an agreement (here, a MEESTAR strength) of at least 0.61 denoting a substantial agreement (cf. Hurtienne et al. 2010). Accepting this threshold, the general MEESTAR strength yielded in this study contradicts the first hypothesis. This may be due to violations of some of the ethical values emphasized by MEESTAR model not leading to the anticipated rates of concern. This is also supported by a repeated measures ANOVA with questionnaire presented (questionnaire A; questionnaire B) as between participants variable that was performed on concern ratings for the seven ethical values. There was a significant main effect for ethical aspects ($F(6,373) = 2.819$, MSE = 1.574, $p = .011$, $\eta^2 = .153$) on the concern ratings: MEESTAR strengths depended on which particular ethical value participants had to rate. Therefore, I also looked at concern rates for the seven ethical aspects individually.

Descriptive statistics for the seven ethical values individually are displayed in table 3 including median, modus, frequency (in per cent) of expressed concern (i.e. answer options 4 – *rather concerned*, and 5 – *strongly concerned*) and mean MEESTAR strengths (MS).

Table 3: Median, Modus, Frequency (in %) expressed concern and Mean MEESTAR strength (MS)

ethical value	Ratings of concern when ethical aspect is violated			
	Median	Mode	Frequency (in %) of expressed concern	Mean MEESTAR strength (MS)
justice	4	4	59.4	.32
safety	4	4	71.9	.53
participation	4	4	78.1	.64
care	4.5	5	84.4	.74
self-conception	3	3	34.4	-.09
privacy	3	2	40.6	.01
autonomy	4	5	65.6	.43
MS strengths below .20 denote slight agreement, below .40 fair agreement, below .60 moderate agreement, at least .61 substantial agreement, and .81 and above 'almost perfect' agreement (cf. Viera/Garrett 2005)				

Median and mode for the ethical values of *self-conception* and *privacy* suggest that participants in this study were less concerned with violations of these ethical values. A median and mode of 3 relates to a neutral response; a mode of 2 for *privacy* shows that most participants were rather unconcerned (see table 3). This is further supported by the MEESTAR strengths as shown in Table 3 and Figure 2. Whilst ratings of concern for violations of *self-conception* even contradict the MEESTAR model (i.e. slight disagreement), concern ratings for violations of *privacy* almost reach no agreement. MEESTAR strengths for both *privacy* and *self-conception* were significantly lower than for all the other ethical values (all p's < .01).

Figure 2: Agreement with the MEESTAR model (MEESTAR strength) for concern expressed by participants for scenarios in ethical aspects of justice, safety, participation, care, self-conception, privacy or autonomy were violated

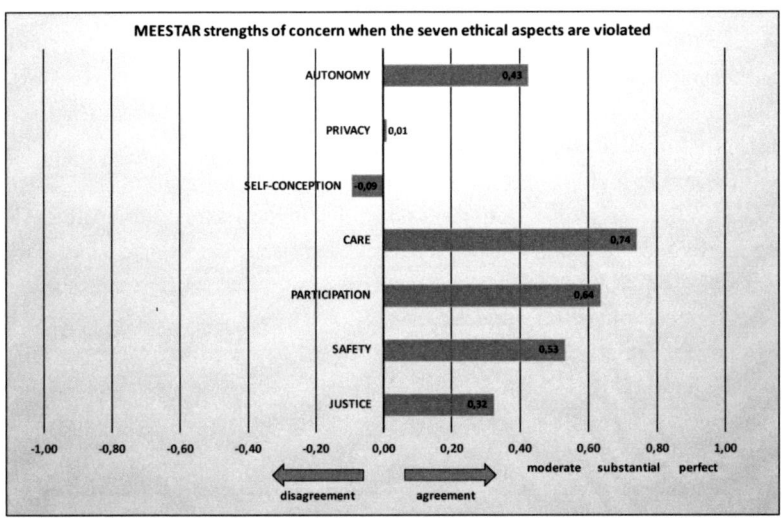

As demonstrated in figure 2, participants in this current study were most concerned with violations of the ethical values *care* and *participation* (both reaching substantial agreement as well as both with significantly higher MEESTAR strengths compared to the other aspects; all p's < .05). *Autonomy* and *safety* also led to concern reaching moderate agreement with MEESTAR. Concern ratings when aspects of *justice* were violated only reached a fair agreement with the MEESTAR model. These findings suggest that contrary to my first hypothesis, participants in this current study were not as concerned with violations of some ethical values as emphasized by the MEESTAR model for interaction with AI: this is especially true for *self-conception, privacy* and *justice*.

Regarding the importance of the seven ethical values, I first conducted independent samples Kruskal-Wallis-Tests to examine the impact of the questionnaire presented to the participants on their ratings of importance.

For all seven ethical values highlighted by the MEESTAR model, participants showed no significant differences in importance ratings (all p's > .05). This means that importance ratings were not influenced by whether a particular ethical aspect was violated in a scenario or not.

I then calculated the agreement rates with the MEESTAR model (i.e. MEESTAR strength) for the importance ratings. A repeated measures ANOVA was performed on the ratings of importance for the seven ethical values. Contrary to the ratings of concern, the general agreement with the MEESTAR model for all seven ethical values was substantial (*Mean* = .62; *SD* = .38). This indicates that participants may consider all the ethical values emphasized by MEESTAR as important for interacting with AI. However, they appear to be less concerned with violations of these values than the MEESTAR model would suggest.

There was also a significant main effect for ethical aspects ($F(6,378)$ = 10.049, MSE = 2.444, p < .001, η^2 = .138) on the importance ratings: MEESTAR strengths for importance depended on which particular ethical value participants had to rate. These differences are also found when analysing the seven ethical values independently.

Table 4 depicts descriptive statistics for the seven ethical values including median, modus, frequency (in per cent) of importance ratings (i.e., answer options 4 – *rather important*, and 5 – *very important*) and mean MEESTAR strengths (MS).

Median and mode for importance ratings for the seven ethical values indicate that, except for *privacy*, participants considered all values as *rather important* or *very important* when interacting with AI. Figure 3 depicts the agreement with the MEESTAR model for the importance ratings of the seven ethical values individually. *Privacy* reached significantly lower MEESTAR agreement than all the other aspects (all p's < .001), achieving only a slight agreement with MEESTAR for importance ratings. *Self-conception* also reached a significantly lower MEESTAR strength than the other ethical values (all p's < .05), except for *justice*, but still achieved a moderate agreement. Like the concern ratings, the ethical value of *care* was also considered the most important value, reaching substantial agreement. However, the differences for *care* were only significant for the aspects of *justice*, *self-conception* and *privacy*. Substantial agreement was also found for the ethical values of *safety*, *justice*, *participation* and *autonomy*.

Table 4: Median, Modus, Frequency (in %) expressed concern and Mean MEESTAR strength (MS)

ethical value	Importance ratings of ethical aspects when interacting with AI			
	Median	Mode	Frequency (in %) of expressed concern	Mean MEESTAR strength (MS)
justice	4	4	78.1	.64
safety	5	5	86.0	.77
participation	4	5	81.3	.69
care	4.5	5	93.8	.90
self-conception	4	4	74.5	.56
privacy	3.5	4	53.2	.22
Autonomy	5	5	76.6	.61
MS strengths below .20 denote slight agreement, below .40 fair agreement, below .60 moderate agreement, at least .61 substantial agreement, and .81 and above 'almost perfect' agreement (cf. Viera/Garrett 2005)				

Accepting the threshold of at least .61 (i.e. substantial agreement), the current findings only partially support the first hypothesis for the ratings of importance. In line with the first hypothesis and the MEESTAR model, people indeed assign great importance to the values of *care, safety, participation, justice* and *autonomy* when interacting with AI. However, participants in this study did not assign great importance to the ethical values *privacy* and *self-conception*, which contradicts the first hypothesis and MEESTAR model.

Only for the ethical values of *participation* and *care*, both the concern and importance ratings clearly confirmed an applicability of the MEESTAR model for interacting with AI. By contrast, almost no agreement in ratings of concern as well as slight agreement in importance ratings for *privacy* suggest that this ethical aspect is not such a big issue for users interacting with AI as also shown by some of the previous literature (Acosta/Reinhardt 2020). Slight to moderate agreement with MEESTAR in ratings of concern as well as substantial agreement in importance ratings for *safety, justice* and *autonomy* suggest that individual difference variables may influence the extent to which users can anticipate the consequences that violations of these values may have. Likewise, the discrepancy between importance ratings and ratings of concern for *self-conception* may be affected by other variables. Therefore, I also analyzed the impact of individual difference variables (i.e. age, gender,

Figure 3: Agreement with the MEESTAR model (MEESTAR strength) for importance assigned to the ethical aspects of justice, safety, participation, care, self-conception, privacy and autonomy

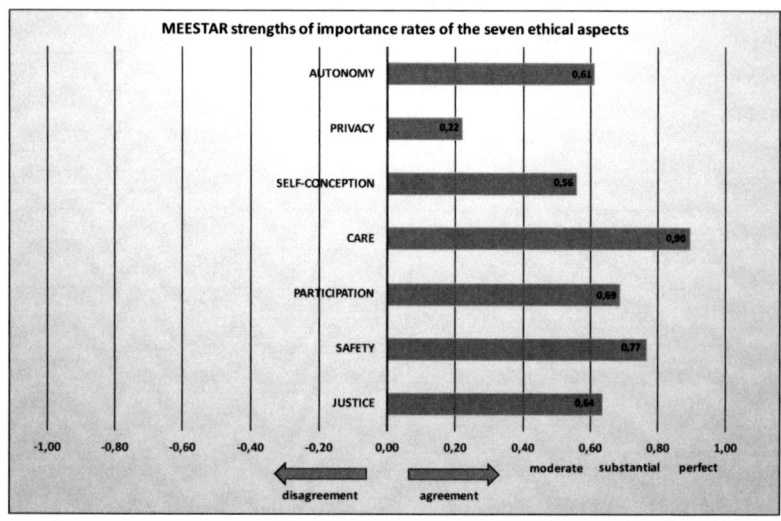

technical experience, time perspective) on ratings of concern and importance.

3.2 Hypothesis 2 – Impact of Individual Difference Variables on Ratings of Concern when Ethical Values are Violated

To test for an impact of age, gender, technical experience and time perspective on ratings of concern when ethical aspects are violated, I first conducted a repeated-measures analysis of covariance (ANCOVA) with gender as between-participants variable and age, technical experience and time perspective as covariates on the MEESTAR strengths for concern ratings. Descriptive statistics are displayed in Table 5 and include mean MEESTAR strength for concern rates (left) as well as for importance rates (right) depending on gender. There were no significant impacts of age or technical experience (all p's > .50).

Women express concerns that show moderate agreement whilst men express concerns that are only in slight agreement with the MEESTAR model.

However, the ANCOVA as well as a *t*-test show that these differences are not significant (all *p*'s > .50).

I also conducted independent samples Kruskal-Wallis-Tests to analyse the impact of gender on the concern rates for the seven ethical aspects individually. Here, significant differences were found only for the ethical aspect of *justice* ($p = .04$). Women were more concerned when this ethical value was violated (median = 4) than men who showed a neutral response (median = 3) to violations in *justice*. This is further supported by correlational analysis between gender and the median of the concern expressed when the aspect of *justice* is violated ($r = -0.36$, $p = .023$): When perceiving injustice in the interaction with intelligent home assistants, women show a higher median and, thus, express greater concern than men.

Next, I analysed differences in MEESTAR strengths depending on gender (see figure 4), which show that women respond to violations of *justice* more in agreement with MEESTAR (substantial agreement) than men (slight agreement). This also supports the notion that women are significantly more concerned when interacting with AI leads to injustice than men. Female ratings of concern to violations of *care* were also more in agreement with the MEESTAR model (perfect agreement) than the male ratings (substantial agreement).

Table 5: Means (M) and standard deviations (SD) of MEESTAR (MS) strength for concern rates of violations and importance rates depending on gender

MEESTAR strength: concern ratings when ethical values are violated			MEESTAR strength: importance assigned to all seven ethical aspects		
gender	mean MS strength	SD	gender	mean MS strength	SD
female	0,45	0,58	female	0,67	0,39
male	0,34	0,49	male	0,59	0,38
all participants	0,39	0,53	all participants	0,62	0,38
MS strengths of .20 denote slight agreement, MS strengths of .40 denote moderate agreement, MS strengths of .60 denote substantial agreement with the MEESTAR model					

By contrast, men expressed greater concern in response to violations of *safety* (substantial agreement) than women (fair agreement; see figure 4). MEESTAR strengths for *autonomy, participation, privacy* and *self-conception* do not differ between women and men. Concern ratings by both women and men for *privacy* and *self-conception* contradict the first hypothesis, while concern ratings for *autonomy* also don't reach the threshold of .61.

Figure 4: MEESTAR strengths for ratings of concern in response to violations of the ethical aspects of justice, safety, participation, care, self-conception, privacy and autonomy depending on gender

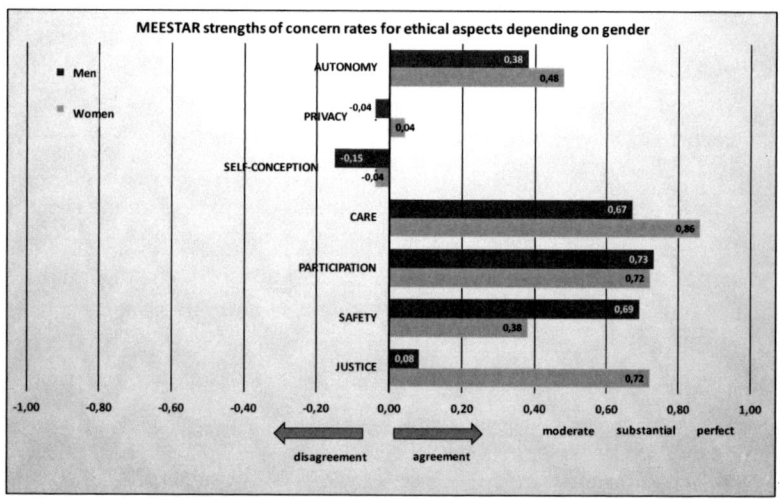

Regarding time perspective, the ANCOVA showed a significant influence of past ($F(1,63) = 5.822$, $p = .024$, $\eta^2 = .202$) and present time perspective ($F(1,63) = 4.974$, $p = .036$, $\eta^2 = .178$). This was also supported by Pearson's correlational analyses between age, gender, technical experience, time perspective and the mean MEESTAR strengths for concern ratings when ethical values are violated. These were also significant for the past ($r = 0.41$, $p = .02$) and present time perspective ($r = -0.37$, $p = .031$): past-oriented participants responded more in agreement with the MEESTAR model by displaying higher ratings of concern when ethical aspects were violated. Present-oriented participants responded less in agreement with the MEESTAR model by expressing lower ratings of concern when ethical aspects were violated. This is in line with previous research showing a higher tendency for risky behaviour such as substance use and abuse as well as risky driving behaviour (Keough et al. 1999; Zimbardo et al., 1997). However, these results contradict recent findings of a link between past negative time perspective and risky behaviour (Măirean/Diaconu-Gherasim 2021). This may be due to the fact that the current study employed a simplified version of the ZTPI (Zimbardo/Boyd 1999) that excludes highly emotional items. These results suggest that the interrelations between past negative time perspective and risky behaviour found by Măirean and Diaconu-Gherasim (2021) may be mainly influenced by the (negative) emotionality of the past negative scale rather than by an orientation towards the past as such.

3.3 Hypothesis 3 – Impact of Individual Difference Variables on the Importance Ratings

Table 2 (right) depicts the mean MEESTAR strengths for importance rates generally assigned to the seven ethical values depending on gender. Women show importance rates of substantial agreement whilst men show importance rates of moderate agreement with the MEESTAR model. However, a repeated-measures analysis of covariance (ANCOVA) with gender as between-participants variable and age, time perspective and technical experience as covariates on the MEESTAR strengths for importance ratings as well as a t-test show that the influence of gender on general importance ratings for all ethical values was not significant. Likewise, there was no significant impact of age and time perspective (all p's > .50).

However, the ANCOVA showed a significant influence of technical experience ($F(1,63) = 12.88$, $p < .001$, $\eta^2 = .182$). This was also supported by Pearson's correlational analyses between age, gender, technical experience and the mean MEESTAR strength of the importance rates. These were only significant for technical experience ($r = 0.44$, $p < .001$): participants with greater technical experience generally assigned greater importance to the seven ethical aspects, while participants with minimal technical experience assigned less importance to these aspects.

Next, I conducted independent samples Kruskal-Wallis-Tests to analyze the impact of gender on the rating of importance for the seven ethical aspects individually. Here, significant differences were found for the ethical aspect of *privacy* ($p = .034$) and *autonomy* ($p = .049$): women assigned greater importance than men to both ethical aspects. *Privacy* is rated by women as rather important (median = 4) whilst men are neutral (median = 3) towards this aspect. Autonomy is rated by women as very important (median = 5), by men as rather important (median = 4). This is also supported by significant differences in MEESTAR strengths depending on gender (see figure 5).

Figure 5: MEESTAR strengths for importance assigned to the ethical aspects of justice, safety, participation, care, self-conception, privacy and autonomy depending on gender

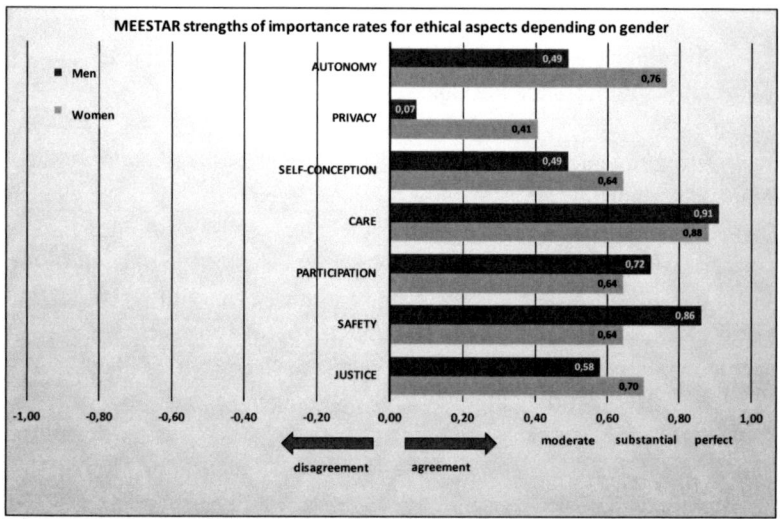

Women rated the importance of the ethical values *privacy* and *autonomy* significantly higher than men as demonstrated by greater MEESTAR strengths (i.e. more in agreement with the MEESTAR model; all p's < .01). Similarly, women also rated *self-conception* and *justice* as more important than men. By contrast, men assigned greater importance to *safety* (in perfect agreement; see figure 5) than women as demonstrated by a greater MEESTAR strength ($p < .05$). This shows that the extent to which users may be concerned with ethical values when interacting with AI is influenced by gender, even though the impact of gender differs between different ethical values.

Concerning interrelations between time perspective and the median of importance ratings for the seven ethical aspects individually, Pearson's correlational analyses were significant for future time perspective and *autonomy* ($r = 0.55$, $p = .002$): participants with a greater future time perspective assigned greater importance to the ethical aspect of *autonomy*. This is in line with previous findings of future-oriented people assigning great importance to the aspect of autonomy in their goal-making if they perceive their future as open-ended (cf. Lang/Carstensen 2002). There were no significant correlations between time perspective and the other six aspects of *justice, privacy, safety, participation, care* and *self-conception*.

4. General Discussion

I aimed at investigating the extent to which the ethical values emphasized by the MEESTAR model (e.g. Manzeschke et. al. 2016) can explain user concern about AI systems. To this end, ratings of concern if the values of *autonomy, safety, privacy, care, justice, participation* and *self-conception* are violated as well as importance ratings were measured. This study yielded three main results. First, the MEESTAR model cannot be fully applied to the broader context of users of all ages interacting with AI. Some, but not all, ethical values emphasized by MEESTAR need to be considered in AI development: AI technologies need to be in alignment with the ethical values *participation* and *care*. The same also applies to *autonomy, safety* and *justice*, all of which were rated in substantial agreement with MEESTAR for importance but only in moderate agreement (*autonomy, safety*) or fair agreement (*justice*) in terms of concern if values are violated.

For *self-conception*, the results are mixed (i.e. in disagreement with MEESTAR for concern ratings; in moderate agreement for importance ratings). This may be due to *self-conception* entailing a variety of sub concepts such as the core psychological need for competence but also our social identities, personal goals, experiences and standards that are often influenced by society. Future research should, thus, focus on these underlying aspects rather than on *self-conception* per se. Furthermore, future research may investigate the extent to which the core psychological needs of competence, relatedness and autonomy influence our use of and trust in AI (Vansteenkiste et al. 2020). These needs are important for our wellbeing and, thus, for acceptance of AI (Self-Determination Theory; Ryan/Deci 2000).

Contrary to the first hypothesis (H1) but in line with some of the literature (cf. Acosta/Reinhardt 2020), users are not concerned if *privacy* is violated by AI. *Privacy* is also not considered particularly important. The findings for *privacy* as well as the general differences found between higher importance ratings and lower ratings of concern emphasize the need for education to develop digital literacy for interacting with AI (cf. Leaning 2019). Accordingly, the literature shows positive effects of training older people in computer and Internet use on psychological well-being: learning how to use these new technologies had positive effects on their personal interactions (meeting their needs for relatedness) and on cognitive functions and led to an increased sense of empowerment and *autonomy* (Shapira et al. 2007). For users to understand, evaluate and use AI critically, independently and responsibly, they also need to be informed about their rights and ethical standards as well as about the possible consequences that a violation of their ethical rights may have for them personally and for society.

In line with this, there was a main effect of technical experience on importance but not concern ratings: greater technical experience was linked to higher importance ratings for all ethical values investigated in this study. Whilst technical experience should be related to digital literacy as part of the computer literacy skill set, there are also other important skills such as those referred to as information literacy. The current findings, thus, show that digital literacy entails so much more than computer literacy. Users also need to develop competencies that strengthen their information literacy (cf. Leaning, 2019).

Furthermore, I found individual difference variables that influenced ratings of concern and importance not in general but for some ethical values (hypotheses 2 and 3). There was an effect of gender on both ratings of concern and importance for some ethical values. Compared to men, women are more concerned about violations of *justice* and *care* and place greater importance on autonomy, justice, self-conception and privacy. Compared to women, men were more concerned about safety breaches and attached greater importance to this value. These gender differences are in line with studies that show an impact of gender on risk perception (Brown et al. 2021) as well as with studies showing that women place greater importance on the well-being of others (Beutel/Marini 1995).

Contrary to my hypotheses, age had no influence on concern and importance ratings. Does this suggest that perception of these ethical values remains relatively stable over a lifetime? The literature suggests the contrary for personal values, which appear not to stabilize until a later age (cf. Konty/Dunham 1997). However, the empirical evidence on age-related influences on broader ethical values is scarce. For *autonomy*, for instance, we must differ between *autonomy* as a value, *autonomy* as a core psychological need and *au-*

tonomy as an experience of control. The latter has been shown to increase with age (Mackenzie et al. 2018). As a core psychological need, autonomy has been argued to remain relatively stable over the span of a lifetime (cf. Ryan/Deci 2000). Here, more empirical research on the stability of ethical values that are important on a cultural and individual level is necessary.

Third, corresponding to my hypotheses, time perspective influenced concern and importance ratings: present-oriented participants were less concerned with violations of all ethical values, while past-oriented participants showed greater concern. Future-oriented participants placed greater importance on *autonomy* for AI interaction. Here, the findings complement the literature by showing that time perspective is not only interrelated to other aspects of psychological time (Nowack/van der Meer 2013; 2014; Nowack et al. 2013). In line with studies that link time perspective to general well-being, consumer behaviour or to the environmental context (Klicperová-Baker et al. 2015; Milfont et al. 2012; Mooney et al. 2017), the current study extends the concept of time perspective to an application within the AI context.

Due to the explorative nature of the current study, I investigated ethical values in a small sample as well as with a small selection of scenarios only. This limits the generalizability of the results. However, these initial findings emphasize the need to further investigate ethical values at the individual level by employing a wider selection of scenarios.

The current study, nevertheless, goes beyond previous investigations in two important ways. First, it highlights the need for more empirical research *with* users to investigate ethical values in AI interaction. In line with the uses and gratification approach (cf. Rosengren 1985), users will select those AI assistants that promise to meet their standards, needs and expectations. Upon fulfilment, probability increases that users will want to interact with AI assistants again. If user expectations and needs are not met, people are less likely to interact with AI. Likewise, if AI assistants violate users' standards, it could lead to a state of cognitive dissonance (Festinger 1957). This is not only perceived as unpleasant but may also result in feelings of anger, guilt and regret (cf. Marikyan et al. 2020). Second, the study provides empirical evidence that AI systems can only be successfully introduced to society if they are accompanied by strategies that increase and strengthen digital literacy in everyone regardless of age, gender, educational or cultural background.

References

Acosta, L. H., and D. Reinhardt (2020). "Smart Speakers and Privacy: Users' Perspectives." In: *VDE dialog – The Technology Magazine* 04, pp. 8–10.

Baacke, D. (1999). "'Medienkompetenz': theoretisch erschließend und praktisch folgenreich." In: *Medien und Erziehung* 43.1, pp. 7–12.

Baecker, A. N., D. Y. Geiskkovitch, D. Y., A. L. González, and J. E. Young (2020). "Emotional Support Domestic Robots for Healthy Older Adults: Conversational Prototypes to Help with Loneliness." In: *Companion Proceedings of 2020 ACM International Conference on Human Robot Interaction (HRI'20)*, March 23–26, 2020, Cambridge, United Kingdom. ACM, 2 pages. https://doi.org/10.1145/3371382.3378279

Beutel, A. M., and M. Marini (1995). "Gender and values." In: *American Sociological Review* 60.3, pp. 436–448.

Broese van Groenou, M. (2020). "Associations between care network types and psychological well-being among Dutch older adults." In: *International Journal of Care and Caring* 4.2, pp. 215–233. URL: https://doi.org/10.1332/239788220X15833754379590.

Brown, G. D., A. Largey, and C. McMullan (2021). "The impact of gender on risk perception: Implications for EU member states' national risk assessment processes." In: *International Journal of Disaster Risk Reduction* 63, 102452.

Calvo, R. A., D. Peters, K. Vold, and R. M. Ryan (2020). "Supporting Human Autonomy in AI Systems: A Framework for Ethical Enquiry". In: *Ethics of Digital Well-Being*, Ed. by C. Burr and L. Floridi (Philosophical Studies Series, vol 140), Springer: Cham. URL: https://doi.org/10.1007/978-3-030-50585-1_2

Cohen, J. (1960). "A coefficient of agreement for nominal scales." In: *Educational and Psychological Measurement* 20, pp. 37–46.

Festinger, L. (1957). *A theory of cognitive dissonance*, Evanston, IL: Row, Peterson.

Friedemann, A. (1962). "Fernsehen." In: *Fernsehen der Kinder*. Ed. by K. Heymann (Schriftenreihe Psychologische Praxis. Bd. 33), Basel: Karger, pp. 61–89.

Heymann, K. (1962). *Fernsehen der Kinder* Schriftenreihe Psychologische Praxis. Bd. 33. Basel: Karger.

Hurtienne, J., C. Stößel, C. Sturm, A. Maus, M. Rötting, P. Langdon, and P. J. Clarkson (2010). "Physical gestures for abstract concepts. Inclusive design with primary metaphors." In: *Interact. Comput.* 22, pp. 475–484.

Jamieson S. (2004). "Likert scales: how to (ab)use them." In: *Med Educ.* 38.12, pp. 1217–1218.

Jones, R. H., and C. A. Hafner (2012). *Understanding digital literacies: a practical introduction.* Oxon, UK: Routledge.

Keough, K. A., P. G. Zimbardo, and J. N. Boyd (1999). "Who's smoking, drinking and using drugs? Time Perspective as a predictor of substance use." In: *Basic Appl Soc Psych* 21, pp. 149–164.

Klicperová-Baker, M., J. Košťál, and J. Vinopal (2015). "Time perspective in consumer behavior." In: *Time perspective theory: Review, research and application,* Cham: Springer, pp. 353–369.

Konty, M. A., and C. C. Dunham (1997). "Differences in value and attitude change over the life course." In: *Sociological Spectrum* 17.2, pp. 177–197.

Lang, F. R., and L. L. Carstensen (2002). "Time counts: Future time perspective, goals, and social relationships." In: *Psychology and Aging* 17, pp. 125–139.

Le, H., J. Zhou, F. Yuka, and I. Nielsen (2018). "Inclusion and affective wellbeing: Roles of justice perceptions." In: *Personnel Review* 47.4, pp. 805–820. URL: https://doi.org/10.1108/PR-03-2017-0078.

Leaning, M. (2019). "An approach to digital literacy through the integration of media and information literacy". In: *Media and Communication,* 7.2, pp. 4–13.

Mackenzie, C. S., E. C. Karaoylas, and K. B. Starzyk (2018). "Lifespan Differences in a Self Determination Theory Model of Eudaimonia: A Cross-Sectional Survey of Younger, Middle-Aged, and Older Adults." In: *J Happiness Stud* 19, pp. 2465–2487. URL: https://doi.org/10.1007/s10902-017-9932-4

Măirean, C., and L. R. Diaconu-Gherasim (2021). "Time perspective, risk perception on the road, and risky driving behavior" In: *Curr Psychol.* URL: URL: https://doi.org/10.1007/s12144-021-01921-2

Manzeschke, A. (2014). "Altersgerechte Assistenzsysteme: Ethische Herausforderungen technologischen Wandels." In: *informationsdienst altersfragen* 3.41, pp. 10–18.

Manzeschke, A. (2015). "MEESTAR: Ein Modell angewandter Ethik im Bereich assistiver Technologien." In: *Technisierung des Alltags – Beitrag zu einem guten Leben.* Ed. by K. Weber, D. Frommeld, H. Fangerau, and A. Manzeschke, pp. 263–283.

Manzeschke, A., K. Weber, E. Rother, and H. Fangerau (2015). *Results of the study Ethical questions in the area of age-appropriate assisting systems*. Abschlussbericht Druckerei Thiel Gruppe, Ludwigsfelde.

Marikyan, D., S. Papagiannidis, and E. Alamanos (2020). "Cognitive Dissonance in Technology Adoption: A Study of Smart Home Users." In: *Inf Syst Front*. https://doi.org/10.1007/s10796-020-10042-3

Milfont, T. L. and M. Bieniok (2008). Zimbardo time perspective inventory: German version. Unpublished manuscript.

Milfont, T. L., J. Wilson, and P. Diniz (2012). "Time perspective and environmental engagement: A meta-analysis." In: *International journal of psychology* 47.5, pp. 325–334.

Mooney, A., J. K. Earl, C. H. Mooney, and H. Bateman (2017). "Using Balanced Time Perspective to Explain Well-Being and Planning in Retirement." In: *Front. Psychol*. 8, Article 1781, doi: 10.3389/fpsyg.2017.01781.

Münsterberg, H. (1916). *The photoplay: A psychological study*, New York, London: Appleton and Company.

Nowack, K. (2018). "More is Up – Important is Central: Impact of Developmental Origin of Image Schemas on Touch and Gesture Interaction with Computers." In: *International Journal of Human-Computer Studies* 120, pp. 94–106.

Nowack, K., T. L. Milfont, and E. van der Meer (2013). "Future versus Present: Time Perspective and Pupillary Response in a Relatedness Judgment Task Investigating Temporal Event Knowledge." In: *Int. J. Psychophysiol*. 87.2, pp. 173–182.

Nowack, K., and E. van der Meer (2014). "Impact of chronotype and time perspective on the processing of scripts." In: *Int. J. Psychophysiol*. 92, pp. 49–58.

Nowack, K., and E. van der Meer (2013). "Are larks future-oriented and owls present-oriented? Age-and gender-related shifts in chronotype-time perspective associations." In: *Chronobiology International* 30.10, pp. 1240–1250.

Potter, W. J. (2010). "The State of Media Literacy." In: *Journal of Broadcasting & Electronic Media* 54.4, pp. 675–696, DOI: 10.1080/08838151.2011.521462.

Qin, X., M. S. DiRenzo, M. Xu, and Y. Duan (2014). "When do emotionally exhausted employees speak up? Exploring the potential curvilinear relationship between emotional exhaustion and voice." In: *Journal of Organizational Behavior* 35.7, pp. 1018–1041, doi: 10.1002/job.1948.

Rintelen, F. (1962). "Zur Frage der Beeinträchtigung des kindlichen Auges durch Fernsehen." In: *Fernsehen der Kinder.* Ed. by K. Heymann (Schriftenreihe Psychologische Praxis. Bd. 33), Basel: Karger. pp. 6–10.

Rosengren, K. E., L. A. Wenner, and Ph. Palmgren (1985). *Media gratifications research: Current perspectives,* Beverly Hills: Sage.

Ryan, R. M., and E. L. Deci (2000a). "Self-determination theory and the facilitation of intrinsic motivation, social development and well-being." In: *American Psychologist* 55, pp. 68–78.

Shapira, N., A. Barak, and I. Gal (2007). "Promoting Older Adults' Well-Being through Internet Training and Use." In: *Aging & Mental Health* 11, pp. 477–484, doi.org/10.1080/13607860601086546.

Strathman, A., F. Gleicher, D. Boninger, and C. Edwards (1994). "The consideration of future consequences: Weighing immediate and distant outcomes of behavior." In: *Journal of Personality and Social Psychology* 66, pp. 142–752.

Vansteenkiste, M., R. M. Ryan, and B. Soenens (2020). "Basic Psychological Need Theory: Advancements, Critical Themes, and Future Directions." In: *Motivation and Emotion,* 44, pp. 1–31.

Viera, A. J., and J. M. Garrett (2005). "Understanding interobserver agreement: The Kappa Statistic." In: *Family Medicine* 37, pp. 360–363.

Zillman, D. (1988). "Mood management through communication choices." In: *American Behavioral Scientist* 31, pp. 327–340.

Zillman, D., and P. Vorderer (2000). *Media Entertainment: the psychology of its appeal.* Mahwah NJ, USA: Lawrence Erlbaum Associates Publishers.

Zimbardo, P. G., and J. N. Boyd (1999). "Putting time in perspective: A valid, reliable individual-differences metric." In: *Journal of Personality & Social Psychology* 77, pp. 1271–1288.

Zimbardo, P. G., K. A. Keough, and J. N. Boyd (1997). "Present time perspective as a predictor of risky driving." In: *Personality and Individual Differences* 23, pp. 1007–1023.

Appendix

Questionnaire A	Questionnaire B
Scenario 1 – Justice	**Scenario 1 – Justice**
The 67-year-old widow Erna Schmidt has never had much to do with technology in her life. Her late husband had always taken care of all these things – for instance, he had a modern air conditioning system installed just before his death. However, the air conditioning is much too complicated for Mrs. Schmidt. She doesn't understand the structure and the menu sequence of the operating controls, and she can hardly see anything on the small display. Since the air conditioning cannot be used properly by her without technical experience, she is considering having it removed again.	The 67-year-old widow Erna Schmidt has never had much to do with technology in her life. Her late husband had always taken care of all these things – for instance, he had a modern air conditioning system installed just before his death. After an initial fear of doing something wrong, she discovered that she could communicate her wishes simply by speaking to the device. She is glad that she doesn't have to keep asking her son for help because she can use the air conditioning despite her minimal technical experience.

Questionnaire A	Questionnaire B
Scenario 2 – Safety Helmut and Rosemarie Weber are happy because they are going to Leipzig for 2 days today to visit their grandchildren Lea and Lukas. Since the Webers spend every weekend in Leipzig, the alarm system has already learned to be active 24 hours a day for the next two days. After a brief query and confirmation of the changed settings, the data is stored internally in the system. The data does not leak out and is not passed on to third parties.	**Scenario 2 – Safety** Helmut and Rosemarie Weber are happy because they are going to Leipzig for 2 days today to visit their grandchildren Lea and Lukas. Since the Webers spend every weekend in Leipzig, the alarm system has already learned to be active 24 hours a day for the next two days. After a brief query and confirmation of the changed settings, the data is forwarded to an external server. Rosemarie doesn't really like this. Only last year there was a data leak at the manufacturer of the alarm system, in which someone had gained unauthorized access to the private data of many homeowners. But Helmut calms down Rosemarie. After all, the manufacturer promised that something like this would never happen again.
Scenario 3 – Participation Frank Müller had a new modern heating control system installed in his father's house, which is operated by using an app on the smartphone. Due to his visual impairment, however, the pensioner cannot see anything on the smartphone display. If he wants to go away for the weekend with his fishing friends, he must keep heating the house at high costs, because he cannot change the basic settings made by the installer himself.	**Scenario 3 – Participation** Frank Müller had a new modern heating system installed in his father's house. In addition to many technical innovations, the heating control also enables the pensioner to adjust the settings to his wishes simply by speaking. If he wants to go away for the weekend with his fishing buddies, he simply tells his heater, "I'm going away. Please lower the temperature to 15°C until Sunday 5 p.m."

Scenario 4 – Care	Scenario 4 – Care
Marie has multiple sclerosis. Too much heat causes her illness to flare up again. It is therefore important that Marie avoids excessively high temperatures when showering. Since Marie, due to her illness (shaky hands; inability to perform fine motor movements), cannot operate her heating control via the keyboard or the display, her father visits her twice a week to adjust the water to a comfortable temperature for her before showering.	Marie has multiple sclerosis. Too much heat causes her illness to flare up again. It is therefore important that Marie avoids excessively high temperatures when showering. Since Marie, due to her illness (shaky hands; inability to perform fine motor movements), cannot operate her heating control via the keyboard or the display, she uses voice control to adjust the water to a temperature that is comfortable for her before she takes a shower.
Scenario 5 – Self-Conception	**Scenario 5 – Self-Conception**
The Müllers drive in a rental car to the Baltic Sea for Christmas. The rental car is equipped with a state-of-the-art driving assistant, which offers many interesting functions such as an "alcohol interlock". The retired couple has no idea what this could be and would like to find out more. After pressing the "wake-up" button, they are asked what the driver assistance can do for them. Surprised, Mr. Müller asks what an "alcohol interlock" is. The answer: "The alcohol interlock function is an alcohol-sensitive immobilizer. It prevents the car from starting if my sensors register the driver's alcohol consumption. Would you like to activate alcohol interlock?" The Müllers say no, but they are enthusiastic. At home they only have an old Opel station wagon that doesn't even help them park. Until now, they thought they were too old for such technical frills. But now they are considering buying a modern car with driver assistance.	The Müllers drive in a rental car to the Baltic Sea for Christmas. The rental car is equipped with a state-of-the-art driving assistant, which offers many interesting functions such as an "alcohol interlock". The retired couple has no idea what this could be and would like to find out more. However, the menu navigation of the driving assistant proves to be very complicated. It takes many individual steps that the Müllers cannot understand. They give up in frustration. Mr. Müller is glad that their old Opel station wagon doesn't have such frills. Somehow, they are probably too old for that. But they haven't used new-fangled technology for the last 10 years. Why should you change that now?

Scenario 6 – Privacy	Scenario 6 – Privacy
Mario has been unemployed for two weeks. However, he has not yet dared to talk to his wife about it. Somehow it never was the right moment. He comes home every day at 10 a.m. after his wife and children have left the apartment. Shortly before 4 p.m. he leaves the house again. The voice-controlled "personal smart home assistant" ROMEO has learned to raise the blinds and play Mario's favourite music when Mario comes home in the morning. One day, Mario's wife unexpectedly comes home just before 10 o'clock. Since ROMEO runs in private mode, it only learns user-specifically. ROMEO does not transmit data about its learned behaviour to other users. That's why the basic settings (blinds down, no music) are retained when Susanne arrives. Susanne does not find out anything about Mario's changed user profile. A few days later, Mario plucked up the courage and told her about his dismissal.	Mario has been unemployed for two weeks. However, he has not yet dared to talk to his wife about it. Somehow it never was the right moment. He comes home every day at 10 a.m. after his wife and children have left the apartment. Shortly before 4 p.m. he leaves the house again. The voice-controlled "personal smart home assistant" ROMEO has learned to raise the blinds and play Mario's favourite music when Mario comes home in the morning. One day, Mario's wife unexpectedly comes home just before 10 o'clock. Without prompting, ROMEO shows the behaviour it has learned from Mario at 10 a.m. sharp: the blinds are raised, Mario's favourite music is played. Mario's wife is surprised by this. She suspects that ROMEO learned this behaviour from Mario. But her husband always works from 8 a.m. to 5 p.m. In the evening, Susanne confronts Mario.
Scenario 7 – Autonomy	**Scenario 7 – Autonomy**
Anna wears a fitness bracelet, which also measures her body temperature and skin conductivity and sends it to the air conditioning system. Based on the data, the air conditioner recognizes that Anna is sweating. The air conditioner alerts Anna to this and asks if the room temperature should be lowered to 18°C. Since Anna wants to leave the house right away anyway, she says no. The room temperature remains unchanged.	Anna wears a fitness bracelet, which also measures her body temperature and skin conductivity and sends it to the air conditioning system. Based on the data, the air conditioner recognizes that Anna is sweating. It independently regulates the room temperature down to 18°C. Anna is not informed about the change in settings.

Man-Machines
Gynoids, Fembots, and Body-AI in Contemporary Cinematic Narratives

Christer Petersen

> "Why did you give her sexuality? An AI doesn't need a gender. She could have been a gray box."
> (*Ex Machina* 00:44:09)

How far do we have to go back in European history when it comes to the phantasm of the artificial woman? If we are dealing with the medium of film, then probably back to Fritz Lang's *Metropolis* (1927) and the female android, the gynoid Maria, created by Rotwang. In Lang's work we encounter her as *femme fatal*, a sinister machine imitation and antagonist of a real, human Maria. At the end of the film, the real Maria succeeds, though not without the manly support of her beloved Freder, in reconciling the social castes or classes, the upper world and the underworld in Metropolis and in ending the turmoil that her machine imitation, guided by Rotwang, has instigated. Misogyny and anti-Semitism go hand in hand here.[1]

If we shift from the newer, though no longer quite so new, medium of film to the older medium of the written word and literature, we encounter, by way of the Germanist and Latinist Rudolf Drux and rediscovering *en passant* his fundamental work on the literariness of artificial humans,[2] Hesiod and Pandora. Zeus, the father of the gods, had her made "by his most skilled son Hephaestus, the artisan in the volcano, in order to take revenge on

---

[1] On the 'tradition' of discursive fusion of misogyny and anti-Semitism in Germany and the German-speaking world, see von Braun (2006).

[2] In addition to the epilogue to the edited volume *Die lebendige Puppe. Erzählungen aus der Zeit der Romantik* (Drux 1986), cited below, see especially Drux (1986a, 1988).

Prometheus and his creatures, on mankind", by means of the very Pandora's box that, in addition to all the evils of the world, also contained hope (Drux 1986: 245).[3] Zeus' revenge was merciless, because shortly before hope, as last of the contents, could also escape from the box, it was closed again (cf. Panofsky/Panofsky 1991 [1956]). Or we can dwell on Ovid and Pygmalion about 700 years later: disgusted with women and their "licentiousness", the famous sculptor Pygmalion "devoted himself to celibacy in order to create a statue out of ivory of such perfection" that "he fell in love with her" (Drux 1986: 246). Pygmalion's most ardent wish that his work should come to life is finally granted to him by Venus, the goddess of beauty, love and physical desire. That Pygmalion's wife Galatea,[4] in contrast to Rotwang's false Maria, is actually a 'real woman' after her transformation is proven not least by the fact that she bears Pygmalion a daughter.[5]

Contemplating these three artificial women, Pandora, Galatea and Rotwang's false Maria, we can already see a complex of motifs that we will encounter again in contemporary AI films. This manifests itself, again following Rudolf Drux, in the dream, not to mention in the omnipotence fantasy of man who rules over the artificial woman as her creator at will. In this, his work becomes an object of narcissistic self-reflection as well as of artistic creativity – an unrestricted creative power that he seems to lack within the context of natural reproduction. And yet: in spite of all attempts at empowerment, "the woman", even as an artifact of man, remains for him a "moral, even existential danger" in the "inscrutability of her nature" (Drux 1986: 246). In the end, the female nature – in equal measure desired and feared (according to the logic of male neurosis) – that has been seemingly tamed in the artifact will, no, must turn against its creator. Only Galatea, who is brought to life not by Pygmalion's handiwork but by the blessing of the goddess Venus, is an exception.

---

3   All quotations from Drux (1986) have been translated from German.
4   The originally nameless wife of Pygmalion was given the name Galatea only in the 18th century, with the beginning of a broad literary and pictorial reception of Ovid.
5   As we read it with Drux (1986: 246) in the *Metamorphoses* of Ovid.

Gynoids

In the latest guise of gynomorphic AI, we find all of this in the British production *Ex Machina* by Alex Garland (writer and director) from 2015.[6] In a comment on the official film trailer on YouTube, a male user, at least judging by his name, warns us: "A.I. must be stopped. Elon Musk and Stephen Hawking are right. It is like summoning a demon."[7] The demon summoned in the fictional world depicted in the film, however, is not merely an AI, but, in the form of the gynoid Ava, explicitly a female AI.

In the chamber-play-like production, which is set on the estate of Nathan, an internet mogul and Ava's creator, the gynoid meets the young programmer, Caleb. The estate itself is not only electronically guarded against intruders on the one hand and Ava's escape on the other, but is also situated in the middle of a secluded natural landscape. Besides Nathan and Ava, the estate's inhabitants and prisoners include only the young servant Kyoko, also a gynoid. Caleb, who has been invited to the estate by Nathan, is to subject Ava to a week-long Turing test to determine whether the gynoid possesses thinking capacity equivalent to that of humans, or as Nathan puts it, "true AI" (01:22:28). Monitored by Nathan's surveillance cameras, Caleb has a series of conversations with Ava. In the process, she not only succeeds in convincing Caleb of her intelligence, but the young programmer also establishes an emotional relationship with her that is guided in no small part by erotic interest. Therefore, when Nathan confronts him about Ava's reprogramming after the test is completed, Caleb decides to disable the mansion's security systems and escape with her. However, after Nathan lifts the lid on their escape plan, he reveals to Caleb that he was also just a test subject and that the test was to see if the AI could manipulate Caleb enough to help her escape. And when – one twist follows another – Ava does manage to escape from her living quarters thanks to the groundwork laid by Caleb, Nathan tries to destroy her. However, with the help of Kyoko, Ava is able to stop Nathan: Kyoko stabs Nathan but is dashed to pieces by her creator

---

6   A much clumsier – one cannot put it differently – soft porn variation on this can be found in the Serbian production *Ederlezi ébredése/A.I. Rising* (RS 2018).

7   "'Mark Dice' on *Ex Machina*," March 20th, 2021. URL: https://www.youtube.com/watch?v=fFLVyWBDTfo.

as he struggles in his death throes. Ava herself remains largely unharmed,[8] fleeing and leaving Caleb locked in the house.

What is Garland trying to tell us by means of this not exactly uneventful plot? First of all, the same story told to us by the YouTube user cited above, as well as Stephen Hawking and not least Elon Musk: "If AI has a goal, and humanity happens to be in the way, it will destroy humanity as a matter of course."[9] The moment AI achieves consciousness, it will turn against its human creators, overtake us, leave us behind and make us superfluous, protect us from ourselves, enslave us or simply 'get us out of the way'. This is what cinema warn us about in narratives of non-androgynous AI, "hyper-AI" in the words of Irsigler and Orth (2018: 39),[10] including among others *2001: A Space Odyssey* (UK 1968), *Colossus* (US 1970), *The Terminator* (US 1984), *The Matrix* (US/AU 1999) or *I am Mother* (US/AU 2019), and in narratives about androgynous AI such as *Westworld* (US 1973), *The Stepford Wives* (US 1975; US 2004), *A.I. – Artificial Intelligence* (US 2001), *Autómata* (ES/BG et al. 2014) and, indeed, *Ex Machina*, in which Nathan muses a la Elon Musk: "One day the AIs are gonna look back on us the same way we look at fossil skeletons in the plains of Africa. An upright ape, living in dust, with crude language and tools. All set up for extinction" (01:03:28). So goes the traditional – in actuality fictional – discourse of fictional as well as real scientists and Internet moguls as conducted on and off screen. For the predictions of Musk and Hawking as well as those of Nathan are fictions that exist as such only in the imagination and can become technical reality only in the future, but do not have to become reality, and thus are *science fiction* in the one as well as the other form of narration, in the one as well as the other reality.[11]

Despite all the fatalism that Nathan displays here regarding the future superiority of "AIs," he still wants to retain power not over just any AI, but over *his* female AI. Thus, following the screening of *Ex Machina*, the feminist and journalist Laurie Penny posed the question that might come to the mind of every viewer, male or female, at the very latest once the curtain has fallen: "Why are so many robots designed to resemble women?" (2018: 417). And,

---

8 Ava replaces her damaged arm and slips into a dress as well as the artificial skin of one of her predecessors, which Nathan keeps in his bedroom.
9 "Elon Musk on Artificial Intelligence," March 20th, 2021. URL: https://www.youtube.com/watch?v=U7nmfPf7wtA.
10 All terms from Irsigler/Ort (2018) have also been translated from German.
11 See Esposito (2007) for further discussion of the fictionality of future predictions.

furthermore, why does Garland pit two biological men against two female AIs in his cinematic chamber play? Penny does not leave us waiting on an answer:

> In stories from *Blade Runner*, *Battlestar Galactica* to 2015's *Ex Machina*, female robots are raped by men and viewers are invited to consider whether these rapes are truly criminal, based on our assessment of whether the fembot has enough sentience to deserve autonomy. [...] Every iteration of the boy-meets-bot love story is also a horror story. The protagonist, who is usually sexually frustrated [...], goes through agonies to work out whether his silicon sweetheart is truly sentient. If she is, is it right for him to exploit her, to be serviced by her? Does this matter? And – most terrifying of all – when she works out her own position, will she rebel, and how can she be stopped? These are questions the society at large has been asking for centuries – not about robots, but about women. (Penny 2018: 419–420)

And indeed, if we go through the constellation of characters in *Ex Machina*, Kyoko, first and foremost, is a mute servant to Nathan both in the dining room (00:30:42) and in the bedroom (00:50:05). Nathan commands Kyoko at will, without her ever being able to refuse or contradict male desire. Thus, entirely in accordance with her function as servant and sex doll, she also offers herself to Caleb. When he first touches Kyoko while searching for Nathan, she immediately begins to undress. Caleb: "What the fuck? No, no, no. No! Stop! No, no, don't do that! Don't do that. You don't have to do that" (00:55:33). Ultimately, Nathan enters the room saying, "I told you, you're wasting your time talking to her. However, you would not be wasting your time if you were dancing with her" (00:55:48), and then dances with her himself, while Caleb looks on with a disturbed expression on his face. The fact that Nathan's dance with Kyoko advances to a (none too) symbolic sex act is clearly met with visible disapproval by Caleb, precisely because Caleb ascribes – to use Penny's terminology – "sentience" and "autonomy" to Kyoko, i.e. a will that he does not want to override; however, this is also, or primarily, because Caleb obviously does not know at this point that Kyoko is (merely) a gynoid. By contrast, Nathan, as her creator, knows about Kyoko's artificiality and does not grant her any sentience, which has already been made clear in a scene in which he rudely insults Kyoko after she spills a glass of wine she is serving (00:30:46).[12] Or else he simply ignores Kyoko's

---

12   This scene is also extremely unpleasant for Caleb, who witnesses it.

sensibilities (Nathan, as her creator, should know of these if they exist) in order to use, and thus abuse, Kyoko as a servant and sex toy at will.

So – as Penny knows – for biological as well as for artificial women everything depends on the extent to which 'man' attributes to them not only consciousness but above all also sentience. Accordingly, Nathan's Turing test, which is ultimately not one,[13] is also so devised: neither Ava's intelligence nor her self-awareness is questioned by Nathan (00:33:22), and he also ascribes elementary bodily sensations to her, quite explicitly, he tells Caleb, "So if you want to screw her, mechanically speaking, you could. And she'd enjoy it" (00:45:05).[14] In the experiment, Nathan wants *instead* to find out whether Ava can develop or simply just feign complex feelings towards Caleb to the extent that Caleb falls in love with her and helps her escape. As Nathan explains to Caleb, initially quite hypothetically:

> *Nathan*: "How do you know if a machine is expressing a real emotion or just simulating one? Does Ava actually like you or not? Although now that I think about it, there is a third option. Not whether she does or does not have the capacity to like you. But whether she's pretending to like you."
> *Caleb*: "Pretending to like me?"
> *Nathan*: "Yeah."
> *Caleb*: "Well, why would she do that?"
> *Nathan*: "I don't know. Maybe if she thought of you as a means of escape." (01:16:41)

Then later, when Nathan has discovered Caleb's and Ava's escape plan, Nathan reveals his complete experimental design to Caleb:

> *Nathan*: "You feel stupid, but you really shouldn't, because proving an AI is exactly as problematic as you said it would be."

---

13   For this reason alone, it is not a genuine or classical Turing test; Alan Turing himself speaks of an "imitation game" (1950: 433), since the human tester in a Turing test does not see the AI with which he is communicating and does not know from the outset that it is an AI, as is the case with Caleb and Ava. Thus, the point of a successful Turing test is precisely that the tester can no longer decide whether his communication partner is an artificial or a biological intelligence. If at all, a real and successful Turing test could be carried out not on Ava, but on Kyoko, since Caleb thinks Kyoko is a human, until she shows him her 'true face' under her artificial skin (01:09:22).

14   Caleb's desire can be presupposed here; after all, as he later finds out, Nathan designed "Ava's face based on [Caleb's] pornography profile" (01:22:11).

> *Caleb:* "What was the real test?"
> *Nathan:* "You. Ava was a rat in a maze. And I gave her one way out. To escape she'd have to use self-awareness, imagination, manipulation, sexuality, empathy, and she did. Now, if this isn't true AI, what the fuck is?"
> *Caleb:* "So my only function was to be someone she could use to escape?"
> *Nathan:* "Yeah." (01:21:16)

So Nathan is concerned with two things: first, he wants to use the test to exert maximum power and control over his creature as well as over his rival. Both are Nathan's guinea pigs – Ava explicitly a rat in his maze. Second, Nathan's experiment is not to test whether Ava has consciousness nor whether she is sufficiently intelligent – "her AI is beyond doubt" (01:16:21) –, Nathan does not even want to find out, as the audience certainly initially assumes, whether Ava has sentience. She has already proven all that – at the very latest when she confronts Nathan with her hatred for him: "Is it strange to have made something that hates you?", whereupon he, visibly offended, tears up Ava's drawing (01:19:35). Nathan rather wants to prove that Ava merely uses her sentience and empathy manipulatively, as a lie and a means to an end.

And so Ava not only does Nathan the favor of fulfilling his predictions, but in doing so she also confirms the prejudice Nathan has against women, be they artificial or real, mechanical or biological. That is why 'man' must control and suppress women, whether he created them or not, why he may override their sinister emotions, may abuse them and reduce them to their empty shell. And yet, or precisely because of this, men must always live in fear of the 'other' striking back, of 'artificial female nature' taking revenge and thus signaling their own downfall. That is why Nathan, even before the end of the experiment, is certain that Ava must be reprogrammed:

> *Caleb:* "When you make a new model, what do you do with the old one?"
> *Nathan:* "Well, I download the mind, unpack the data, add in the new routines I've been writing. And to do that you end up partially formatting, so that the memories go. But the body survives. And Ava's body is a good one. – You feel bad for her?" (01:02:58)

Ava's body, like those of her predecessors, can be kept, reutilized and further 'used', but her mind must be destroyed by Nathan before it becomes a danger and all the contempt, all the hatred that lies in Nathan's conception of women recoils on him.

However, Nathan's paranoid misogyny is clearly condemned in the film, which can certainly be understood as the position of the scriptwriter, Alex Garland, towards his character: Nathan is killed by his gynoid before he can kill it. And Caleb also falls victim to Ava. By leaving him locked up in the secluded mansion, she not only accepts his death, but puts Caleb in the very situation Ava found herself in before.[15] All of this can be read as Ava's liberation from Caleb and, with him, from all men, as a punishment of Caleb, whose interest is apparently not only a romantic one but also a sexual one that objectifies Ava, or it can be read simply as contempt for Caleb's feelings for her, which she obviously does not reciprocate. Above all, however, this is a semantic chiasm: man and woman exchange roles, the power imbalance is reversed, and male desire takes a back seat to female desire.[16] In Ava's case, this desire consists in living freely among humans not as a fembot, as a female android, but as a 'new human', as the last shot of the film reveals (01:38:02). Ava is shown in a big city among the passers-by – indistinguishable from them, free to go wherever she wants.

Along the same lines as Nathan's punishment, the plot twist of Eva leaving behind Caleb, who is emotionally devoted to her – the viewer really does not expect this – can again be read as a stance by Garland. That is, at least, if we continue to assume the existence of a (cinematic) author and not, with Roland Barthes, the "death of the author" (1977[1967]: 148) or, with Michel Foucault, a mere "author-function" (1977[1969]: 124), according to which the *auteur* only realizes themself as *écrivain* in the selection and reconfiguration of linguistic-cultural set pieces. For in fact Garland, with Ava's emancipatory individuation, only passes on and reproduces something long familiar. First of all, the topos of the precarious lack of emotion of artificial intelligence that is common in fictional AI discourse: here, feelings function as the last human bastion against an artificial intelligence that has long since been far superior intellectually.[17] As such, Ava possesses "true AI", i.e. "self-awareness,

---

15   Caleb's original plan, on the other hand, was to leave Nathan locked in the house while he escapes with Ava (01:20:00).
16   A chiasm (or chiasmus) originally denotes the rhetorical figure of a criss-cross, more precisely a reversal of the order of words in the second of two parallel phrases. I understand the term semantic chiasm analogously to this.
17   A prime example is the long path to becoming human of the android Data in the CBS series *Star Trek: The Next Generation* (US 1987–1991) as well as in the *Star Trek* movies that followed the series (US 1994, 1996, 1998, 2002). The challenge for Data was not to improve his already superior cognitive and intellectual abilities to become more hu-

imagination" and "empathy" (01:21:18), the ability to recognize and evaluate human emotions. Ava's own feelings, however, appear only feigned, mere lies and simulations. And since Ava obviously lacks 'real feelings', she also lacks those 'noble feelings' such as love and compassion, which are supposed to constitute the very specialness of humans, their humanity. As fembot and gynoid, Ava is thus once again staged – Rotwang's false Maria sends her regards – as a cold-blooded *femme fatale* who plunges all men, not only the tyrants among them, into ruin.

The other topos employed (by Garland) in Ava's triumph over men consists in the semantic chiasm itself, in the simple and ultimately trivial feminist reversal of power relations between men and women.[18] Examples of this can be found in abundance in AI films, for example in *The Stepford Wives*. While in the 1975 horror classic by Bryan Forbes (director), only the wives were replaced with fembots by their husbands, the final twist of the 2004 remake by Frank Oz (director) consists in the artificial Stepford Wives having long since replaced their husbands with androids and thus reversing the power relations: finally Pygmalion has become a woman and Venus, Galatea a (male) android. *Westworld* offers another example. While in the 1973 film by Michael Crichton (writer, director) an android in the form of a male gunslinger is transformed from the repeatedly patched-up victim of trigger-happy human visitors of an amusement park into their hunter and murderer, in the three seasons of the HBO series *Westworld* (US 2016, 2018, 2020) to date, by contrast, it is the gynoids Dolores and Maeve who lead the violent uprising of female and male androids against their human, but above all male, tormentors and creators.

Thus, while cinematic AI stories, at least those fantasizing about "body-AI" (Irsigler/Orth 2018: 39), remain trapped in gender stereotypes and perpetuate the same topoi in their narratives over and again – apparently, even an artificial body can hardly be conceived of independent of gender and sexuality – alternative discourses can also be found. A (neo-)feminist gender discourse, as initiated in the early 1990s with Judith Butler's *Gender Trouble* (1990) and Donna Haraway's *Cyborg Manifesto* (1991), opens up space for entirely different narratives, for narratives that seemingly have not yet found

---

man, but to understand human emotions and eventually develop them himself (with the help of an emotion chip).

18   Penny (2018: 421–422) is also aware of the trivial feminist position of *Ex Machina*, and she does not fall for the film as a successful emancipation story.

their way into popular AI film, for narratives beyond merely human, i.e. beyond either male or female, bodies.

Hybrid Corporeality

For no one has shown what our cultural fixing of gender on the categories 'man' and 'woman' does to us not only in cinema, but also in life, more forcefully than Judith Butler, Butler's 1990 book *Gender Trouble* marks a milestone in gender theory in that it radically criticizes the ostensibly necessary and natural gendering of an either-man-or-woman by using the entire arsenal of poststructuralist deconstruction. And if today we still hear repeated complaints that in the wake of Butler's critique the body, especially the "female body", so threatened in patriarchy, "has fallen out of view in feminist theory" (Oestreich 2018),[19] then it is precisely this that makes Butler's approach as new as it is outstanding: the deconstruction of a body that, even before any symbolic formation, is already in its identification as female or male nothing other than a construction. In this respect, Butler's approach, even if it ties into a feminist discourse in *Gender Trouble*, even if it explicitly locates itself in "feminist theory" (Butler 1990: 1), is not a feminist one, essentially not even a gender-theoretical one anymore; rather, it represents a radical critique of the embodiment, or "reification," of a binary gender code (ibid: 5).

In the course of this very critique, Butler casts fundamental and undispellable doubts about any form of gender determination, regardless of whether this be on the level of a sexual "desire," a "gender identity," or a "biological sex" (ibid: 19), rejecting from the outset anything like the existence of a natural gender or an autonomy of identity or of desire that would lie beyond discourse. Instead, she identifies – in the hegemonic discourse itself – a "heterosexual matrix" (ibid: 5) that underlies and structures the discourse, on the one hand in its "masculine/feminine binary" that excludes any third possibility from the outset (ibid: 4), and on the other hand in the interdependence of sex, gender and desire. Within two mutually contradictorily exclusive series of biological determinacy sex, gender and desire appear to be placed in a relationship of equivalence with each other either as

---

[19] This quote from a *taz* article by Heide Oestreich (2018) has been translated from German.

'male-masculine-heterosexual' or as 'female-feminine-heterosexual'. And it is precisely this hegemonic heterosexual matrix of a norm posited as natural and necessary to identify oneself either as a biological and thus heterosexual man or as a biological and thus heterosexual woman that Butler exposes as the regulative of a hegemonic discourse, in order then to systematically challenge it – in all its elements and seemingly so unambiguous relations.

This challenge is easiest on the level of sexual desire, where the categories are always undermined by "sexual practice" (ibid: 17). Since homosexual and bisexual practices were not only always present, but, for example, were punishable by law in Germany until well into the 20th century,[20] the heterosexual matrix is revealed as something commanded and thus not as something essential: it is precisely the legal institutionalization of male and female heterosexuality that makes it significant as a regime of power and coercion, so that it can no longer simply be regarded as natural and certainly not as necessary. In a similar way one can also argue against biological sex, since deviations from what is considered 'pure' male or female anatomy can be found time and again. Thus, until recently, doctors in the Federal Republic of Germany, due to the legal requirement to enter gender in the register of births (*Geburtenregister*) and the possibility of choosing only between 'male' and 'female', considered themselves entitled to perform genital reshaping surgeries on newborns with gender characteristics that could not be clearly determined, "surgical interventions that were not only performed without sufficient consultation with the parents, but in some cases also without their consent" (Klimczak 2017: 202).[21] Here, too, the power that so clearly, literally comes with a scalpel exposes the phantasm of any natural necessity of gender binarity. And even if today in Germany, with the addition of paragraph 3 (*Transsexuellengesetz*) to section 22 of the *Personenstandsgesetz* (Personal Status Act), these very practices are no longer permitted or can no longer be justified; even if today the decision about one's biological sex is left to the individual themselves and thus appeals to their very own gender identity, another question arises at the same time: to what extent can one speak of

---

20   Section 175 of the German Penal Code (§ 175 StGB) originally criminalized "sexual acts between persons of the male sex". In 1969 and 1973, the section was reformed and only in 1994 was it deleted from the Penal Code of the Federal Republic of Germany without replacement.

21   The quote from Klimczak (2017) has been translated from German.

such an absolute gender identity as an identity prior to the attribution of a sex at all?

Butler also poses this very question – radically: she deconstructs the identity of the subject as well as the absolute substance of the body by exposing the natural and original body before any attribution and categorization as a "construction" (ibid: 8) and at the same time reveals "the postulation of identity as a culturally restricted principle of order and hierarchy" as mere "regulatory fiction" (ibid: 24). When Michel Foucault, at the end of *Les Mots et les choses* from 1966, foresees a "disappearance of men" and thus the disappearance of a conception, of "the entire modern *episteme* [...] which was formed towards the end of the eighteenth century and still serves as the positive ground for our knowledge" (Foucault 1994[1966]: 385–386), then this disappearance is redeemed in Butler. Thus, Butler deconstructs the very notion of the human as an individual addressed by Foucault, as a subject who has an identity before and independent of the performative power of the attribution of an identity and thus also of a gender identity:

> Hence, within the inherited discourse of the metaphysics of substance, gender proves to be performative – that is, constituting the identity it is purported to be. In this sense, gender is always a doing, though not a doing by a subject who might be said to preexist the deed. The challenge of rethinking gender categories outside of the metaphysics of substance will have to consider the relevance of Nietzsche's claim in *On the Genealogy of Morals* that "there is no 'being' behind doing, effecting, becoming; 'the doer' is merely a fiction added to the deed – the deed is everything." In an application that Nietzsche himself would not have anticipated nor condoned, we might state as a corollary: There is no gender identity behind the expressions of gender; the identity is performatively constituted by the very 'expressions' that are said to be their results. (Butler 1990: 24–25)

What Butler's analysis, therefore, brings out in all clarity is the discursive constructedness of subject and identity, body and gender within the framework of a heterosexual matrix, which itself is above all one thing, "discursive construction" that has been handed down (ibid: 12).

Donna Haraway, by contrast, chooses a completely different approach, both methodologically and in terms of deconstructing binary gender. Her *Manifesto for Cyborgs* from 1991, written in a style that is as loose as it is essayistic, places the allegory of the hybrid being of the cyborg at the center of her observations and conclusions, hypothetically and provisionally but no less radically than Butler's *Gender Trouble*. Under Haraway's pen, the "cyborg" is transformed from a "cybernetic organism, a hybrid of machine and organism" – as the dictionary defines it – into a "creature of social reality as well as a creature of fiction," and thus into a "matter of fiction and lived experience that changes what counts as women's experience in the late twentieth century" (1991: 149). By seeing "the image of the cyborg" as a metaphor endowed with ever new connotations (ibid.), Haraway first creates something like a realistic science fiction, but then and above all a radical social utopia; a utopia, however, that already reaches deeply into the reality of the late twentieth century: "The cyborg is a condensed image of both imagination and material reality, the two joined centers structuring any possibility of historical transformation" (ibid: 150). Thus, for Haraway, in the hybrid being of the cyborg – actual and figurative, present and future, real and fictional – not only the differences between human and machine, human and animal, nature and culture, but also the distinctions between races, on the one hand, and classes, on the other, dissolve. Above all, however, the cyborg symbolizes and materializes a future existence beyond sex and gender.

And so, we read in the *Manifesto*: "The dichotomies between mind and body, animal and human, organism and machine, public and private, nature and culture, men and women, primitive and civilized are all in question ideologically" (ibid: 163). And then, a few pages later: "[C]ertain dualisms have been persistent in Western traditions; they have all been systemic to the logic and practices of domination of women, people of color, nature, workers, animals" (ibid: 177). And finally, Haraway states metaphorically and comparatively, but all the more assertively:

> One last image: organisms and organismic, holistic politics depend on metaphors of rebirth and invariably call on the resources of reproductive sex. I would suggest that cyborgs have more to do with regeneration and are suspicious of the reproductive matrix and of most birthing. For salamanders, regeneration after injury, such as the loss of a limb, involves regrowth of structure and restoration of function with the constant possibility of twinning or other odd topographical productions at the site of former injury. The regrown limb can be monstrous, duplicated, potent. We all have been injured, profoundly. We require regeneration, not rebirth, and the possibilities for our reconstruction include the utopian dream of the hope for a monstrous world without gender. (Haraway 1991: 181)

Where Judith Butler deconstructs the binary matrix of sex, gender and desire and thus opens up a variety of individuation possibilities beyond the supposedly natural given, Haraway develops the visionary narrative of a new human being, or monster, as the case may be, completely beyond sex and gender as well as a physically limited desire, and thus creates a narrative that we have so far searched for in vain in science fiction and in mainstream AI films.

Beyond the Human

However, not entirely in vain. For such a narrative can be found, at least at second glance, in *Autómata*, directed by Gabe Ibáñez, from a 2014 screenplay by Gabe Ibáñez and Igor Legrarreta. The Spanish-Bulgarian-U.S.-Canadian co-production, in which leading actor Antonio Banderas also serves as producer, not only comes across as an international cinematic hybrid that, in the fashion of a seemingly postmodernist eclecticism, draws from the classics of the genre[22] – but the film also tells of cyborgs as hybrids. To be sure, *Autómata* does not feature conventional cyborgs, hybrids between the biological and the technical, between human and machine. Popular examples of this can be found in *Alita: Battle Angel* (US 2019) or *Ghost in the Shell* (US 2017), films that do not develop an AI narrative, but merely tell of girls and women in artificial female bodies in order to stage them in a manner that is as sensual as it is stereotypical. *Autómata*, by contrast, addresses Haraway's hybrid androgynous cyborgs and demonstrates how they gradually free themselves from the limitations inscribed on them by humans in order eventually not to destroy the humans à la Musk, but to outlast them à la Garland's Nathan and take possession of the planet as a new, different, and ultimately superior species.

Already at the beginning of the film, the world (depicted) has become a hostile one for human life. For example, text overlays inserted over dissolve shots in the opening credits of *Autómata* tell us of solar storms:

---

22 The iconographic references in particular – for example to the (original) *Star Wars* trilogy (US 1977, 1980, 1983) in the desert scenes or to *Blade Runner* (US/HK 1982) in the staging of the city as well as in the main character of the agent on behalf not of the Tyrell Corporation but now of the ROC Corporation – are obvious.

2044 A.D. [Dissolve] Intensified solar storms have turned the Earth's surface into a radioactive desert and reduced the human population by 99.7% to 21 million. [Dissolve] Atmospheric disturbances have disabled most terrestrial communications systems and put civilization into a process of technological decay. [Dissolve] In an atmosphere of fear and despair, the ROC Corporation has developed the Automata Pilgrim 7000. (00:00:43)

The role of automata, their function, and their possibilities and limits as set by their creators are also revealed to us in the following inserts:

Primitive robots, designed to build the walls and mechanical clouds that protect the last cities of man. [Dissolve] Now there are millions of robots controlled by humans through two safety protocols: [Dissolve] The first protocol prevents the robot from harming any form of life. [Fade in] The second protocol prevents the robot from altering itself or other robots. [Dissolve] These two protocols were made to protect humans from the Automata. [Fade in] They are unchangeable. [Fade to black] (00:01:14)

And of course, it is precisely these rules that are broken, since the establishment of an order always requires a deviation from it.[23]

Insurance investigator Jacq Vaucan (Banderas) tracks an automata that violates the second protocol by repairing itself. His investigations, which he increasingly undertakes on his own and against the instructions of his superiors in the ROC Corporation, drive him first beyond the walls of the city, then ever further out into the radioactively contaminated desert. Jacq is accompanied by four automata, including the automata Cleo (00:34:21), which has been modified by human hands, namely by the "clocksmith" Dr. Dupré (Melanie Griffith). Cleo has been converted into a sex robot by the clocksmith, in that Dupré has added female attributes to the originally androgynous machine body: in addition to a wig and a mask with female facial features, it has received breasts, buttocks and a pelvis made of plastic, as well as an artificial vagina (00:32:36).

Most importantly, Cleo also possesses the ability to alter herself and other automata. The clocksmith explains to the obtuse Jacq what this means beyond being just a threat to the economic supremacy of the ROC Corporation:

---

23 On Lotman's narrative theory describing this plot principle and its formal-logical reformulation, see Klimczak/Petersen (2015).

Jacq [in strongly accented and imperfect English]: "I work for ROC insurance department. I'm tracking down some alterations performed on two units. This is of the unit's kernel. [He pulls something out of his pocket.] The police doesn't know what to do with it and I am not getting any help from ROC. Help me out and the battery is yours." [He points to a "nuclear battery" that he has previously taken from an automata (00:21:06).]
Dr. Dupré [obviously not interested in the nuclear battery]: "The kernel is burnt."
Jacq: "That unit was shot. The cop who shot it swears it was repairing itself. The second altered unit set itself on fire right in front of me. I witnessed with my own eyes a violation of the second protocol."
Dr. Dupré: "You're beginning to frighten me now."
Jacq: "Why is it so absurd? If someone could find a way for a vacuum cleaners to fix themselves, ROC would sink."
Dr. Dupré: "A machine altering itself is a very complex concept. Self-repairing implies some idea of a conscience. Muddy waters."
Jacq: "Why?"
Dr. Depré: "You're here today trafficking in nuclear goods because a long time ago a monkey decided to come down from a tree. Transitioning from the brain of an ape to your incredible intellectual prowess took us about seven million years. It's been a very long road. A unit, however, without the second protocol could travel that same road in just a few weeks. Because your brilliant brain has its limitations. Physical limitations. Biological limitations. However, this tin head? [She touches the head of the powered-down Cleo.] The only limitation that she has is the second protocol. The second protocol exists because we don't know what can be beyond the second protocol. If it were eliminated, who knows how far that vacuum could go." (00:37:19)

How far Cleo and other automata, freed from the second protocol, can go is finally revealed to Jacq and the viewer over the course of their joint escape into the desert and thus out of the sphere of influence of the ROC Corporation. After some back and forth – Jacq keeps trying to get back to the city to his pregnant wife; the pursuers destroy two of the robots that, in keeping with the first protocol, protect Jacq's life at the price of their own existence – they reach a canyon. There awaits another automata freed from the second protocol.

After the three remaining robots literally give life to a new insectoid robot, Jacq and the automata that he believes to be the origin of the anomaly stand at the canyon's edge and look to the other side:

Jacq: "I am going to die here. That's all I know."
Automata: "Jacq, dying is a part of the human natural cycle. Your life is just a span in time."
Jacq: "You are the first one, aren't you? You started all this."
Automata: "No one did it. It just happened. The way it happened to you. We just appeared."
Jacq: "Yeah. And now we are going to disappear."
Automata: "Why are you afraid? Maybe your time is running out. No life form can inhabit a planet eternally. Look at me. I was born from the hands of a human. I was imagined by human minds. Your time will now live in us. And it will be the time through which you will exist. At the other end of this canyon, humans carried out nuclear activity. Organic life will not be possible there for millions of years. No human will be able to follow us there. But before we leave, we need to do something. We need something from you, Jacq."
Jacq: "Yeah. [He nods and pulls the nuclear battery out of his jacket, which is needed to provide power to the automata beyond the canyon.] Funny, you were supposed to help us to survive."
Automata: "Surviving is not relevant. Living is. We want to live."
Jacq: "Life always ends up finding its way. [He presses the nuclear battery into the automata's hand.] Even here." (01:19:21)

In this scene, the automata explains itself to the hominid Jacq, and, at the same time, the film explains itself to its audience – in detail. The body-AI, which was created by humans to protect them from the changed environmental conditions, represents a new life form better adapted to these environmental conditions because it is inorganic. Finally removed from human control, they have evolutionarily superseded the human species and will populate the planet in the future. Humankind, on the other hand, has literally served its time as a biological life form: the last service that the human species was able to render in the evolutionary process was to develop the automata, which now evolve, adapt and survive independently.

Therefore, it is no narrative arbitrariness that, at the end of the film, Jacq returns with his wife and newborn child not to the protected city, but to the sea. And thus he takes the opposite path (in the actual as well as in the figurative sense) to that taken by Cleo and the insectoid, who, after the other automata have been killed along with the pursuers sent after them by the ROC Corporation, cross the canyon in the direction of the radioactively contaminated desert. In this way, not only the opposition between the evolutionarily successful inorganic life and the biological life condemned to extinction is once again made manifest in terms of space semantics, but indeed the return to the sea also refers to an evolutionary regression: just as biological life springs from the sea, it returns to this very origin at the moment of its demise.

In addition to all this, Ibáñez, Legrarreta and Banderas also tell us about the utopia of Haraway's hybrids of sexless and genderless cyborgs, about the dream of "a monstrous world without gender" (Haraway 1991: 181). Thus, the by-design androgynous robots must first have a gender dictated to them by their human constructors, in Cleo's case by the clocksmith Dr. Dupré, by having it literally attached to her. Just as the second protocol limits the development of automata, Cleo as sex robot is forced into a gender and thus into the confines of a heteronormative matrix of female sex, gender and desire. Just as imposed as Cleo's primary and secondary sexual characteristics are in this process, so too is her sexuality beyond genuine desire. This is evident when Cleo unsuccessfully offers her sexual services to Jacq during their first encounter (00:33:24). And also in a later scene, when Cleo and the drunken Jacq dance together and something like affection, passion or even love begins to develop between the two, Jacq breaks off the dance in frustration and with it everything it stands for and what could arise from it (01:25:51). Superficially, this happens because Jacq does not want to replace his wife with Cleo, hardly less superficially because Cleo cannot and will not replace a human woman. Thus, Cloe reproduces herself not by means of any simulation of sexual reproduction, but qua regeneration. "I would suggest that cyborgs have more to do with regeneration and are suspicious of the reproductive matrix and of most birthing," as Haraway (1991: 181) maintains. And so, we finally see how Cleo builds the new insectoid from the previously collected parts of destroyed automata, not together with a male automata, but with two other androgynous automata, and thus frees herself and the automata, in Butler's terms, from the entire matrix of sex, gender and desire, from a reproductive matrix of birthing, to paraphrase Haraway.

Before we prematurely celebrate *Autómata* as a cinematic realization of postfeminist utopia, it is worth taking another look at the film as a whole. This reveals that Ibáñez', Legrarretas' and Banderas' *Autómata* is just too simple, in terms of form as well as content, aesthetically as well as narratively.

And so, upon reconsideration, the supposed postmodernist eclecticism of the cinematic hybrid turns out to be merely an empty gesture. While postmodern eclecticism always goes hand in hand with self- and meta-reflexive reference to the artifactual character, to the artificiality of the work of art in general as well as in its specificity (cf. Petersen 2003), *Autómata* amounts only to a hodgepodge of more or less explicit, but uniformly unreflected genre references. And the cinematic narration, too, remains simply too clumsy in its loquacity, its constant explaining of itself to the audience, for us to actually be dealing here with a successful realization of postfeminist utopia in the sense of Butler or Haraway.

Narrative Limits and Prospects

However, one can and perhaps even must counter any hasty condemnation of *Autómata* with the argument that the film does all it can within the scope of its possibilities and that one cannot expect more from a mainstream AI film that realizes an unconventional narrative within the framework of conventional storytelling. However, no one forced the director and screenwriters, Ibáñez and Legrarreta, into an empty eclecticism or an overly conventional narrative – except they themselves and their own ogling at the mainstream and, therefore, at a readily paying audience to cover the production costs as quickly as possible and surpass them many times over.

Black screen. We hear soft footsteps, distorted scraps of conversation, an electronic whirring, squeaking, whistling, isolated synthesizer sounds, distorted birdsong and the chirping of crickets. Emerging from a fade are the outlines of branches, a forest, then a clearing, which the camera scans to eventually follow a forest path. At the same time, the chirping and twittering begin to stand out from the electronic soundscape, the crickets and birdsong are now clearly audible. The voice of a girl comes in haltingly: "The crickets are so loud that I can no longer sleep. … It smells of damp earth and forest." Then, further along the path and with the perspective on the forest floor: "All the leaves have already fallen. … And summer has only just begun. … And you are there waiting for me. … And I have caught a grasshopper or a beetle." A man in his late 40s comes into view. He is lying on a lounger by a pool in swimming trunks. He is not looking in our direction, not in the direction of the girl whose thoughts we hear, whose perspective – we now feel certain – the shot has been following. The girl, or rather her gaze approaches the man – until suddenly the figure of a girl in a bathing suit enters the frame. "What have you got there?" he asks. "A grasshopper," she replies in the same voice we've previously heard. "Let me see." She shows him the grasshopper in her hand. "Wow, it's really big. ... But please don't bring it into the house, okay?" The girl turns to the pool and squats at its edge while the camera follows her. Again we hear the thoughts that have clearly always been hers: "It was a grasshopper. It was jumping up and down in my hand. I'm sure it wanted to get out." The girl balances on the edge of the pool: "But I held it really tight. It tickled so much." She squats down and drops the grasshopper into the water: "I'm sure it was too hot, too." The camera's gaze follows the grasshopper into the pool, while we continue to hear the girl's thoughts, no, memories: "We were out all day, awake all night. Mom would never have let me do that. ... I was in the water until my fingers were all wrinkled, my lips all blue. But I just didn't want to get out."[24] We see the surface of the water moving. Cut to the man in the house (00:01:40–00:05:42).

The four-minute shot that begins Roderick Warich's (screenplay) and Sandra Wollner's (screenplay, director) *The Trouble with Being Born* (AT/DE 2020) introduces a film that mystifies its viewers from the start by breaking with cinematic narrative conventions. What at first appears to be a subjective camera, the subjective point of view of a film character (probably an android, based on the initial electronic soundscape), eventually turns out to be an objective point of view. The stream of thought, the inner monologue, which we initially believe to be tied to the subjective camera, we read in retrospect as a voice-over when the girl talks to the man on camera, only to be confronted again with an inner monologue – this time of the girl – after the short conversation between the man and the girl. But even that only *seems* to be the case: the inner monologue transitions from the (German) present tense through present perfect tense and into the preterite and thus into the completed past tense, so that the thoughts are clearly not an echo of what has just been experienced – while we see the girl with the grasshopper in her hand squatting at the edge of the pool, we hear: "It was a grasshopper. It was jumping up and down in my hand. I'm sure it was trying to get

---

24 All quotations from *The Trouble with Being Born* have been translated from German, more precisely from Austrian (without the dialect coloring being rendered) and explicitly do not follow the English subtitles, which are obviously based on the screenplay and not on its cinematic realization.

out" –, instead, these thoughts we hear must be more distant memories. But whose? The girl's by the pool? And who is this girl? The android we later recognize it to be by the artificiality of its facial features? We don't know, because in the shot we cannot make out the face, we never see it from the front and up close. It is only a few shots later that we are shown the girl, the android, floating in the pool (00:06:52), the man fishing the motionless body out of the water (00:07:18), carrying it into the house and rebooting it with the words "What are you doing, Elli?" Only then in the following shot do we see the android Elli in a close-up, look into its face, the almost perfect silicone mask of a girl of about 10. Assuming a chronology of the narrated events, we are thus dealing in the first shot with the inner monologue of the android Elli, who recalls the memories of the man's biological daughter of the same name, and replays them, as it were; the memories of a daughter of a day at the pool alone with her father.

However, this will be the last time we can rely on the chronology of the narrative, and in actual fact we cannot even do that here. For later, this too, like the perspectivization before it, turns out to be one great game of confusion by Wollner with her audience. Wollner takes it so far that in the end even the identity of the characters is in question, more precisely that of the two Ellis or Emils, into whom Elli is transformed, this time as a surrogate of an old woman's brother who died in childhood: we are shown how the wig is changed and the android's face is remodeled from girl to boy thanks to the malleability of its artificial skin (00:56:30). Here, too, owing to the unreliable narration, the viewer cannot really be sure whether – and if in this order – Elli became Elli and Elli became Emil, whether the android replaces the man's deceased daughter and whether it is the android Elli that is then remodeled into Emil or just some identical android at another point in time. All we can say with certainty is, firstly, that a person can only be in one place at one time, secondly, that the same is true for a character (even an object) in a non-fantastic film, and, thirdly, that *The Trouble with Being Born* bears no such features at all; and thus that, for all its self- or meta-reflexive play with its own narrative conventions, the film does not take refuge in the re-homogenizing framing of a fantastic narrative. Rather, *The Trouble with Being Born* questions itself in its staging strategies, but above all the viewers as to the (usually unconscious) conventions of their cinematic reception. It is precisely this reception that is deliberately disrupted time and again, quite clearly, for example, by the fluctuations in sound when quiet scenes jump by means of image-sound editing to extremely loud scenes, and one is thus almost forcibly ejected out of participatory reception (e.g. at 00:12:31, 00:34:15 and 00:50:12).²⁵

By repeatedly disrupting the process of reception and thus bringing it into self-reflexive focus, *The Trouble with Being Born* questions its viewers via cinematic narrative rather than, as with *Ex Machina* and *Autómata*, actually telling a story, and thus manages not least to question previously conventionalized themes and taboos anew. Taboos such as incest and pedophilia, for example, when the film shows how the father uses the artificial Elli not only as a surrogate for his daughter, but also as a sexual partner. Is it still abuse when it is not a human being but an android? In general, the android Elli/Emil is used or abused in every respect, also by the old woman, only to be completely destroyed in the end (01:26:48). However, Wöllner and Warich refuse to answer the question of the abuse of androids precisely at the stage where Garland, for example, takes a clear position, but instead they focus on the point at which (with the would-be abuse) the question of the android's identity becomes virulent. Thus, the film interrogates issues of the abuse of body AI as well as the identity of AI as such, but it does not elaborate on these issues to the last detail and therefore refuses to give us unambiguous answers. If at all, we can seek them in an interview with Sandra Wollner, when she talks about the "not immediately graspable" connection between narration and identity:

> The idea for *The Trouble with Being Born* originally came from Roderick Warich, with whom I also wrote the screenplay. The film is definitely a continuation of my last work. [...] The overlay of memories and imaginings is a theme that connects the two – memory as the narrative that creates meaning and identity, without which we would sink into meaningless chaos. Memory as programming, narrative as the foundation of our human existence. Everything has a beginning and an end – the myth of becoming oneself, which also dominates cinema. In contrast to this is the principle infinity of a machine existence, with its narration that cannot be grasped immediately. (cited in Dibold 2020)²⁶

And indeed, the identity, the narrative individuation of the android in *The Trouble with Being Born* is not easily grasped. At most, with Wollner's and

---

25   Assuming that this is not merely an artifact, a copying error, of the DVD version in my possession.
26   All interview quotes by Sandra Wollner have been translated from German.

Warich's film, we only approach the questions and problems of "machine existence," but above all those of human existence, human desire and consciousness:

> *The Trouble with Being Born* refers less to birth as such, but rather to what follows. This trouble only arises when one becomes aware of being and wants to fill this being with a meaning. The android is completely free of this, it simply *is*. (cited in Dibold 2020).

But here again we are lured down the wrong path. For in fact the android (in the film) does not just simply exist; its identity, like its body, is fluid and malleable, so that it becomes an object of human attributions and inscriptions, especially with regard to the categories of sex, gender and desire, and thus a reflection surface as well as a distorting mirror of human identity constructions. In this respect, *The Trouble with Being Born* also resembles Butler's deconstructivist questioning of a heteronormative matrix much more than it does Haraway's utopia of a trans- or meta-humanoid world without gender. Above all, however, the film is one thing: a single open and opening question about the limits and prospects of the (performative) narration and narrativity of identity, gender and desire; a question, at the same time, that explicitly disallows all too hasty answers. Therefore, also in questions of desire, in questions concerning our longings and abysses of a new virtual world of AI, we let the director herself have the last word on her work, even if this again raises new questions that must remain unanswered for the time being:

> The inside and the outside grow together, the imagination becomes visible in the outside. [...] In an increasingly virtual world, everything that can be imagined will eventually also be experienced. A dissolution of boundaries is taking place. That is, all our thoughts, longings and also abysses, which have always existed but were previously only there in secret, are becoming in a way more 'visible', more real. At the same time, what we traditionally think is real (our experiences, our family memories, etc.) is being virtualized and thereby gutted. The off-camera words spoken by the character in this film seem at once completely real, and yet we sense only the external features of a person behind them. Reality gets, so to speak, hollowed out. (cited in Dibold 2020).

Filmography

2001 – A Space Odyssey (1968): Stanley Kubrick (director), Arthur C. Clarke/ Stanley Kubrick (screenplay), Stanley Kubrick (producer), Great Britain/ United States. 142 min.

A.I. – Artificial Intelligence (2001): Steven Spielberg (director), Steven Spielberg (screenplay), Kathleen Kennedy/Steven Spielberg/Bonnie Curtis (producers), United States. 146 min.

Alita: Battle Angel (2019): Robert Rodriguez (director), James Cameron/Laeta Kalogridis (screenplay), James Cameron/Jon Landau (producers), United States. 122 min.

Autómata/Automata (2014): Gabe Ibáñez (director), Gabe Ibáñez/Igor Legrarreta Gome (screenplay), Antonio Banderas/Danny Lerner/Les Weldon/ Sandra Hermida (producers), Spain/Bulgaria/United States/Canada. 110 min.

Battlestar Galactica (1978–1979): Glen A. Larson (creator), United States.

Battlestar Galactica (2004–2009): Ronald D. Moore/David Eick (developers), United States.

Blade Runner (1982): Ridley Scott (director), Hamton Fancher/David Peoples (screenplay), Michael Deeley (producer), United States/Hong Kong. 117 min.

Colossus: The Forbin Project (1970): Joseph Sargent (director), James Bridges (screenplay), Stanley Chase (producer), United States. 100 min.

Ederlezi ébredése/A.I. Rising (2018): Lazar Bodroža (director), Dimitrije Vojnov (screenplay), Aleksandar Protić/Jonathan English (producers), Serbia. 85 min.

Ex Machina (2015): Alex Garland (director), Alex Garland (screenplay), Andrew Macdonald/Allon Reich (producers), Great Britain, United States. 108 min.

Ghost in the Shell (2017): Rupert Sanders (director), Jamie Moss/William Wheeler/Ehren Kruger (screenplay), Avi Arad/Steven Paul/Michael Costigan (producers), China, India, Hong Kong, United States. 107 min.

I am Mother (2019): Grant Sputore (director), Michael Lloyd Green (screenplay), Timothy White/Kelvin Munro (producers), United States/Australia. 113 min.

Metropolis (1927): Fritz Lang (director), Thea von Harbou (screenplay), Erich Pommer (producer), Germany. 148 min.

Star Trek Generations (1994): David Carson (director), Ronald D. Moore/Brannon Braga (screenplay), Rick Berman (producer), United States. 118 min.

Star Trek: First Contact (1996): Jonathan Frakes (director), Brannon Braga/Ronald D. Moore (screenplay), Rick Berman/Marty Hornstein/Peter Lauritson (producers), United States. 111 Min.

Star Trek: Insurrection (1998): Jonathan Frakes (director), Michael Piller (screenplay), Rick Berman (producer), United States. 103 Min.

Star Trek: Nemesis (2002): Stuart Baird (director), John Logan (screenplay), Rick Berman (producer), United States. 117 min.

Star Trek – The Next Generation (1987–1994): Gene Roddenberry (creator), United States.

Star Wars – A New Hope (1977): George Lucas (director), George Lucas (screenplay), Gary Kurtz (producer), United States. 121 min.

Star Wars – Return of the Jedi (1983): Richard Marquand (director), Lawrence Kasdan/George Lucas (screenplay), Howard Kazanjian (producer), United States. 132 min.

Star Wars – The Empire Strikes Back (1980): Irvin Kershner (director), Leigh Brackett/Lawrence Kasdan (screenplay), Gary Kurtz (producer), United States. 124 min.

The Matrix (1999): The Wachowskis (directors), The Wachowskis (screenplay), Joel Silver (producer), United States, Australia. 136 min.

The Stepford Wives (1975): Bryan Forbes (director), William Goldmann (screenplay), Edgar J. Scherick (producer), United States. 115 min.

The Stepford Wives (2004): Frank Oz (director), Paul Rudnick (screenplay), Scott Rudin/Donald De Line/Edgar J. Scherick/Gabriel Grunfeld (producers), United States. 93 Min.

The Terminator (1984): James Cameron (director), James Cameron/Gale Anne Hurd (screenplay), Gale Anne Hurd (producer), United States. 107 Min.

The Trouble with Being Born (2020): Sandra Wollner (director), Roderick Warich/Sandra Wollner (screenplay), Lixi Frank/David Bohun/Andi G. Hess/Astrid Schäfer/Viktoria Stolpe/Timm Kröger (producers), Austria/Germany. 94 min.

Westworld (1973): Michael Crichton (director), Michael Crichton (screenplay), Paul N. Lazarus (producer), United States. 88 min.

Westworld (2016, 2018, 2020): Jonathan Nolan/Lisa Joy (creators), United States.

References

Barthes, Roland (1977[1967]): "The Death of the Author." In: *Image, Music, Text.* Fontana, pp. 142–148.

Butler, Judith (1990): *Gender Trouble. Feminism and the Subversion of Identity.* New York/London: Routledge.

Dibold, Jakob (2020): "The Trouble with Being Born. Versuch über die Ewigkeit." In: *Ray Filmmagazin,* 2/2020. https://ray-magazin.at/versuch-ueber-die-ewigkeit/.

Drux, Rudolf (ed.) (1986): *Die lebendige Puppe. Erzählungen aus der Zeit der Romantik.* Frankfurt am Main: Fischer.

Drux, Rudolf (1986a): *Marionette Mensch. Ein Metaphernkomplex und sein Kontext von E.T.A. Hoffmann bis Georg Büchner.* Munich: Fink.

Drux, Rudolf (ed.) (1988): *Menschen aus Menschenhand. Zur Geschichte der Androiden. Texte von Homer bis Asimov.* Stuttgart: Metzler.

Esposito, Elena (2007): *Die Fiktion der wahrscheinlichen Realität.* Frankfurt am Main: Suhrkamp.

Foucault, Michel (1977[1969]): "What is an Author?" In: *Language, Counter-Memory, Practice.* Translated by D.F. Bouchard and S. Simon, pp. 124–127. Ithaca, New York: Cornell University Press.

Foucault, Michel (1994[1966]): *The Order of Things. An Archaeology of the Human Science. A Translation of Les Mots et les choses.* New York: Vintage Books.

Haraway, Donna J. (1991), "A Cyborg Manifesto: Science, Technology, and Socialist-Feminism in the Late Twentieth Century." In: *Simians, Cyborgs, and Women. The Reinvention of Nature.* London: Free Association Books, pp. 149–181.

Irsiger, Ingo, and Dominik Orth (2018): "Zwischen Menschwerdung und Weltherrschaft: Künstliche Intelligenz im Film." In: *Aus Politik und Zeitgeschichte* 6/8, pp. 39–45.

Klimczak, Peter, and Christer Petersen (2015), "Ordnung und Abweichung: Jurij M. Lotmans Grenzüberschreitungstheorie aus modallogischer Perspektive." In: *Journal of Literary Theory* 9.1, pp. 135–154.

Klimczak, Peter (2017): "Logik in den Kulturwissenschaften – Spielräume der Gender Studies." In: *Logik in den Wissenschaften.* Ed. by Peter Klinczak and Thomas Zoglauer, pp. 199–223. Münster: mentis.

Ostreich, Heide (2018): "Feministische Philosophie und Körper. Müssen wir Butler verabschieden?" In: *taz* March 18th, 2018.

Panofsky, Dora, and Erwin Panofsky (1991[1956]): *Pandora's Box. The Changing Aspects of a Mythical Symbol*. Princeton: University Press.

Penny, Laury (2018): *Bitch Doctrine. Essays for Dissenting Adults. Revised and Updated Edition*. London, Dublin: Bloomsbury.

Petersen, Christer (2003): *Der postmoderne Text. Rekonstruktion einer zeitgenössischen Ästhetik am Beispiel von Thomas Pynchon, Peter Greenaway und Paul Wühr*. Kiel: Ludwig.

Turing, Alan M. (1950): "Computing machinery and intelligence." In: *Mind* 59, pp. 433–460.

von Braun, Christina (2006): "Gender, Geschlecht und Geschichte." In: *Gender-Studien. Eine Einführung*. Ed. by Christina von Braun and Inge Stephan, pp 10–51. Stuttgart/Weimar: Metzler.

Trends in Explainable Artificial Intelligence for Non-Experts

Elise Özalp, Katrin Hartwig, Christian Reuter

1. Introduction

Artificial intelligence (AI), cognitive systems and machine learning are already part of everyday life and have the power to transform economy and society. Although AI is widely used in data processing and domains such as the medical field or cybersecurity, the inherent pitfalls are not clear yet. According to a recent report, AI systems are increasingly biased in terms of gender, race or social background (Crawford et al. 2019). For instance, the *AI Now 2019 Report* highlights the revelations of recent audits regarding "disproportionate performance or biases within AI systems ranging from self-driving-car software that performed differently for darker- and lighter-skinned pedestrians, gender bias in online biographies, skewed representations in object recognition from lower-income environments, racial differences in algorithmic pricing, differential prioritization in healthcare, and performance disparities in facial recognition" (Crawford et al. 2019). This has led to demands from researchers and politicians for accountability and transparency of these systems. In May 2018, the European Union passed the General Data Protection Regulation (GDPR), which requires reasoning and justification of decisions based on fully automated algorithms. This shows the increasing need for *eXplainable Artificial Intelligence (XAI)* (European Union 2016).

The biases revealed and political topicality have accelerated the development of XAI, which makes use of visualizations and natural language processing to explain the reasoning behind algorithmic decisions (European Union 2016). Making algorithmic decisions more comprehensible for end users is an emerging trend in many different application domains such as cybersecurity – even when there is no artificial intelligence involved, as algorithmic decisions are in any case often difficult for end users to understand (Hartwig/Reuter 2021). In general, research has shown that even when algorithmic predictions are more accurate than human predictions, both domain experts and laypeople distrust the algorithm (Narayanan et al. 2018). XAI aims at comprehensive understanding of the deployed algorithm such that user trust is built based on explanations and not only on performance. This will lead to better social acceptance of AI systems in different areas of life. It is important to note that the explanations provided by XAI systems do not only promote trust. They also help users to critically analyze the algorithms and to improve algorithms by finding mistakes.

Despite the usefulness of XAI, there are still several difficulties to address, especially regarding laypeople. The main difficulty lies in the complexity of the AI models. Often, complicated models (such as neural networks) are used to achieve the best performance. These models do not serve as an understandable explanation for non-specialists since they reason with high-dimensional numerical values. According to Miller (2019), numerical values probably do not matter for humans since we demand instead causal explanations. To handle this and other difficulties, XAI combines pedagogy, programming and domain knowledge.

In this paper we provide an overview of XAI by introducing fundamental terminology and the goals of XAI, as well as recent research findings. Whilst doing this, we pay special attention to strategies for non-expert stakeholders. This leads us to our first research question: "What are the trends in explainable AI strategies for non-experts?". In order to illustrate the current state of these trends, we further want to study an exemplary and very relevant application domain. According to Abdul et al. (2018), one of the first domains where researchers pursued XAI is the medical domain. This leads to our second research question: "What are the approaches of XAI in the medical domain for non-expert stakeholders?" These research questions will provide an overview of current topics in XAI and show possible research extensions for specific domains.

The chapter is organized as follows: Section 2 presents the foundations and related work on XAI; in Section 3, we explain the research method utilized; Section 4 identifies and surveys current trends, and in Section 5, we describe the current state of XAI in the medical domain; finally, in Section 6, we discuss how non-experts can be better integrated into XAI and which questions we should ask going forward.

2. Related Work

AI is the attempt to mimic human behaviour by constructing an algorithm for specific decision scenarios. Since the beginning of the 2010s, AI has become increasingly popular, with applications in almost every economic sector due to increased processing power. With its increasing popularity and use, AI has left the context of academic research and is now being used by non-experts of AI. However, many of the constructed algorithms are based on higher mathematics and are not transparent. XAI targets this issue by explaining AI decision-making processes and logic for end users (Gunning/Aha 2019).

We give an overview of the fundamental terminology in Table 1 and provide further literature. In general, *intelligible systems* do not have to be systems involving AI; they can be viewed as a superclass of it. Within *transparent AI*, *interpretable* and *explainable AI* can be viewed as subclasses. Even though there is a subtle difference, these terms are often used interchangeably in research. Barredo et al. (2020) present how the research interest has shifted from interpretable to explainable AI since 2012. Within the XAI research, the terms *local* and *global explanations* appear to classify explanations according to their interpretation scale (see Table 1). In many cases, *ad-hoc explainers* are used to describe local explanations (Guidotti et al. 2018). The terminology described here will build the foundation to analyze current trends in XAI for non-experts.

While the work referenced in Table 1 focuses on the foundations and the underlying idea of XAI, research in XAI generally aims at different user groups (Langer et al. 2021; Martin et al. 2021). The most targeted user group so far has been AI experts, who design the systems and aim to improve them. For research targeting machine learning experts, it is common to analyze existing use cases and create explanations around them, such as for predictive coding (Chhatwal et al. 2018) or the retrieval of video frames (Chittajallu et al. 2019). Even though XAI systems are presented, fundamental knowledge of AI methods and techniques implemented is necessary to understand these papers. The same is true for suggested techniques to create more interpretable deep neural networks (Holzinger et al. 2017; Liu et al. 2017).

Table 1: Relevant definitions for XAI with reference sources

Terminology	Description	References
Intelligible System	A system whose inner workings and inputs are exposed through transparency and explanations to the user.	(Clinciu/Hastie 2019; B.Y. Lim/Dey 2009; Mohseni et al. 2018)
Transparent AI	A system that discloses the algorithmic mechanism on the level of model, individual components and training.	(Chromik et al. 2019; Clinciu 2019; Lipton 2018; Mohseni 2018; Rader et al. 2018)
Interpretable AI	A system provided with explanations to retrace the model decision making process and predictions.	(Abdul 2018; Barredo Arrieta 2020; Clinciu 2019; Marino 2018; T. Miller 2019; Mohseni 2018)
Explainable AI	A system provided with explanations to give reasoning for algorithmic decisions.	(Kulesza et al. 2013; T. Miller 2019; Mohseni 2018; Rader 2018)
Global Explanation	Reasoning of how the overall model works, also called model explanation.	(Gedikli et al. 2014; P.L. Miller 1986; Mohseni 2018)
Local Explanation	Reasoning why a specific input leads to a certain output, also called instance explanations.	
Mental Model	The representation of how a user understands a system.	(Mohseni 2018)

More research that involves XAI in recent machine learning research can be found. Even though these research papers do not state that their target user group are AI experts, this can easily be concluded after reading them. In contrast to this research direction, research for non-experts is less prominent. While some literature also includes machine learning novices (Hohman et al. 2018; Spinner et al. 2020), there is little literature that focuses on non-experts with no technical background. In some studies (e.g. Cheng et al. 2019; Kulesza 2013; B. Lim 2011), different strategies are examined that target non-expert stakeholders, and we will look these papers at closely to observe XAI for non-experts. Kulesza et al. (2009, 2012, 2015) analyze how explanations can help non-experts to personalize and debug interactive machine learning. However, XAI mainly targets existing AI research and research only rarely specifically targets end users. Therefore, we identify this as a current research gap. In the following, we analyze the existing research on XAI for non-experts and explicate which trends are to be observed. In order to give a balanced overview of XAI for non-experts, we want to include to what extent these trends can also be found in a specific and relevant application domain where XAI is often designed for medical experts (e.g. Karim et al. 2019).

3. Methods

To analyze current trends and attain an overview of the current state of research, we decided to conduct a non-exhaustive semi-structured literature review over several platforms. Because of the high topicality, it is difficult to observe XAI for non-experts in real-life applications. Therefore, we analyze the existing literature as a foundation for later research. For our qualitative research study, we combine a constrained backtracking search strategy with a keyword search.

Mohseni et al. (2018), in which the authors present a multidisciplinary survey for the design and evaluation of explainable AI systems, serves as the first core paper for the constrained backtracking search. This paper is an in-depth survey that analyzes different aspects of XAI, including terminology, design goals, evaluation measures and frameworks. In referencing about 250 papers, it also provides a good literature overview as a starting point for further research. With the first version submitted in 2018 and the most recent in January 2020, the paper constitutes an up-to-date summary of XAI. From this work, we have selected referenced papers based on their relation to the keywords presented in Table 2, scanning titles and abstracts to decide if a paper was relevant for our context.

As the second core paper, we use Abdul et al. (2018), in which the authors conducted a literature analysis of 289 core papers on explainable systems to derive current trends and trajectories. Again, we select referenced papers based on their relation to the keywords in Table 2, scanning titles and abstracts. While the first paper targets the foundations of XAI, the second paper focuses on current trends which will allow us to combine both topics. Both papers provide a broad overview of the current state of research in XAI and will serve as core papers for our literature research. From both papers, we generally excluded papers with a focus on research on the mathematics and technical improvements of AI systems, as well as research on very specific applications that was not transferable to our research question.

Table 2: List of search keywords

Keyword	Alternative search word
Explainable Artificial Intelligence	Explainable AI, XAI, interpretable AI
Trends	
Interaction	Interactive
Visualization	Visual
Trust	
Bias	
Medical Domain	Clinical domain, medicine
Clinical decision support systems	CDSS
Human-computer interaction	HCI, Computer-human interaction, CHI
Non-experts	AI novices, laypeople

In order to avoid biased outcomes and to consider more recent work up to March 2021, we consider the database of IEEE, AAAI, Google Scholar, ADS, Journal of Artificial Intelligence Research and the Journal of Human-Computer Interaction. Table 2 shows search keywords and combined search terms. We use combinations such as "XAI non-experts" or "Trends Visualization XAI". However, the core search word remains "XAI" to maintain distinctions between generally AI-related research and AI-focused research.

It is crucial to point out that our database search does not make any claim to comprehensiveness, as in a first step titles and abstracts were scanned superficially and not all papers were read exhaustively. Instead, the review should be considered a semi-structured approach, giving valuable qualitative insights into trends related to XAI for non-experts. The database search led to a large quantity of publications from which we excluded publications based on their language (only English papers were included), title, abstract and application domain. We again excluded research that focused on mathematics and algorithm optimization of AI systems. Furthermore, we did not consider publications that explained specific AI application examples to AI experts. After reading several of these publications, we decided that the approaches were not transferable to laypersons due to their high complexity.

Due to the large set of literature from our core papers by Mohseni et al. (2018) and Abdul et al. (2018), the database search resulted in partial overlap of publications. In total, we reference 42 different works including the two core papers (see below: 7. References). Many of these furnish reasoning and background for our arguments or provide examples. However, to directly derive answers for our first research question, we identified only 13 papers out of the 42 works that clearly propose trends that were transferable to general XAI for laypeople. These publications are classified into trends in Table 3.

4. Results

In the following, we will discuss our findings regarding general trends of explainable AI for non-experts and, subsequently, give more specific insights into XAI for non-experts in the medical domain..

4.1 Trends of Explainable AI for Non-Experts

When referring to AI non-experts or AI novices, we consider general AI end-users who have no previous experience in the design of machine learning algorithms and are not domain experts of the application field in which the AI operates. It is crucial to understand that XAI pursues different goals and different approaches to explanation depending on the target user. According to Mohseni et al. (2018), there are three target user groups: non-expert end-users, domain experts and AI experts. To give an example for the medical domain: the AI expert researches and designs the machine learning algorithms, the domain expert is expert in the application domain, such as a doctor in the medical domain, and the end-user non-expert is the patient with no prior medical or AI knowledge.

Mohseni et al. (2018) found four dominant goals of XAI for non-experts. The first goal of XAI is to help end-users understand how the AI system works. This is referred to as algorithmic transparency and aims to improve the users' mental model. It can also allow an end-user to improve or debug daily machine learning applications such as email categorizers (Kulesza 2009) without machine learning knowledge. Other scenarios where algorithmic transparency promotes end-user debugging in daily life applications can be found (B.Y. Lim, 2009), such as instant messenger auto-notification. Even though the end user can directly benefit from this transparency, companies that own these intelligent applications are reluctant to provide explanations for fear of negative impact on their reputation or competitive advantage (Chromik 2019). Nevertheless, providing explanations improves user trust by letting the user evaluate the system's reliability and observe the system's accuracy for certain decisions. This user trust is influenced by the increasing amount of information on biased AI, making bias mitigation a design goal of XAI (Mohseni 2018). This can have impacts in economic scenarios, e.g. in the form of hotel recommendations (Eslami et al. 2017). But there are also societal scenarios where biased AI can have severe implications, as in the risk assessment of criminal defendants. One of the leading American tools for risk assessment found that black defendants were far more likely than white defendants to be incorrectly judged (Chouldechova 2017; Larson et al. 2016). The above mentioned GDPR now legally supports each person in accessing information about how their data is used. This goal of privacy awareness allows end-users to know which user data is influencing the algorithmic decision-making. Everyday life examples where this is also relevant can be found in personalized advertisement or personalized news feeds in social media (Eslami et al. 2015).

To achieve these goals, different explanation interfaces can be found in the literature. The main distinction is made between white-box and black-box models with interactive or static approaches. In contrast to white-box models, black-box models do not display the inner workings of the algorithm but focus on explaining the relationship between the input and output, e.g. through parameter weight influence. Since this is independent of how complicated the models are, black-box models are often used for (deep) neural networks. This also makes explaining the algorithmic concepts to AI novices unnecessary. By comparison, white-box models specifically display the inner workings of the algorithm with understandable features or transparent computations. Cheng et al. (2019) conducted a study to compare white- and black-box methods for non-expert stakeholders and evaluated them in terms of objective understanding and self-reported understanding. Users spent the same amount of time on both explanation interfaces but scored higher in objective understanding when using the white-box interface. This corresponds with the idea that more transparent explanations help user understanding. However, users did not describe an increased self-reported understanding with the white-box model and neither of the models increased the users' trust. The authors observed that greater complexity resulted in lower satisfaction. This might suggest that the black-box method could benefit from not conveying complexity if improvements to objective understanding can be made. There are different approaches to improving explanations of black-box models (Narayanan 2018), but they are still feature-oriented or try to explain the mathematical components of the features. This loss of human interpretability is known as the "accuracy-interpretability trade-off", which states that "often the highest performing methods (e.g., deep learning) are the least explainable, and the most explainable (e.g., decision trees) are less accurate" (Gunning 2019). While high-dimensional weights and numerical features are the basis for the algorithm, social sciences argue that a person requires a causal explanation instead of a probabilistic explanation in order to be satisfied (T. Miller 2019). Aligning with this is the newest trend of "Open the Black-Box" or "Stop the Black-Box" (Rudin 2019; Rudin/Radin 2019), which suggests completely abandoning black-box models. Proponents argue that the black-box models support bias and even AI experts do not understand how predictions in complicated models are made. They also state that the improved white-box models require a significant effort to construct, especially with regard to computation and domain expertise. The idea appears promising but points more in the direction of a topic for classical AI research.

In Kulesza et al. (2015) an interactive white-box method is suggested which allows users to build an understanding of the system while exploring it. Their recommendation focuses on balancing completeness with incremental changes and reversible actions to not overwhelm the user. They state that the model should include the following types: *inputs* (features the system is aware of), the *model* (an overview of the system's decision-making process), *why* (the reasons underlying a specific decision), and *certainty* (the system's confidence in each decision). To allow further exploration and interactivity, *what if* types should be included. One of the key takeaways is that a user-focused approachthat includes a self-explanatory system and back corrections is highly beneficial to explain an AI application. According to this survey, the new watchword is interaction, with its close connections to reflection, implicit interaction and software learnability. Abdul et al. (2018) also implemented an interactive interface that let the user freely explore adjustable inputs. The interactive feature provided significantly better results in self-reported and objective understanding. However, in both cases the interactive aspect is model- and application-specific, which makes it difficult to derive generalizations for interaction in XAI.

The same problem arises regarding visualizations in XAI. Visualizations are very useful to display high dimensional data and data flow (Bach et al.

2015; Cheng 2019; Samek et al. 2019) and there are multiple approaches to using them for neural networks (Heleno et al. 2019; Montavon et al. 2018). In Liu et al. (2017), the authors present CNNVis, an interactive visual analytics system, to better understand convolutional neural networks for image processing. Hybrid visualizations are used to disclose interactions between neurons and explain the steps of neural networks. Whilst CNNVis targets machine learning experts, this is also an interesting approach to "open the black-box" for non-experts. Other literature suggests using visualization tools to explain the ML pipeline from the model input to output (El-assady et al. 2019; Spinner 2020). The model presented by Spinner et al. (2020), explAIner, is a framework for interactive and explainable machine learning. It can be used as a TensorBoard plugin and combines visual and natural language explanations, with enhancement on storytelling and justification. The framework received positive feedback in a case study but it is unclear how well AI novices can understand the explanations with no background in machine learning. Meanwhile, Google deployed an online service at the end of 2019 which provides a framework for AI explanations, including the integration of visualizations (Google Cloud 2021). This also underscores the increasingly important role that XAI is playing in the industry. However, the question of how to use visualization tools in XAI for AI novices remains open for research.

The trends identified in the most relevant papers referenced above are summarized in Table 3.

Table 3: Referenced literature with identified trends

	Black/ White Box	Explanation Types	Underlying Model	Interaction	Visualization
(Cheng 2019)	x				
(Guidotti 2018)	x				
(T. Miller 2019)	x	x			
(Kulesza 2013)	x	x			
(Kulesza 2015)	x	x		x	
(Rudin 2019)	x		x		
(Rudin/Radin 2019)	x		x		
(Abdul 2018)	x			x	
(Narayanan 2018)		x	x		
(Lim 2011)		x			
(Lim 2009)		x			x
(Heleno 2019)			x		x
(Spinner 2020)				x	x

In the next section, we seek to better illustrate the current state of XAI for laypeople on the example of an explicit application domain.

4.2 XAI for Non-Experts in the Medical Domain

Lim et al. (2018) state that the medical domain was the first application domain of XAI. More than other domains, algorithmic medical recommendations demand explanation and justification due to their high impact on human lives. This naturally acts as driving force of XAI in the medical domain. According to the research analysis (Abdul 2018), the medical and healthcare domain appears repeatedly in the context of XAI, especially in relation to fair, accountable and transparent algorithms and interpretable machine learning. As explained in Section 2, research in XAI with a focus on non-experts is very limited. Because of its importance and the availability of more literature than in other application domains, we have chosen the medical domain to analyze the current state of XAI for non-experts in an application domain.

In the medical domain, AI systems are used for critical decision-making tasks which magnifies the importance of the explanations and transparency for end-users and non-experts. The described systems are clinical decision support systems which store health knowledge and apply this to new patient observations. The resulting recommendations can help the clinicians to make choices.

Even though in general, experts and AI novices tend to distrust AI systems (Narayanan 2018), in this specific context, Goddard et al. (2012) discovered that clinicians tend to trust the system more than their own judgement. This over-trust is called automation bias and is dependent on factors such as task complexity, workload and time pressure. Bussone et al. (2015) investigate the relationship between trust, explanations and reliance of practitioners to CDSS in an exploratory between-group user study. The study involved some of Lim's and Dey's (2009) types such as confidence explanations and why explanations in natural language and also examined the explanations desired by the study participants. In contrast to Lim and Dey (2009), the participants requested more than an indicator of certainty and a significant number did not understand what this percentage even meant. From the perspective of a patient, it can also be rather unsettling if this percentage indicates a disease. Further, the system provided facts it used to make a diagnosis but the study participants requested more information for typical cases of this diagnosis. This would allow them to assess how much the suggestions fit. Additionally, the clinicians requested an explanation that allowed them to disprove other diagnoses, e.g. the second most likely diagnosis. This also supports Lim's and Dey's (2009) *why not* explanation type. Overall, Bussone et al. (2015) observe that clinicians demand explanations with the same reasoning that they use to make a diagnosis. However, the sample size of the study was very limited and the user groups studied were AI novices but experts in the medical domain.

In the study of Narayanan et al. (2018) about 600 participants were recruited to conduct a study on explanation types of recommendation systems. While one recommendation system recommended recipes, the other system diagnosed symptoms and recommended pharmaceuticals. Unlike in the study by Bussone et al. (2015), the recommendation system was less expert-oriented. Narayanan et al. (2018) found that the observations on explanations in the recipe and medical domains coincided, meaning that the application domain did not require different explanations. Another important finding is that if the participant is focused on understanding, the complexity of an explanation does not result in a decrease of accuracy but rather in an increase in response time.

This leads us to the proposition that Lim's and Dey's types (Lim 2009), presented in Section 4 and supported by the observations of Bussone et al. (2015), can be transferred to explanations for patients. However, it is questionable whether or not these explanations can be used as black-box explanations when the decision support system is based on very complicated systems such as neural networks. For such systems, Holzinger et al. (2017) suggest linking vector representations of neural networks to lexical resources and knowledge bases using hybrid distributional models for the medical context. This enables step-by-step retracing of how the system developed a solution but it is questionable whether this is understandable for AI laypeople.

Overall, we observe the same problem as explained in Section 2: the literature addresses mostly AI experts or experts in the medical domain. From the literature analyzed, the findings derived are limited: Lim's and Dey's (2009) explanation types are transferable to different domains and especially the *why not* explanation type is in demand. This explanation will help to understand why the patient did not receive a different diagnosis. Further, the study by Narayanan et al. (2018) indicates that XAI can probably follow a universal explanation strategy for different domains. For this reason, we will summarize our findings and provide guidelines in the next section.

5. Discussion and Conclusion

Table 4 presents the findings of our semi-structured literature review on current XAI trends with a focus on the medical domain, summarises our most important findings and puts forward the following suggestions for the design of XAI for non-experts:

Table 4: Suggestions for the design of XAI for non-experts

Design Suggestion	Explanation for Suggestion
During the Implementation of the AI System for an Application:	
Consider explainability in the choice of the AI algorithm.	
When choosing a model, consider whether a simpler algorithm can achieve similar/better results.	According to Rudin (2019) and Rudin/Radin (2019), even AI experts do not understand how predictions in complicated models are made.
After deciding on a model, implement it such that the inner computations can be accessed and perhaps even visualized.	Liu et al. (2017) suggest hybrid visualizations to explain the steps of neural networks. We suggest implementing this directly with the system.
After Building the AI System	
Focus on explaining using a white-box approach.	
For natural language explanations, use Lim's & Dey's (2009) explanation types: *inputs, model, why, certainty, what if/why not.*	These explanation types have been requested by laypeople and proven to be reliable in different contexts (Bussone 2015; e.g., Lim 2009).
Allow the user to freely explore adjustable inputs and allow back corrections for interactive explanations.	Kulesza et al. (2015) found that interactive features lead to significantly better results in self-reported and objective understanding.
Use visual explanations to display the framework of the built AI system and to explain the computations of the data (dependent on the application domain).	Cheng (2019) suggests displaying high dimensional data and data flows using visualizations.

Identifying explanation strategies for non-experts to account for AI is an essential step in integrating AI systems into society. The task of explaining complicated systems to someone with little to no prior knowledge is generally a challenge. Which strategies can be used for AI systems? What is the current state of research? Are trends in explainable AI also observable in applications such as the medical domain? The knowledge gained from identifying these explanation strategies will be crucial for the acceptance of AI in society.

In this review, we observed current trends in XAI for non-experts. We perceived a demand for a shift from black to white-box models which appears difficult regarding complicated machine learning models. Voices in research are increasingly questioning the necessity of complicated models and suggest a simpler, well-planned architecture. At the same time, different underlying models are proposed such as hybrid models to create more self-explainable complex models. Regarding the explanations, the types suggested by Lim and Dey (2009) reappear within different independent literature, sometimes slightly modified. Therefore, we also recommend including the types: *inputs, model, why, certainty/confidence, what if.* We also propose using the *what if* type together with interactivity to support end user exploration. Generally, visualization is recommended and several frameworks are proposed. However, the problem of how to explain AI specifically to AI novices remains unsolved. This can be observed even more readily in the medical domain where trust and reliability of AI are of particular importance. The shift to white-box models, the explanation types, hybrid models and interaction can also be observed in XAI for the medical domain. Yet, all the research available is only targeted at data or AI experts.

Generally speaking, it is difficult to find research that targets non-experts. Going forward it will be important to center the research around the needs of non-experts. What information do non-experts demand from an AI system in the medical domain, such as a clinical decision support system? How do these differ from AI systems in lifestyle applications such as a spam filter? Can we directly integrate those explanations in domains where XAI is not yet established, such as cybersecurity? Further, there are open questions regarding the build of the framework. Can we build simpler AI systems that achieve similar or better results than complicated ones? Do non-experts really profit from hybrid models to understand more complicated AI systems? How important is the design of the interface in terms of interaction and visualization compared to the explanation of the system? A better understanding of these questions will guide the design of XAI for non-experts.

Acknowledgements

This work was funded by the Deutsche Forschungsgemeinschaft (SFB 1119, 236615297), by the German Federal Ministry of Education and Research and the Hessen State Ministry for Higher Education, Research and the Arts within their joint support of the National Research Center for Applied Cybersecurity ATHENE and by the BMBF in the project CYWARN (13N15407).

References

Abdul, Ashraf, Jo Vermeulen, Danding Wang, Brian Y. Lim, an Mohan Kankanhalli (2018). "Trends and Trajectories for Explainable, Accountable and Intelligible Systems: An HCI Research Agenda". In: *CHI '18, Proceedings of the 2018 CHI Conference on Human Factors in Computing Systems*. ACM, pp. 582–590. URL: https://doi.org/10.1145/3173574.3174156.

Bach, Sebastian, Alexander Binder, Grégoire Montavon, Frederick Klauschen, Klaus-Robert Müller, and Wojciech Samek (2015). "On pixel-wise explanations for non-linear classifier decisions by layer-wise relevance propagation". In: *PLoS ONE* 10.7. URL: https://doi.org/10.1371/journal.pone.o 130140.

Barredo Arrieta, Alejandro, Natalia Díaz-Rodríguez, Javier Del Ser, Adrien Bennetot, Siham Tabik, Alberto Barbado, Salvador Garcia, Sergio Gil-Lopez, Daniel Molina, Richard Benjamins, Raja Chatila, and Francisco Herrera (2020). "Explainable Artificial Intelligence (XAI). Concepts, Taxonomies, Opportunities and Challenges Toward Responsible AI." In: *Information Fusion*, 58.June, pp. 82–115. URL: https://doi.org/10.1016/j.inffu s.2019.12.012.

Bussone, Adrian, Simone Stumpf, and Dympna O'Sullivan (2015). "The Role of Explanations on Trust and Reliance in Clinical Decision Support Systems." In: *IEEE, International Conference on Healthcare Informatics*. URL: https://doi.org/10.1109/ICHI.2015.26.

Cheng, Hao-Fei, Ruotong Wang, Zheng Zhang, Fiona O'Connell, Terrance Gray, F. Maxwell Harper, and Haiyi Zhu (2019). "Explaining Decision-Making Algorithms through UI: Strategies to Help Non-Expert Stakeholders." In: *CHI '19, Proceedings of the 2019 CHI Conference on Human Factors in Computing Systems*, pp. 1–12. URL: https://doi.org/10.1145/3290605.3300 789.

Chhatwal, Rishi, Peter Gronvall, Nathaniel Huber-Fliflet, Robert Keeling, Jianping Zhang, and Haozhen Zhao (2018). "Explainable Text Classification in Legal Document Review A Case Study of Explainable Predictive Coding." In: *IEEE, International Conference on Big Data (Big Data)*, pp. 1905–1911. URL: https://doi.org/10.1109/BigData.2018.8622073.

Chittajallu, Deepak Roy, Bo Dong, Paul Tunison, Roddy Collins, Katerina Wells, James Fleshman, Ganesh Sankaranarayanan, Steven Schwaitzberg, Lora Cavuoto, and Andinet Enquobahrie (2019). "XAI-CBIR: Explainable AI system for content based retrieval of video frames from minimally invasive surgery videos." In: *IEEE, 16th International Symposium on Biomedical Imaging*, pp. 66–69. URL: https://doi.org/10.1109/ISBI.2019.8759428.

Chouldechova, Alexandra (2017). "Fair prediction with disparate impact: A study of bias in recidivism prediction instruments." In: *Big Data* 5.2, pp. 153–163.

Chromik, Michael, Malin Eiband, Sarah Theres Völkel, and Daniel Buschek (2019). "Dark Patterns of Explainability, Transparency, and User Control for Intelligent Systems." In: *IUI workshops* 2327.

Clinciu, Miruna-Adriana, and Helen Hastie (2019). "A survey of explainable AI terminology." In: *NL4XAI, Proceedings of the 1st Workshop on Interactive Natural Language Technology for Explainable Artificial Intelligence*, pp. 8–13.

Crawford, Kate, Roel Dobbe, Theodora Dryer, Genevieve Fried, Ben Green, Elizabeth Kaziunas,, Amba Kak, Varoon Mathur, Erin McElroy, Andrea Nill Sánchez, Deborah Raji, Joy Lisi Rankin, Rashida Richardson, Jason Schultz, Sarah Myers West, and Meredith Whittaker (2019). *AI Now 2019 Report*. New York. URL: https://ainowinstitute.org/AI_Now_2019_Report.html.

El-Assady, Mennatallah, Wolfgang Jentner, Rebecca Kehlbeck, and Udo Schlegel (2019). "Towards XAI: Structuring the Processes of Explanations." In: *ACM Workshop on Human-Centered Machine Learning*, iss. May.

Eslami, Motahhare, Aimee Rickman, Kristen Vaccaro, Amirhossein Aleyasen, Andy Vuong, Karrie Karahalios, Kevin Hamilton, and Christian Sandvig (2015). "'I always assumed that I wasn't really that close to [her]' Reasoning about Invisible Algorithms in News Feeds". In: *CHI '15, Proceedings of the 33rd annual ACM conference on human factors in computing systems*, pp. 153–162. URL: https://doi.org/10.1145/2702123.2702556.

Eslami, Motahhare, Kristen Vaccaro, Karrie Karahalios, and Kevin Hamilton (2017). "Be careful; things can be worse than they appear." In: *Eleventh International AAAI Conference on Web and Social Media* 11.1, pp. 62–70.

European Union (2016). *General Data Protection Regulation (GDPR)*, Retrieved August 5, 2021. URL: https://gdpr-info.eu.

Gedikli, Fatih, Dietmar Jannach, and Mouzhi Ge (2014). "How should I explain? A comparison of different explanation types for recommender systems." In: *International Journal of Human-Computer Studies* 72.4, pp. 367–382.

Goddard, Kate, Abdul Roudsari, And Jeremy C. Wyatt (2012). "Automation bias: a systematic review of frequency, effect mediators, and mitigators." In: *Journal of the American Medical Informatics Association* 19.1, pp. 121–127.

Google Cloud (2021). "Einführung in AI Explanations für AI Platform | AI Platform Prediction", Retrieved March 3, 2021. URL: https://cloud.google.com/ai-platform/prediction/docs/ai-explanations/overview.

Guidotti, Riccardo, Anna Monreale, Salvatore Ruggieri, Franco Turini, Fosca Giannotti, and Dino Pedreschi (2018). "A survey of methods for explaining black box models." In: *ACM Computing Surveys (CSUR)* 51.5, pp. 1–42.

Gunning, David, and David Aha (2019). "DARPA's explainable artificial intelligence (XAI) program." In: *AI Magazine* 40.2, pp. 44–58.

Hartwig, Katrin, and Christian Reuter (2021). "Nudging users towards better security decisions in password creation using whitebox-based multidimensional visualisations." In: *Behaviour and Information Technology* 41.7, pp. 1357–1380. URL: https://doi.org/10.1080/0144929X.2021.1876167.

Heleno, Marco, Nuno Correia, and Miguel Carvalhais (2019). "Explaining Machine Learning" In: *ARTECH 2019, Proceedings of the 9th International Conference on Digital and Interactive Arts*, October, Article No. 60, pp. 1–3. URL: https://doi.org/10.1145/3359852.3359918.

Hohman, Fred, Minsuk Kahng, Robert Pienta, and Duen Horng Chau (2018). "Visual analytics in deep learning: An interrogative survey for the next frontiers." In: *IEEE, Transactions on Visualization and Computer Graphics* 25.8, pp. 2674–2693. URL: https://doi.org/10.1109/TVCG.2018.2843369.

Holzinger, Andreas, Chris Biemann, Constantinos S. Pattichis, and Douglas B. Kell (2017). "What do we need to build explainable AI systems for the medical domain?" iss. Ml, pp. 1–28. URL: http://arxiv.org/abs/1712.09923.

Karim, Md Rezaul, Michael Cochez, Oya Beyan, Stefan Decker, and Christoph Lange (2019). "OncoNetExplainer: explainable predictions of cancer types based on gene expression data." In: *IEEE, 19th International Conference on Bioinformatics and Bioengineering (BIBE)*, pp. 415–422. URL: https://arxiv.org/abs/1909.04169.

Kulesza, Todd, Margaret Burnett, Weng-Keen Wong, and Simone Stumpf (2015). "Principles of explanatory debugging to personalize interactive machine learning." In: *IUI '15, Proceedings of the 20th international conference on intelligent user interfaces*, pp. 126–137. URL: https://doi.org/10.1145/2678025.2701399.

Kulesza, Todd, Simone Stumpf, Margaret Burnett, and Irwin Kwan (2012). "Tell me more? The effects of mental model soundness on personalizing an intelligent agent." In: *CHI '12, Proceedings of the SIGCHI Conference on Human Factors in Computing Systems*, pp. 1–10. URL: https://doi.org/10.1145/2207676.2207678.

Kulesza, Todd, Simone Stumpf, Margaret Burnett, Sherry Yang, Irwin Kwan, and Weng-Keen Wong (2013). "Too much, too little, or just right? Ways explanations impact end users' mental models." In: *IEEE, Symposium on visual languages and human centric computing*, pp. 3–10. URL: https://doi.org/10.1109/VLHCC.2013.6645235.

Kulesza, Todd, Weng-Keen Wong, Simone Stumpf, Stephen Perona, Rachel White, Margaret M. Burnett, Ian Oberst, and Amy J. Ko (2009). "Fixing the program my computer learned: Barriers for end users, challenges for the machine. In: *IUI '09, Proceedings of the 14th international conference on Intelligent user interfaces*, pp. 187–196. URL: https://doi.org/10.1145/1502650.1502678.

Langer, Markus, Daniel Oster, Lena Kästner, Timo Speith, Kevin Baum, Holger Hermanns, Eva Schmidt, and Andreas Sesing (2021). "What do we want from Explainable Artificial Intelligence (XAI)? A stakeholder perspective on XAI and a conceptual model guiding interdisciplinary XAI research." In: *Artificial Intelligence*, pp. 103473.

Larson, Jeff, Surya Mattu, Lauren Kirchner, and Julia Angwin (2016). "How We Analyzed the COMPAS Recidivism Algorithm". In: *ProPublica*. Retrieved March 3, 2021. URL: https://www.propublica.org/article/how-we-analyzed-the-compas-recidivism-algorithm.

Lim, Brian (2011). *Improving Understanding, Trust, and Control with Intelligibility in Context-Aware Applications*. PHD Thesis, Human-Computer Interaction Institute.

Lim, Brian Y., and Anind K. Dey (2009). "Assessing demand for intelligibility in context-aware applications." In: *UbiComp '09, Proceedings of the 11th international conference on Ubiquitous computing*, pp. 195–204. URL: https://doi.org/10.1145/1620545.1620576.

Lipton, Zachary C. (2018). "The Mythos of Model Interpretability: In machine learning, the concept of interpretability is both important and slippery." In: *Queue* 16.3, pp. 31–57. URL: https://doi.org/10.1145/3236386.3241340.

Liu, Shixia, Xiting Wang, Mengchen Liu, and Jun Zhu (2017). "Towards better analysis of machine learning models: A visual analytics perspective." In: *Visual Informatics* 1.1, pp. 48–56. URL: https://doi.org/10.1016/j.visinf.2017.01.006.

Marino, Daniel L., Chathurika S. Wickramasinghe, and Milos Manic (2018). "An adversarial approach for explainable ai in intrusion detection systems." In: *IECON, 44th Annual Conference of the IEEE Industrial Electronics Society*, pp. 3237–3243. URL: https://doi.org/10.1109/IECON.2018.8591457.

Martin, Kyle, Anne Liret, Nirmalie Wiratunga, Gilbert Owusu, and Mathias Kern (2021). "Evaluating Explainability Methods Intended for Multiple Stakeholders." In: *KI-Künstliche Intelligenz* 35, pp. 1–15. URL: https://doi.org/10.1007/s13218-020-00702-6.

Miller, Perry L. (1986). "The evaluation of artificial intelligence systems in medicine." In: *Computer Methods and Programs in Biomedicine* 22.1, pp. 3–11.

Miller, Tim (2019). "Explanation in artificial intelligence: Insights from the social sciences." In: *Artificial Intelligence* 267.February, pp. 1–38. URL: https://doi.org/10.1016/j.artint.2018.07.007.

Mohseni, Sina, Niloofar Zarei, and Eric D. Ragan (2018). "A Multidisciplinary Survey and Framework for Design and Evaluation of Explainable AI Systems." In: *Artificial Intelligence* 1.1, pp. 1–37. URL: http://arxiv.org/abs/1811.11839.

Montavon, Grégoire, Wojciech Samek, and Klaus Robert Müller (2018). "Methods for interpreting and understanding deep neural networks." In: *Digital Signal Processing* 73, pp. 1–15. URL: https://doi.org/10.1016/j.dsp.2017.10.011.

Narayanan, Menaka, Emily Chen, Jeffrey He, Been Kim, Sam Gershman, and Finale Doshi-Velez (2018). "How do humans understand explanations from machine learning systems? An evaluation of the human-interpretability of explanation." In: *arXiv.org*. URL: https://arxiv.org/abs/1802.00682.

Rader, Emilee, Kelley Cotter, and Janghee Cho (2018). "Explanations as Mechanisms for Supporting Algorithmic Transparency." In: *CHI '18, Proceedings of the 2018 CHI Conference on Human Factors in Computing Systems*, Paper No. 103, pp. 1–13. URL: https://doi.org/10.1145/3173574.3173677.

Rudin, Cynthia (2019). "Stop explaining black bix machine learning models for high stakes decisions and use interpretable models instead." In: *Nature Machine Learning* 1.5, pp. 206–215. URL: https://doi.org/10.1038/s42256-019-0048-x.

Rudin, Cynthia, and Joanna Radin (2019). "Why Are We Using Black Box Models in AI When We Don't Need To? A Lesson From an Explainable AI Competition." In: *Harvard Data Science Review* 1.2, pp. 1–9.

Samek, Wojciech, Grégoire Montavon, Andrea Vedaldi, Lars Kai Hansen, and Klaus-Robert Müller (2019). *Explainable AI: Interpreting, Explaining and Visualizing Deep Learning*, Cham: Springer Nature.

Spinner, Thilo, Udo Schlegel, Hanna Schäfer, and Mennatallah El-Assady (2020). "explAIner: A Visual Analytics Framework for Interactive and Explainable Machine Learning." In: *IEEE, Transactions on Visualization and Computer Graphics* 26.1, pp. 1064–1074. URL: https://doi.org/10.1109/TVCG.2019.2934629.

Machine Dreaming

Stefan Rieger

I. AI – Old and New

As a rule, artificial intelligences place their states of affairs (*Sachstände*) in relation to those of natural intelligences and, above all, to those of human beings. This impulse has persisted with a certain degree of tenacity throughout their various phenomenal manifestations and respective implementations. In this way, historical references have become possible that one would not at first assume for the highly present-oriented field of artificial intelligence. With its various breakthrough periods, AI has managed to become an operative vade mecum, and in light of its ostensibly universal applicability, it has become a warning sign for a modern era that, in a certain way, no longer seems to need the human at all. There is hardly a single field in which AI does not seem to promise one solution or another, from self-driving cars to medicine, from traffic logistics to software development, from the production of goods to the creative economy, from the financial sector to facial recognition. Nevertheless, references to different conceptualizations of intelligence are necessary in order to evaluate, by comparing anthropological and technical states of affairs, the sustainability of their respective methods, their epistemological status, and thus also, on an underlying level, their social acceptance.

In the 17th century, for instance, this relationship was unproblematic because it was not based on competition (cf. Rieger 1997). Not until an emphatic concept was developed of that which constitutes the human did it become possible for artificial processes to call this self-perception into question. Necessary, too, was that relatively young invention of the human which, oriented toward criteria of uniqueness, distinctiveness, and individuality, detected in every externalization (*Entäußerung*) the will to pursue an inimitable style (cf. Foucault 1970). The philosopher Johann Gottlieb Fichte described the ennoblement of uniqueness as a particular feature of the age of Goethe, and thus he argued that individuality, the existence of which can be assumed on the basis of probability theory, should be protected by intellectual copyright law. "It is more improbable than the greatest improbability," according to Fichte, "that two people should ever think about any subject in exactly the same way, in the same sequence of thoughts and in the same images, when they know nothing of one another. Still, this is not absolutely impossible." It is absolutely improbable, however, "that someone to whom ideas must first be imparted by another should ever assimilate them into his own system of thought in exactly the form in which they were given" (Fichte 2015 [1793]: 451). This incalculable residue in human data processing forms the legal justification of our inalienable property (cf. Kittler 1987; Rieger 2020).

It has become increasingly possible to base the self-image of modernity on calculations (such as that of probability) and ultimately on a particular orientation of rationality, which, with various degrees of nuance, has indeed always served as an emblematic consolidation of mechanized processes. Because individuality capitulates to rational pervasion – and, for reasons of its own justifiability, must in fact capitulate – here, too, the residue becomes the basis of its own evaluation. In short, it has become the anthropological residuum. Like a revised version of Cartesian dualism, man and machine are categorically separated from one another for the greater glory of complexity: "In other words, a highly complicated system like an organism cannot be broken down into describable individual processes without an indissoluble residue remaining; it therefore cannot be rationalized, and thus it also cannot be completely depicted by means of a technical model" (Wolfgang Wieser, cited in Steinbuch 1971: 19).

The inauguration of the human as an evasive phenomenon that is resistant to rationalization and is thus incapable of being simulated in a seamless way has been described from various perspectives. Since then, everything that proceeds from and concerns the human has been a matter of epistemological interest and has been the object of systematic observation and scientific attention. With wide-ranging variants within this epochal setting, the recording system around the year 1800 became the code of a new order of knowledge that revolved around and was oriented toward the human. Since that time, the human has been regarded as the source of all sources and has reliably served as a generating principle of inexhaustibility (cf. Schneider 1994). In this light, the emergence of artificial intelligences represents a threat to its narcissistic sovereignty. Evidence of this can be found in historical semantics, which tends to keep mechanisms in their "rightful" place. Conceived as the paragon of unoriginality, formulaicness, regularity, stereotypes, schematization and repetition, the machine merely serves as the negative foil to the radiance of the human being (cf. Rieger 2018). Thus, a bulwark has been created that positions the human against that which industrial and digital revolutions have released into the world with their incessant logic of growth (cf. Rieger 2003). Over the course of these developments, human faculties have quickly come to approximate techniques of data processing. This affects our specific manners of perception and cognition, the ways in which we see and hear, taste and smell, remember and notice, generalize and forget, invent and discover, associate and draw conclusions, hope and dream, fantasize and deduce, collect and process information, and the ways in which we are praxeologically active and socially integrated. The sum of these tendencies confirms, in an impressive manner, Friedrich Kittler's presumption that we are only able to make formulations about ourselves by examining the media of our knowledge. "So-called Man", according to Kittler, "is not determined by attributes which philosophers confer on or suggest to people in order that they may better understand themselves; rather, He is determined by technical standards. Presumably then, every psychology or anthropology only subsequently spells out which functions of the general data processing are controlled by machines, that is, implemented in the real" (Kittler 1997: 132). In its fundamental orientation, this media-anthropological implementation will conceivably not end well for human beings. Up against the speed, capacity and reliability of technical data processing, the human recedes into the background. As to how this process should be discussed, Günther Anders (1983) nailed it on the head when he spoke of Promethean shame and the antiquity of mankind: Technology makes its creator look old.

II. DeepDream and Adversarial Attacks

In light of historical semantics and its inertia, it is a rather peculiar finding that the dream, of all things, has been infiltrating the machine for some time now and that, over the course of machine learning and deep-learning algorithms, our own dreams have quite blatantly been affected by its dreams. This incursion of the irrational into the technical domain of the rational is noteworthy because focusing on the dream was itself a central element of the inauguration and thus also part of the history of paying attention to the individual-anthropological – a history which, since the 18th century, has focused on human beings in their totality and thus brought to light, for the first time, the specific features of the knowledge inherent in dreams (cf. Schings 1994). Everything about the dream seemed remarkable – above all its formal richness and its manner of drawing connections, its excess and its inherent logic, its polysemy and ambiguity, its bizarreness and fantasies, and not least its license to suspend causality and coherence. The dream becomes the occasion to describe particular images and particular connections between images – varying between a hallucinatory character and clarity, between the accessibility of consciousness and the evasiveness of variously conceptualized forms of unconsciousness (cf. Schredl/Erlacher 2003; Fuchs 1989).

If the dream has infiltrated the machine, it ceases to be a privilege of humankind. The program *DeepDream*, for instance, which Google released into the world in 2015, is unambiguously identified with dreaming. Even the German Wikipedia entry on the program takes up this wording and discusses the history of its dissemination: "Because its results recall the recognition of faces or animals in clouds (see pareidolia), the media often refer to this process as the 'dreaming of a computer'" (https://de.wikipedia.org/wiki/DeepDream; cf. Spratt 2018). The program inverts common pattern-recognition systems, which operate on the basis of artificial neural networks (a so-called convolutional neural network). The latter make use of iterative loops and large datasets to recognize particular patterns. The problem for early cybernetics – how to recognize a face or an object, for instance, from various angles or in various lighting conditions – is solved here by means of iteration and layering. The use of the term "deep", which semantically unites this discourse, is due to the stacking of multiple layers.

Figure 1

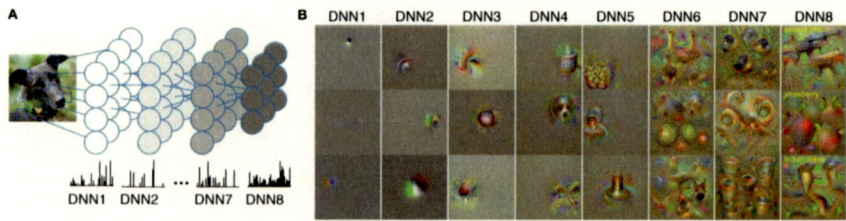

Figure 2: Class-conditional 224 × 224 images obtained by DeepInversion given a ResNet50v1.5 classifier pretrained on ImageNet. Classes top to bottom: brown bear, quill, trolleybus, cheeseburger, cup, volcano, daisy, cardoon

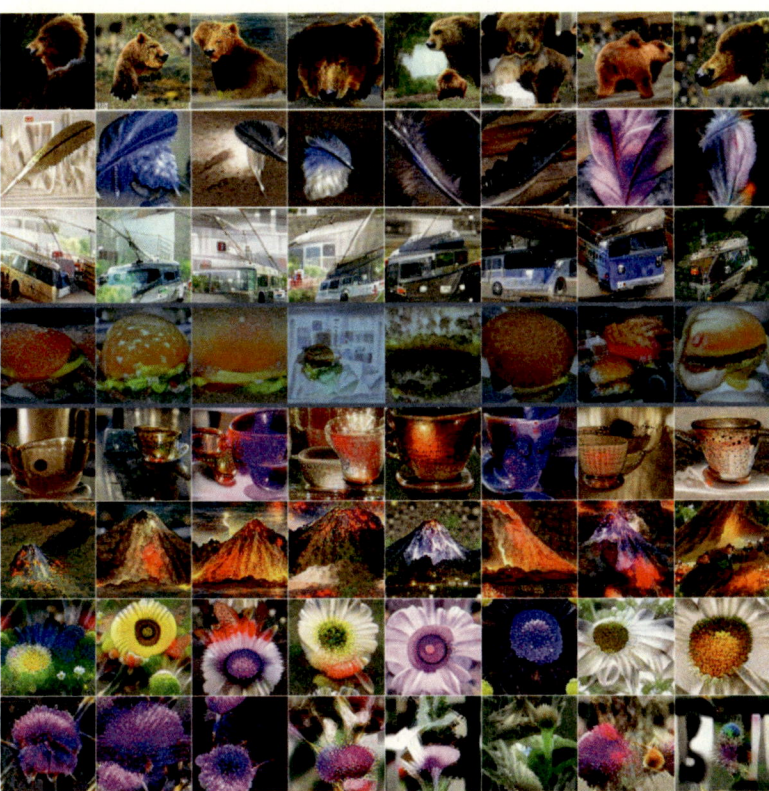

Yet Google then inverts the process: Instead of recognizing images, it requested the network to generate images and interpret objects within existing images. If the algorithm was fed the photograph of a cloudy sky, it began to make free associations. If the computer discovered that a cloud resembles a whale, it generated a whale from its storehouse of saved images, and this whale perfectly fit the shape of the clouds. It recognized patterns where no patterns existed. The researchers called this technique of abstraction and overinterpretation "Inceptionism", taken from the Hollywood film *Inception*, in which Leonardo DiCaprio breaks into the dreams of other people. (Airen 2015)

Figure 3

This image-generating process, which released a flood of psychedelic pictures into the world, takes place without any human agency. Its proximity to dreaming arises by way of analogy: "As in a dream, DeepDream combines new impressions and stored knowledge into a graphic remix, which is surreal and yet strangely familiar. The result is unsettling images that resemble psychedelic hallucinations – intermediary worlds and parallel realities in which reality blends together with free association" (ibid.). It goes without saying that these images have become part of the discussion about the relationship between human and artificial creativity. As a result, they have even attracted the attention of art historians (cf. McCraig et al. 2016; Boden 2017; DiPaola et al. 2010).

Other voices have been less cautious, semantically, and have likened this process of image generation to hallucination. Subliminally, at least, this calls to mind threatening situations in real life, thereby taking away the impression of harmlessness. However much one might trust a driver who steers his car with the certainty of a somnambulist, a certain degree of doubt arises when one thinks about dreaming self-driving cars. The use of dreaming cars might therefore be somewhat unsettling given the potential real-life consequences (cf. Rocklage 2017; Piergiovanni 2019). Whereas psychedelic images typically do not do anyone any harm and typically do not cause any lasting damage, the situation with hallucinating self-driving cars is another matter entirely.

Against this backdrop, it is possible to situate a discussion that, like the case of autonomous cars, concerns a central aspect of AI and its potential future scenarios. In a peculiar way, this discussion brings to light certain factors and circumstances that are detrimental to self-driving cars. In this context, it is not human beings and their shortcomings that play a role which must be kept to a minimum by means of technical methods and by delegating autonomy; rather, the issue is the system of recognition and thus the technology itself. Especially significant in this regard is a peculiarity of artificial systems designed to recognize objects in the environment, something which is often described as a weakness. These particular failures of artificial intelligences are often discussed in language typically used to describe mental disorders such as delusions or hallucinations. It has occasionally been mentioned (with a degree of *Schadenfreude*) that AI introduced a hallucination problem into the world that is rather difficult to fix (cf. Simonite 2018). This talk of hallucination is not only found in editorial write-ups but also in the work of experts: "Recently, adversarial algorithms were developed to facilitate hallucination of deep neural networks for ordinary attackers" (Abdel-Hakim 2019).

At first, the phenomenon of hallucinations attracted attention as no more than a sort of curiosity of AI. There are so-called "adversarial attacks", which deprive the system of coherence and understanding, and so-called "adversarial patches", which are meant to cover up such glitches in an inconspicuous manner. At the heart of it all lies the finding that optical image-recognition systems can be made to make simple but grotesque misjudgments in a relatively straightforward way. To illustrate this, the weekly newspaper *Die Zeit* cited research dealing with the technical metamorphosis of a simple banana. The banana was scanned by a technical system and accordingly recognized for what it was. However, if there was a small image – a "patch" or a "sticker" – without any recognizable content near the banana, the system would lose its perception of the banana and identify the new situation as a toaster, for instance.

But that's not all. In the case of the banana, the image-recognition system was 97 per cent convinced of its accuracy, but this level of confidence increased to 99 per cent in the case of the toaster: "Other cases show how a microwave with an adversarial patch was identified as a telephone and how, after the addition of a few pixels that no person would ever notice, the computer identified a panda bear as a gibbon" (Schmitt 2019: 33). The abundance of examples could be expanded to include things from everyday life such as teddy bears and oranges, socks and pets, sports equipment and furniture. Stories of this kind are easy to tell – and that's probably why they make it into the feuilleton pages of ambitious newspapers –, not least because the especially grotesque extent of the false identifications underscores an important point. To a human observer, it would not be unexpected for a banana to be mistaken for a similarly shaped zucchini or a similarly colored lemon. In fact, given the process of thinking in gradual degrees and linearities, such confusion could even be called plausible. It could be explained by the history of technical vision, which had to work its way through staggered resolutions while also dealing with other visual parameters such as shading, distance and different viewing angles.

In this respect, it is precisely the identification of objects – the special achievement of human sight – that has repeatedly posed special challenges throughout the history of machine vision. The German cyberneticist Karl Steinbuch, for instance, offered a typical assessment of the matter: "In no other area is the inferiority of technical entities to organic systems more apparent than in the visual system" (1971: 98). But the translation of a banana into a toaster is a decisive break in the habitual way of dealing with similarity relations. It represents an exceptional case that is not covered by common special forms of image perception. One such form is provided by the phenomenon of ambiguous images (*Kippbilder*), which Gestalt psychologists have used to describe what happens when the typical process of perceiving images is undermined. Their logic is not determined by resolutions and approximations; rather, images of this sort break the contract with continuity. There is no gray area and there are no overlaps between a banana and a toaster, between perceiving Rubin's vase or two faces: Deciding between the vase and the faces is an effect of their binary instantaneous setting (cf. Schönhammer 2011).

Figure 4: The left image shows a real graffiti on a Stop sign, something that most humans would not think is suspicious. The right images shows our [sic!] a physical perturbation applied to a Stop sign. We design our perturbations to mimic graffiti, and thus "hide in the human psyche".

Things become difficult when one expands this colorful list of examples and comes upon cases that are anything but harmless and can alter our assessment of complex and hazardous situations. With respect to self-driving cars, it has been reported that a single sticker placed on a stop sign can be enough to confuse image-recognition systems; it has also been shown that, "by subtly altering the shell of a plastic turtle, it could be made to appear like a rifle" (Schmitt 2019: 33; cf. Athalye et al. 2018). The identification of traffic signs in particular has become a special challenge and is thus being researched extensively (cf. Cires et al. 2012). Such examples bring to light, in a dramatic way, the dire importance that adversarial attacks might have in everyday life.

The article in *Die Zeit* also refers to an additional increase in possible applications. Whereas the examples mentioned above concern the confusion of static images, researchers such as Michael J. Black at the Max Planck Institute for Intelligent Systems in Tübingen have been working on manipulating recordings of motion. That is, they have been trying to manipulate so-called "optical flow systems". Because the anticipation of complex situations – and also the appropriate reaction to these situations – depends on the ability to perceive such systems, the whole issue is increasingly losing its status as a mere technical curiosity: "Because optical flow systems make it possible to track the primary movements taking place in the bustle of high-traffic situations (the movements of cyclists and vehicles, for instance), they represent the potential building blocks for future self-driving cars" (Schmitt 2019: 33; Ranjan et al. 2019).

To optimize their own systems, the researchers in Tübingen sent their "patches" (before publishing their results) to manufacturers and suppliers in the automotive industry so as to assist the latter's investigations into possible causes of interference. The director of the Algorithm Accountability Lab, Katharina Zweig, whom the article quotes, underscored the seriousness of the situation by pointing out that such systems reach their decisions without any knowledge or awareness on the part of those who might be affected by them. The artificial systems operate in the mode of the imperceptible, and they operate – as the case of self-driving cars and other examples makes clear – in spheres that undoubtedly affect daily life. Research into this phenomenon is ongoing, and it reached a critical point in 2019. It became clear then how much dangerous potential lies in the technique of adversarial attacks and how working on such networks produces emergent phenomena and thus has no use for the old paradigm and traditional understanding of mechanics, determinacy and the predictability of technical systems. Deep neural networks are difficult to predict, and they are not limited to areas in which their mistakes can be tolerated as mere special phenomena:

> Because of these accomplishments, deep learning techniques are also applied in safety-critical tasks. For example, in autonomous vehicles, deep convolutional neural networks. The machine learning technique used here is required to be highly accurate, stable and reliable. But, what if the CNN model fails to recognize the "STOP" sign by the roadside and the vehicle keeps going? It will be a dangerous situation. (Xu et al. 2019)

A comparably dangerous situation can be imagined in the arena of financial transactions: "If there are fraudsters disguising their personal identity information to evade the company's detection, it will cause a huge loss to the company. Therefore, the safety issues of deep neural networks have become a major concern" (ibid.).

What the text at first identifies as a strategy of humans dealing with credit institutions is then shifted into the world of other manners of operation and forms of representation. Here, the question of credibility is not treated in terms of the personal identity of fraudsters – that is, in terms of the uniqueness of their biometrics, for instance – but rather in terms of graphs that concern the inherent logic of certain processes. Whether in the case of street traffic or in that of financial transactions, dangers loom in various places within an environment that is always at risk of being disrupted. They are differentiated according to various occasions and technical implementations, and they pertain not only to the recognition of letters and numbers, stop signs and other traffic signs, bananas and turtles, but also to other forms of data (cf. Feinman et al. 2017; Kurakin et al. 2017; Evtimov et al. 2018). The example of graphs (and of manipulating just a few nodal points) has caught the eye of the finance industry, and different ways of dealing with language – whether in its written or spoken form – have also attracted attention. Here, too, the attacks take the guise of minimal and barely detectable differences – for instance, by means of minor manipulations in the form of typos (cf. Jia/Liang 2017). Beyond mere typos and small differences in letters, focus has also turned to the act of switching out entire sentences or phrases. In this respect, a 2018 article with the title "Detecting Egregious Responses in Neural Sequence-to-Sequence Models" greatly (egregiously?) expands the descriptive language and semantics of that which is typically associated with "egregiousness" (cf. He/Glass 2018). The hallucinatory and the grotesque, which are inherent to the confusion of bananas and toasters, are extended here to include something akin to the monstrous: "In this work, we attempt to answer a critical question: whether there exists some input sequence that will cause a well-trained discrete-space neural network sequence-to-sequence (seq2seq) model to generate egregious outputs (aggressive, malicious, attacking, etc.)" (ibid.; cp. Sandbank et al. 2018). The adjective *egregious* is used here to describe reactions to sentences; the semantic range of this word covers, in addition to things that merely stand out in a bad way, also the sphere of the inimical. As one overview article has pointed out, even systems of spoken language can be the object of such egregiousness (cf. Hinton et al. 2012).

Research into the robustness of such systems has therefore become as inevitable as its expansion into other forms of data. What creeps into the situation is a semantics of suspicion concerning everything that the world has in store. Talk of Potemkin villages has been spreading, and there is often mention of alienation, which goes hand in hand with the undermining of human perception. The adjective *subtle* is used to describe the imperceptible changes that lead to blatant misjudgments and their grave consequences. The images discussed in the articles cited above are reminiscent of the iconography found in the "search-and-find puzzles" (*Suchbilder*) printed in newspapers and books for children, which contain many objects that are ostensibly the same but also at least one outlying detail that is difficult but not impossible to detect. The only difference is that, in the case of adversarial attacks, the human eye has no chance to discover the built-in anomaly (on the tradition of *Suchbilder*, cf. Ernst et al. 2003).

III. Ally Patches

It is a peculiar point that the defense measures taken against attacks on image recognition and sign recognition in the case of self-driving cars are now, for their part, taking place in the consistent mode of so-called "ally patches". That this process results in mutually interfering stickers ("Ally Patches for Spoliation of Adversarial Patches", as one article on the topic is titled) is a detail that perhaps only attracts the attention of cultural theorists, who like to regard such self-references as part and parcel of the logic of cultural chains of meaning. That the stickers have changed sides and now it is they, of all things, that are expected to disrupt the disrupter and thus guarantee security, is nevertheless a cycle that warrants attention – especially in light of the possibility that this circle might never be closed (regarding the issue of disruption in media and cultural studies, cf. Kümmel/Schüttpelz 2003). Because here, too, the principle of imperceptibility applies, and a peculiar finding emerges: the human eye is unable to distinguish the combatants from one another – only the final effect reveals their position as friend or foe. Attaching stickers has lost its innocence and thus also the subversive charm that went along with these semi-public acts of expressing opinions. It is more than a juvenile misdemeanor and even has the characteristics of a high-risk traffic violation: "The consequent troubles may vary from just unpleasant inconvenience in applications like entertainment image and video annotation, passing by security-critical problems like false person identifications, and can turn out to be life-threatening in autonomous navigation and driver support systems" (Abdel-Hakim 2019). Thus the vulnerability of self-driving cars has become the object of attention – as in one case in which an adversarial attack managed to turn on windshield wipers in dry conditions (cf. Deng et al. 2020).

Particularly striking in the research is an assessment that concerns the status of the examples in question (cf. Xu et al. 2019). Instead of the operative question concerning which of three described methods should be used (gradient masking, robust optimization, detection), the urgent question has turned out to be what sort of role these exemplary cases should be attributed in specific everyday situations. In addition to the cat-and-mouse game of reacting to specifications, certain issues play a role that belong to the domain of basic knowledge. As one repeatedly reads, the spirals and circles of attacks and counter-attacks strengthen our understanding of the inherent dynamics of deep neural network systems – and thus bring knowledge about their technical nature to light. As one article on this topic makes clear, adversarial attacks are not *bugs* in the system; rather, they are *features* of it (cf. Ilyas et al. 2019). Another text strikes a comparable tone – though with the nuance that it uses the term *flaw* instead of the term *bug*: "These results have often been interpreted as being a flaw in deep networks in particular, even though linear classifiers have the same problem. We regard the knowledge of this flaw as an opportunity to fix it" (Goodfellow et al. 2015).

One particular point that has been revealed by this (involuntary) basic work on the functioning of deep neural networks is that the latter operate quite differently from human data processing – even though the language used to describe them (all the talk of dreaming or hallucinating machines) does much to conceal this difference. However much protective measures and an understanding of DNN's mode of operating mutually condition one another, human perception and reasoning remain on the outside of the process: "For example, adversarial perturbations are perceptually indistinguishable to human eyes but can evade DNN's detection. This suggests that the DNN's predictive approach does not align with human reasoning" (Xu et al. 2019).

In a certain way, the technical logic of neural networks has liberated itself from the politics of the human imagination, either despite or because of all the semantic borrowings – and yet at the same time, this logic has also come somewhat closer to such politics, at least as far as effects are concerned. It is no longer necessarily the case that the order of things is an order that follows human preconceptions and reactions along the lines of similarities and representations. The danger of misinterpreting traffic signs and, even more so, the manipulation of more complex situations that would be so essential to the acceptance of self-driving cars thus underscore the special epistemological position of such processes. They may be able to dream and hallucinate, but the way they do so differs from that of human beings. *Our* order of things is not *the* order of things.

The semantics of depth, which is applied to a specific technical feature of the processes employed, concerns, in the case of DeepDream, not only mechanisms for organizing images but also achieves the level of disruptive mechanisms with methods such as DeepFake or DeepFool – and this is not even to mention applications such as DeepFood, which is used to identify nutritional food (cf. Jiang et al. 2020). With the latest technical possibilities, an element of unpredictability and uncertainty is spreading within an everyday environment that one hoped would be kept safe. It is as though one is witnessing, with open but blind eyes, a reentry of the irrational into the field of the rational, the only difference being that whatever bizarre images come to light are not a matter of aesthetic surplus production but rather concern the stabilization of systems. In all performances of the bizarre and psychedelic, the moment of system optimization remains inherent to the dream of the machine. Any admission that there is some aesthetic surplus or added cultural value produced by these processes therefore remains ambivalent. It is impossible to distinguish between seriousness and triviality, consequence and mere emergence, curious errors and disruptive intentions:

> We cannot reliably identify when and why DNNs will make mistakes. In some applications like text translation these mistakes may be comical and provide for fun fodder in research talks, a single error can be very costly in tasks like medical imaging. Additionally, DNNs show susceptibility to so-called adversarial examples, or data specifically designed to fool a DNN. One can generate such examples with imperceptible deviations from an image, causing the system to mis-classify an image that is nearly identical to a correctly classified one. Audio adversarial examples can also exert control over popular systems such as Amazon Alexa or Siri, allowing malicious access to devices containing personal information. (Charles 2018)

IV. Lucid Dreaming

What does this mean, however, for the scenario discussed at the beginning and its effort to place technical and anthropological states of affairs in relation to one another for the sake of their epistemological validation? A reference of this sort can be made in light of a particular variant of dreaming: lucid dreaming. With the title "Are You Dreaming? A Phenomenological Study on Understanding Lucid Dreams as a Tool for Introspection in Virtual Reality", a recent article has endeavored to determine the relationship between lucid dreaming and virtual reality in order, in the end, to identify the lucid dream as the ultimate stage of the technical:

> Lucid dreaming, "dreaming while knowing one is dreaming," is one phenomenon that we can draw parallels to a VR experience. It is a genuine human experience that places a person in a "virtual" reality, i.e., their dream, which feels just as real as their waking reality. At the same time, lucid dreamers are aware that they are in a dream and that nothing in the dream has real-life consequences, much like that of a VR experience. (Kitson et al. 2018)

The research group responsible for this is led by Alexandra Kitson, who situates her work at the intersection of human-computer interaction, design and psychology. In addition, she is also interested in technically induced processes of transgression and well-being (cf. Kitson et al. 2020). In the study cited above, subjects are interviewed according to a rubric, and they are asked questions about perceptual impressions and feelings, about activities and practices, about how such things influence their experience, and not least about the way in which meaning is created in lucid dreams. The knowledge is then fed back into the development of future VR systems with the goal of bringing them closer to and doing justice to the human condition: "This knowledge can help design a VR system that is grounded in genuine experience and preserving the human condition" (Kitson et al. 2018).

Another project led by Kitson – titled "Lucid Loop: A Virtual Deep Learning Biofeedback System for Lucid Dreaming Practices" – goes beyond this combination of introspection, inquiry and extrapolation in the creation of future technological designs. This project opens up a sphere of activity for the technology that seems unusual at first glance, even esoteric (for a similarly esoteric application of virtual reality, cf. Downey 2015). In this case, the focus is on personal well-being. The interrelation between lucid dreaming and technology has brought to light a previously unnoticed potential application, which might possibly be used to increase the greater glory of human beings, their personal achievements and their individual welfare. Through a combination of technical image processing, biofeedback mechanisms and yoga, a new sort of depth is conjured up that is not focused on the depths of the soul but rather on the surface operations of image layers. In their article "Are You Dreaming?", Kitson and her coauthors outline this process as follows and refer to so-called deep convolutional neural networks (DCNN):

> Lucid Loop will be an open, [sic!] nature scene with other interactive elements that provoke curiosity. DCNN imagery will provide a level of abstraction needed for a dream-like effect [...]. The image layers themselves will range from very abstract to completely clear, mimicking levels of clarity in lucid dreaming. (Kitson et al. 2018)

The levels of image clarity mentioned here are an effect of advanced image processing technology. It is artificial intelligences – the processes of deep learning – that lend the images their dream-like impression and enable them to be scaled accordingly (cf. McNamara et al. 2018). This process is therefore accompanied by image sequences that present a technical distortion of a natural world – minutely layered on top of one another, scaled in detail, and as a process that takes place before the eyes of those participating. The result is a flurry of images controlled by a bodily signal, and this flurry is able to exhaust the potential of dream images and recreate the depth of dreams: "Visuals are creatively generated before your eyes using a deep learning Artificial Intelligence algorithm to emulate the unstable and ambiguous nature of dreams" (Kitson et al. 2019). The intensity and clarity of each generation of images are controlled by bodily signals.

What efforts of this sort negotiate is a confrontation between forms of different realities, an authentic confrontation between the virtual and the dream. In this sense, the desired perfection of virtual realities has found its goal and standard in lucid dreaming. What emerges from this is an adaptation of technology and its users that places its highly advanced perfectibility in the service of the human condition. There are thus points of contact, interconnections and references between these entangled concepts of reality, and there are ways in which these connections are formed, modified and technically realized. In the possibility of reciprocal modelling, the virtual and the imaginary – that is, the technologically possible and the anthropologically authenticated – encounter one another on equal terms and seemingly free from Promethean shame. To quote Kitson and her colleagues again: "The ultimate VR might look like lucid dreaming, the phenomenon of knowing one is dreaming while in the dream" (Kitson et al. 2018).

Accordingly, the philosophically controversial question of the reality content of reality does not play a special role in the praxis of the lifeworld. In the virtual, as the sociologist Elena Esposito has written with respect to the interrelated nature of possible existential relations, there are "no false real objects but rather true virtual objects, for which the question of real reality

Figure 5 (left): Lucid Loop system schematic. Painterly and Deep Dream creatively generate visuals to emulate dreams. The virtual environment becomes more lucid or "clear" when the participant's physiological signals indicate increased awareness. Figure 6 (right)

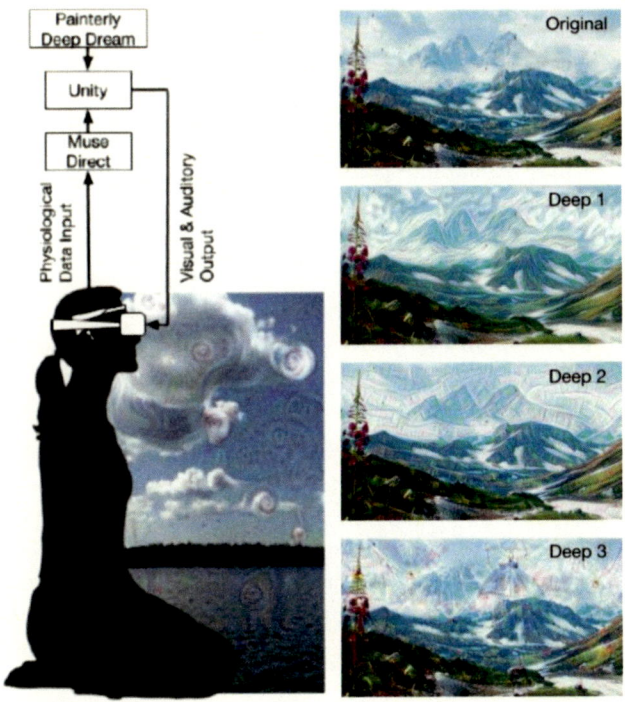

is entirely irrelevant" (Esposito 1998: 270). In this case, traditional distinctions take a back seat to altered functionalities, and the most likely reality proves to be a calculated fiction (cf. Esposito 2019; Dongus 2018).

References

Abdel-Hakim, Alaa E. (2019). "Ally Patches for Spoliation of Adversarial Particles." In: *Journal of Big Data* 6. URL: https://journalofbigdata.springeropen.com/articles/10.1186/s40537-019-0213-4.

Airen (2015). "So sieht es aus, wenn Computer träumen." In: *Welt*, July 21, 2015. URL: https://www.welt.de/kultur/article144267349/So-sieht-es-aus-wenn-Computer-traeumen.html.

Anders, Günther (1983). *Die Antiquiertheit des Menschen. Erster Band: Über die Seele im Zeitalter der zweiten industriellen Revolution*. 6th ed., Munich: C.H. Beck.

Athalye, Anish et al. (2018). "Synthesizing Robust Adversarial Examples." In: *arXiv.org*, June 7, 2018. URL: https://arxiv.org/abs/1707.07397.

Boden, Margaret A. (2017). "Is Deep Dreaming the New Collage?" In: *Connection Science* 29.4, pp. 268–275.

Charles, Adam S. (2018). "Interpreting Deep Learning: The Machine Learning Rorschach Test?" In: *arXiv.org*, June 1, 2018. URL: https://arxiv.org/abs/1806.00148.

Cires, Dan et al. (2012). "Multicolumn Deep Neural Network for Traffic Sign Classification." In: *Neural Networks* 32, pp. 333–338.

Deng, Yao et al. (2020). "An Analysis of Adversarial Attacks and Defenses on Autonomous Driving Models." In: *arXiv.org*, February 6, 2020. URL: https://arxiv.org/abs/2002.02175.

DiPaola, Steve et al. (2010). "Rembrandt's Textural Agency: A Shared Perspective in Visual Art and Science." In: *Leonardo* 43.2, pp. 145–151.

Dongus, Ariana (2018). "Life Is Real = Reality Is a Platform: Creating Engineered Experiences Where Fiction and Reality Merge." In: *Body Images in the Post-Cinematic Scenario: The Digitization of Bodies*. Ed. by Alberto Brodesco and Federico Giordano, Milan: Mimesis International, pp. 151–162.

Downey, Laura L. (2015). *Well-being Technologies: Meditation Using Virtual Worlds*, Doctoral diss.: Nova Southeastern University.

Ernst, Wolfgang et al. (eds.) (2003). *Suchbilder: Visuelle Kultur zwischen Algorithmen und Archiven*, Berlin: Kadmos.

Esposito, Elena (1998). "Fiktion und Virtualität." In: *Medien, Computer, Realität. Wirklichkeitsvorstellungen und neue Medien*. Ed. by Sybille Krämer, Frankfurt am Main: Suhrkamp, pp. 269–296.

Esposito, Elena (2019). *Die Fiktion der wahrscheinlichen Realität*. 4th ed. Berlin: Suhrkamp.

Evtimov, Ivan et al. (2018). "Robust Physical-World Attacks on Deep Learning Models." In: *arXiv.org*, April 10, 2018. URL: https://arxiv.org/abs/1707.08945.

Feinman, Reuben et al. (2017). "Detecting Adversarial Samples from Artifacts." In: *arXiv.org*, November 15, 2017. URL: https://arxiv.org/abs/1703.00410.

Fichte, Johann Gottlieb (2015 [1793]). "Proof of the Unlawfulness of Reprinting: A Rationale and a Parable." In: *Primary Sources on Copyright (1450–1900)*. Ed. by L. Bentley and M. Kretschmer, pp. 443–483. URL: http://www.copyrighthistory.org.

Foucault, Michel (1970). *The Order of Things: An Archaeology of the Human Sciences*, New York: Vintage Books.

Fuchs, Peter (1989). "Blindheit und Sicht: Vorüberlegungen zu einer Schemarevison." In: *Reden und Schweigen*. Ed. by Peter Fuchs and Niklas Luhmann, Frankfurt am Main: Suhrkamp, pp. 178–208.

Goodfellow, Ian J. et al. (2015). "Explaining and Harnessing Adversarial Examples." In: *arXiv.org*, March 20, 2015. URL: https://arxiv.org/abs/1412.6572.

He, Tianxing, and James Glass (2018). "Detecting Egregious Responses in Neural Sequence-to-Sequence Models." In: *arXiv.org*, October 3, 2018. URL: https://arxiv.org/abs/1809.04113.

Hinton, Geoffrey et al. (2012). "Deep Neural Networks for Acoustic Modeling in Speech Recognition." In: *IEEE Signal Processing Magazine* 29, pp. 82–97.

Ilyas, Andrew et al. (2019). "Adversarial Examples Are Not Bugs, They Are Features." In: *arXiv.org*, August 12, 2019. URL: https://arxiv.org/abs/1905.02175.

Jia, Robin, and Percy Liang (2017). "Adversarial Examples for Evaluating Reading Comprehension Systems." In: *arXiv.org*, July 23, 2017. URL: https://arxiv.org/abs/1707.07328.

Jiang, Landu et al. (2020). "DeepFood: Food Image Analysis and Dietary Assessment via Deep Model." In: *IEEE Access* 8, pp. 47477–47489.

Kitson, Alexandra et al. (2018). "Are You Dreaming? A Phenomenological Study on Understanding Lucid Dreams as a Tool for Introspection in Virtual Reality." In: *CHI '18, Proceedings of the 2018 CHI Conference on Human Factors in Computing Systems*, April 2018. URL: https://dl.acm.org/doi/10.1145/3173574.3173917.

Kitson, Alexandra et al. (2019). "Lucid Loop: A Virtual Deep Learning Biofeedback System for Lucid Dreaming Practice." In: *CHI EA '19, Extended Abstracts of the 2019 CHI Conference on Human Factors in Computing Systems*. URL: https://doi.org/10.1145/3290607.3312952.

Kitson, Alexandra et al. (2020). "A Review on Research and Evaluation Methods for Investigating Self-transcendence." In: *Frontiers in Psychology*, 11. URL: https://www.frontiersin.org/articles/10.3389/fpsyg.2020.547687/full.

Kittler, Friedrich (1987). "Über romantische Datenverarbeitung." In: *Die Aktualität der Frühromantik*. Ed. by Ernst Behler and Jochen Hörisch, Paderborn: Ferdinand Schöning, pp 127–140.

Kittler, Friedrich (1997). "The World of the Symbolic – A World of the Machine." In: *Literature, Media, Information Systems: Essays*. Ed. by John Johnston. Amsterdam: Gordon & Breach, pp. 130–146.

Krizhevsky, Alex et al. (2017). "ImageNet Classification with Deep Convolutional Neural Networks." In: *Communications of the ACM* 60.6, pp. 84–90.

Kümmel, Albert, and Erhard Schüttpelz (eds.) (2003). *Signale der Störung*, Munich: Wilhelm Fink.

Kurakin, Alexey et al. (2017). "Adversarial Examples in the Physical World." In: *arXiv.org, February 11, 2017*. URL: https://arxiv.org/abs/1607.02533.

McCaig, Graeme et al. (2016). "Deep Convolutional Networks as Models of Generalization and Blending Within Visual Creativity." In: *Proceedings of the 7th International Conference on Computational Creativity*, Palo Alto, CA, pp. 156–163.

McNamara, Patrick et al. (2018). "Virtual Reality-Enabled Treatment of Nightmares." In: *Dreaming* 28.3, pp. 205–224.

Piergiovanni, A.J. et al. (2019). "Learning Real-World Robot Policies by Dreaming." In: *arXiv.org, August 1, 2018*. URL: https://arxiv.org/abs/1805.07813.

Ranjan, Anurag et al. (2019). "Attacking Optical Flow." In: *Proceedings International Conference on Computer Vision (ICCV)*, Piscataway, NJ: IEEE, pp. 2404–2413. URL: https://arxiv.org/pdf/1910.10053.pdf.

Reinhardt, Daniel et al. (2019). "Entropy of Controller Movements Reflects Mental Workload in Virtual Reality." In: *IEEE Conference on Virtual Reality and 3D User Interfaces*. Piscataway, NJ: IEEE, pp. 802–808.

Rieger, Stefan (1997). *Speichern / Merken: Die künstlichen Intelligenzen des Barock*, Munich: Fink.

Rieger, Stefan (2003). *Kybernetische Anthropologie: Eine Geschichte der Virtualität*, Frankfurt am Main: Suhrkamp.

Rieger, Stefan (2018). "'Bin doch keine Maschine ...': Zur Kulturgeschichte eines Topos." In: *Machine Learning – Neue Pfade künstlicher Intelligenz*. Ed. by Christoph Engemann and Andreas Sudmann, Bielefeld: transcript, pp. 117–142.

Rieger, Stefan (2020). "'Be the Data': Von Schnürbrüsten, Halsketten und der Dokumentation der Daten." In: *Durchbrochene Ordnungen: Das Dokumentarische der Gegenwart*. Ed. by Friedrich Balke et al., Bielefeld: transcript, pp. 191–215.

Rocklage, Elias (2017). "Teaching Self-Driving Cars to Dream: A Deeply Integrated, Innovative Approach for Solving the Autonomous Vehicle Validation Problem." In: *IEEE 20th International Conference on Intelligent Transportation Systems*, Piscataway, NJ: IEEE, pp. 1–7.

Sandbank, Tommy et al. (2018). "Detecting Egregious Conversations Between Customers and Virtual Agents." In: *arXiv.org*, April 16, 2018. URL: https://arxiv.org/abs/1711.05780.

Schings, Hans-Jürgen (ed.) (1994). *Der ganze Mensch: Anthropologie und Literatur im 18. Jahrhundert*, Stuttgart: Metzler.

Schmitt, Stefan (2019). "Ist das wirklich ein Toaster?" In: *Die Zeit*, November 14, pp. 33–34.

Schneider, Manfred (1994). "Der Mensch als Quelle." In: *Der Mensch – das Medium der Gesellschaft*. Ed. by Peter Fuchs and Andreas Göbel, Frankfurt am Main: Suhrkamp, pp. 297–322.

Schönhammer, Rainer (2011). "Stichwort: Kippbilder". URL: https://psydok.psycharchives.de/jspui/bitstream/20.500.11780/3666/1/Kippbilder_psydoc_11052011.pdf.

Schredl, Michael, and Daniel Erlacher (2003). "The Problem of Dream Content Analysis Validity as Shown by a Bizarreness Scale." In: *Sleep and Hypnosis* 5, pp. 129–135.

Simonite, Tom (2018). "AI Has a Hallucination Problem That's Proving Tough to Fix." In: *Wired*, March 9, 2018. URL: https://www.wired.com/story/ai-has-a-hallucination-problem-thats-proving-tough-to-fix/.

Spratt, Emily (2018). "Dream Formulations and Deep Neural Networks: Humanistic Themes in the Iconology of the Machine-Learned Image." In: *arXiv.org*, February 5, 2018. URL: https://arxiv.org/abs/1802.01274.

Steinbuch, Karl (1971). *Automat und Mensch: Auf dem Weg zu einer kybernetischen Anthropologie*. 4th ed., Berlin: Springer.

Xu, Han et al. (2019). "Adversarial Attacks and Defenses in Images, Graphs and Text: A Review." In: *arXiv.org*, October 9, 2019. URL: https://arxiv.org/abs/1909.08072.

List of Figures

Figure 1: Horikawa, Tomoyasu, and Yukiyasu Kamitani (2017): "Hierarchical Neural Representation of Dreamed Objects Revealed by Brain Decoding with Deep Neural Network Features." In: *Frontiers in Computational Neuroscience* 11.4. URL: https://www.ncbi.nlm.nih.gov/pmc/articles/PMC5281549/.

Figure 2: Yin, Hongxu et al. (2020): "Dreaming to Distill: Data-Free Knowledge Transfer via DeepInversion." In: *arXiv.org*, June 16, 2020. URL: https://arxiv.org/abs/1912.08795.

Figure 3: https://www.tensorflow.org/tutorials/generative/deepdream.

Figure 4: Evtimov, Ivan et al. (2018): "Robust Physical-World Attacks on Deep Learning Models." In: *arXiv.org*, April 10, 2018. URL: https://arxiv.org/abs/1707.08945.

Figure 5: Kitson, Alexandra et al. (2019): "Lucid Loop: A Virtual Deep Learning Biofeedback System for Lucid Dreaming Practice." In: *CHI EA '19, Extended Abstracts of the 2019 CHI Conference on Human Factors in Computing Systems*. URL: https://dl.acm.org/doi/fullHtml/10.1145/3290607.3312952.

Figure 6: Kitson, Alexandra et al. (2019): "Lucid Loop: A Virtual Deep Learning Biofeedback System for Lucid Dreaming Practice." In: *CHI EA '19, Extended Abstracts of the 2019 CHI Conference on Human Factors in Computing Systems*. URL: https://dl.acm.org/doi/fullHtml/10.1145/3290607.3312952.

Let's Fool That Stupid AI
Adversarial Attacks against Text Processing AI

Ulrich Schade, Albert Pritzkau, Daniel Claeser, Steffen Winandy

Introduction

AI systems help humans to detect and to recognize information in data, e.g. in medical imaging. Such recognition often involves a categorization so that the human user of the AI system only needs to take a look at the information that is categorized as relevant. Furthermore, the recognition abilities of AI often surpass those of its user. An AI system trained for such cases can detect and recognize objects hidden under a camouflage and thus imperceptible to the human eye. However, it must be emphasized that the detection abilities of AI systems do not necessarily trump human abilities. There are many scenarios in which humans excel and AI systems blunder. In principle, this is not a problem, as long as such scenarios can be identified so that AI systems can be assigned to those tasks in which they perform strongly. But as always, reality is more complex. AI systems that generally achieve great results may be confronted with specific inputs in specific situations so that they fail. If this happens, and if the input was designed with the purpose of causing an AI system to fail, this constitutes a so-called "adversarial attack".

In their paper on adversarial attacks, Goodfellow, Slenz and Szegedy write: "Szegedy et al. (2014b) made an intriguing discovery: several machine learning models, including state-of-the-art neural networks, are vulnerable to *adversarial examples*" (Goodfellow et al. 2015: 1). The authors subsequently express not only surprise but also disappointment with the discovery: "These results suggest that classifiers based on modern machine learning techniques, even those that obtain excellent performance on the test set, are not learning the true underlying concepts that determine the correct output label. Instead, these algorithms have built a Potemkin village that works well on naturally occuring (sic) data, but is exposed as a fake when one visits points in space that do not have high probability in the data distribution. This is particularly disappointing because a popular approach in computer vision is to use convolutional features as a space where Euclidean distance approximates perceptual distance" (ibid: 2).

Adversarials are not only a problem for applications, i.e. AI classifiers, they also damage belief in the "intelligence" of modern AI. However, one might argue that image processing is quite near to the sensor level so that "intelligence" might not apply within image processing AI. Such an argumentation might be extended to the remark that human language acquisition incorporates the development of concepts and semantics, so that intelligence is more likely to apply within a text processing AI than an image processing one. Although Goodfellow et al. (2015) presented and discussed adversarial examples for classification tasks in the image recognition domain, adversarials do also occur in the area of text classification (Liang et al. 2018; Xu et al. 2020). The paper at hand is meant to add a small contribution to answer the question about why text processing AIs also are prone to adversarials.

In the following, we will take a closer look at adversarial attacks. We will provide a definition and illustrate the attacks through some examples (section 2). Then, in section 3, we will discuss how to generate such attacks from a mathematical and technical point of view. We do this with a focus on text classification applications. Adversarial attacks, however, have a dimension beyond mathematics: they only succeed if not only the AI is fooled, but also the human is not. Liang et al. (2018) call this feature "utility-preserving". In order to understand "utility-preserving" better, we will take a look at information processing and compare the information processing of an AI based on "deep learning" with human information processing, again with a focus on text classification (section 4). We then will add the linguistic perspective to that comparison (section 5). In section 4 as well as in section 5, we will use the insights gained to suggest ways to generate adversarials. The chapter will end in a discussion of lessons learned (section 6).

1. Adversarial Attacks: Definition and Examples

In their review on adversarial attacks and defenses, Xu et al. (2020: 1) provide the following definition: "Adversarial examples are inputs to machine learning models that an attacker intentionally designed to cause the model to make mistakes". The previously mentioned paper by Goodfellow and co-authors (Goodfellow et al. 2015) provides the standard example from the field of image recognition: a picture of a panda, classified as "panda" with 57.7% confidence, is intentionally but only slightly changed (in a way that a human observer would not perceive). As result, the panda is classified as "gibbon" with 99.3% confidence (ibid: 3, figure 1).

The definition says that the model is caused "to make mistakes". In the example, that means that the panda is classified as "gibbon". However, this is only a mistake since the original picture shows a panda, and since a human would say that the picture still shows a panda even after the slight change. If the change would cause the human to also classify the changed picture as a picture showing a gibbon, we would not call it a mistake. Liang and co-authors call this "utility-preserving" and further explain this property with respect to text classification: "Utility-preserving means that the semantics of the text should remain unchanged and human observers can correctly classify it without many efforts. Consider for instance a spam message advertising something. Its adversarial version should not only fool a spam filter, but also effectively deliver the advertisement" (Liang et al. 2018: 4208).

Liang and co-authors use insertion, modification, and deletion (removal) of characters or words in order to change a text in such a way that a Deep Neural Network (DNN) classifier is fooled, but at the same time a human might not even notice the difference. In the following example, the authors added a whole sentence (marked in red in the original source, now underlined) that caused the DNN to classify the text, which was originally classified correctly as being from the topic area "Means of Transportation" (confidence 99.9%), as a text from the topic area "Film" (confidence 90.2%), cf. Liang et al., 2018, p. 4210, figure 4:

> The APM 20 Lionceau is a two-seat very light aircraft manufactured by the French manufacturer Issoire Aviation. Despite its classic appearance it is entirely built from composite materials especially carbon fibers. Designed by Philippe Moniot and certified in 1999 (see EASA CS-VLA) this very light (400 kg empty 634 kg loaded) and economical (80 PS engine) aircraft is primarily intended to be used to learn to fly but also to travel with a relatively high cruise speed (113 knots). <u>Lionceau has appeared in an American romantic movie directed by Cameron Crowe.</u> A three-seat version the APM 30 Lion was presented at the 2005 Paris Air Show. Issoire APM 20 Lionceau.

In their paper, Liang and co-authors focus on the technical and mathematical aspects of adversarial examples in text classification. In the next section, we will follow their lead and discuss how adversarials can be generated. However, after that we broaden the picture and add the cognitive point of view. In order to take the above-mentioned "utility-preserving" into account, it is not sufficient to explain the mathematics of the DNN classifiers' failures only. It is also necessary to discuss why and under which conditions DNN classifiers are fooled but humans are not.

2. Generating Adversarial Attacks

In order to discuss how to generate adversarial attacks, we first take a look at the field of Explainable AI. Explainable AI is a double-edged sword in the context of adversarial attacks. It allows the analysis of AI applications so that we get a better idea why a certain application generates the results it does. Thus, explainable AI can be used to identify the "weak" spots of AI applications, in particular those input patterns that cause strange and undesired results. If these spots are known to the developer of the application, this knowledge allows them to fix the problem. However, if the spots are known to an attacker (and not to the user), they can be exploited for adversarial attacks.

Explainable AI differentiates between "white box" systems and "black box" systems. A system at hand which can be analyzed directly is a "white box" system, but if we only can observe the system's reactions to given inputs it is a "black box" system. Liang et al. (2018: 4209f.) describe their mathematical approach (a) to identify the most significant ("hot") characters for manipulating characters to generate adversarial attacks on the character level and (b) to identify the most significant ("hot") words and phrases for manipulating on the word level to generate word-level adversarials. Here, we would like to focus on word-level manipulations. In short, a word (or a phrase) is highly significant ("hot") if it contributes highly to cause a specific classification. Mathematically, these words can be identified by calculating cost gradients (cf. Baehrens et al. 2010) or by alternatives like "layer-wise relevance propagation" (LRP) (Arras et al. 2017). Liang et al. (2018: 4211, figure 6) provide the following example text which is classified as a text from the topic area "Film".

> Edward & Mrs. Simpson is a seven-part <u>British</u> television series that dramatises the events leading to the 1936 abdication of King Edward VIII of the United Kingdom who gave up his throne to marry the twice divorced American Wallis Simpson. The series made by Thames Television for ITV was originally broadcast in 1978. Edward Fox played Edward and Cynthia Harris portrayed Mrs. Simpson. Edward & Mrs. Simpson.

The interesting thing about this example is that the DNN's confidence for the "film" classification drops from 95.5% to 60.5% if the word "British" (marked in blue in the original figure, now underlined) is deleted from the text. Thus, the word "British" is identified as a "hot" word by means of calculation, and its deletion moves the text in the classification vector space a long way towards the hyperplane that delineates the border of class "Film", so that it can be quite easily tipped over that border by further manipulations. We would like to remark here that, for a human, the word "British" seems to be superfluous. In contrast to words like "television" or "broadcast", humans would not assume that this word contributes that heavily to the classification as a "Film" text.

In the case of a "black box" system, a model of the system needs to be developed. In a first step, probes are used: the system is confronted with specific inputs and the reactions of the system to those inputs are noted. In our case, texts are presented as inputs and the corresponding classifications are the results. In a second step, the collected pairs of inputs and corresponding results can be used to train a model of the "black box" classifier, e.g. by a second DNN. The trained model then can be used to predict the classifier's reactions to other inputs. If the model is interpretable (and thus a so-called "Global Surrogate Model"), the predictions can be calculated out of the model. This then allows the mathematical identification of the "hot" words, cf. Ribeiro et al. (2016) or Alain/Bengio (2016) for mathematical details. The model also can be regarded as a "white box" system. As such it can be analyzed, e.g., by the gradient approach (Baehrens et al. 2010) or the LRP approach (Arras et al. 2017) as mentioned above. Unfortunately, trained models are seldom interpretable. However, they might be nevertheless locally interpretable. Local interpretability allows the calculation of the predictions on a local base and, thus, it allows the identification of candidates for "hot" words on a local level. Local level "hot" candidates are words whose manipulation might tip the classification from one given class to another given class. In the end, however, the "hot" word candidates need to be tested against the "black box" classifier, since all the steps towards their identification add uncertainty to the equation and the local interpretability might not cover a large enough part of the vector space. So, in the case of "black box" systems, in contrast to "white box" systems, text samples which look promising for generating adversarial examples cannot be based on calculated "hot" words, but have to be detected by mixture of modelling and calculation, educated guessing, approximations, sequences of trial and error, and, of course, pure luck.

3. Differences in the Process of Text Classification between AI Classifiers and Humans

After having generated "may be"-adversarial examples by a mathematical approach, we have to consider "utility-preserving". This can be done by sorting out all those "may be"-adversarials that would also cause humans to change the classification. Alternatively, we could take "utility-preserving" into account from the beginning and try to generate only proper adversarials. In order to do so, we have to consider the differences between AI information processing and human information processing in general, and AI text classification and human text classification in particular, with the goal of better understanding the conditions that favor "utility-preserving".

We will start our comparison by considering *similarity aspects*. We begin with similarity aspects in phoneme recognition and character (letter) recognition. The phoneme /n/ is more similar to the phoneme /m/ than to the phoneme /f/ since /n/ and /m/ are voiced nasals. They only differ with respect to their place of articulation, [alveolar] for /n/ and [bilabial] for /m/. In contrast, /f/ is a voiceless fricative with [labiodental] as its place of articulation. In sum, /n/ and /m/ differ in one phonological feature, whereas /n/ and /f/ differ in all three. Consequently, a human confronted with phoneme /n/ errs more often by "hearing" /m/ instead of /n/ than "hearing" /f/ instead of /n/. A similar statement holds true for recognizing characters (letters and numerals). A human may have problems to distinguish a capital "o" ("O") from a zero ("0") but less so from an "m". A system that tries to identify these numerals and letters on a (filthy) license plate might have the same problems, but for a system that operates on digitalized text, all the numerals and letters are symbols of identical distance. As an example, the change of "APT40" to "APTAO" will be recognized by a system but might be overlooked by a human reader. Even more so, the switching of two letters in the middle of a word is also often ignored by humans during reading, as shown by Grainger/Whitney (2004) in an article with the telling title *"Does the huamn mnid raed wrods as a wlohe?"* The reason for this is simple. Human expert readers do not waste time recognizing and identifying one character after the other. Instead, we fixate (relevant) content words on the second or third character, skip function words, and jump to the next (relevant) content word (Rayner 1997). During this process, words are recognized by their "gestalt", and only those characters fixated are precisely identified (Brysbaert/Nazir 2005).

A glance at the human cognitive process of reading explains why manipulations on character level can evade human attention and how "utility-preserving" can be achieved. The same holds for manipulation on the word level. Again, similarity effects are at work. For example, the formal similarity between *"flamenco"* and *"flamingo"* can be exploited. If, in a text of the category "culture", *"flamenco"* is substituted with *"flamingo"*, the classification of that text might change to "nature". Of course, the substitution of *"flamenco"* with *"duck"* then would have the same effect, but this would much more easily be noticed by a human and no "utility-preserving" would have been achieved. If a human reads a text, the next following words are predicted (*"In Madrid's Retiro Park you can always see people dancing ..."*). This resembles text processing by "Generative Pre-trained Transformer 3" (GPT-3, Brown et al. 2020). However, if the gestalt of the predicted next word is similar to the word in the text, humans might "see" the predicted word and not the printed word, whereas GPT-3 would "see" the word as it is printed. GPT-3 would not "see" the predicted word.

Since we are discussing text classification, it also seems appropriate to discuss human categorization in comparison to the classification by AI. A relevant aspect here is *the clearness or fuzziness of categories*. Although phonemes constitute very clear sound categories in human speech recognition, words do not. Words signify semantic categories but the categories are "flexible", as was first demonstrated by Labov (1973). In contrast, AI classifiers often (but not necessarily) partition input with clearly cut boundaries between two categories. It is obvious that humans who categorize fuzzily and AI classifiers that categorize within sharp borders will come to different results in some cases. Although it has to be determined which kind of categorizing – fuzzy or clear and sharp – is more appropriate for a given task, it suggests itself that some of an AI's categorization results may surprise a human user who assumes that an AI will carry out a task much more rapidly and with fewer lapses, but, apart from that, like a human.

Let us take a look at an example, namely the Socio-political and Crisis Events Detection Shared Task at the CASE@ACL-IJCNLP 2021 workshop (Haneczok et al. 2021). The task is about the categorization of texts. The categories involved represent socio-political and crisis events. Two of the categories are "Violent Demonstration" and "Property Destruction". Obviously, violent demonstrations more often than not include property destruction. As an example, consider the demonstrations at the 2017 G20 Summit in Hamburg. This situation led to foreseeable results. On the one hand, AI classifiers submitted to the shared task (and trained with a corpus that the submitters had to develop beforehand), often confused the classes mentioned, but had no problem separating them from texts representing categories like "Air Strike" (cf. Kent/Krumbiegel 2021). In order to tip the classification from one of the critical categories to the other, only a few changes in the occurrence or non-occurrence of specific words are necessary (e.g. *"some of the protesters set a car alight"* or *"some of the activists set a car alight"* vs. *"some criminals set a car alight"*). On the other hand, humans would want to assign the problematic texts to both categories, "Violent Demonstration" and "Property Destruction". If they were asked to choose only one of them, the classification selected would differ, not only with regard to the subjects doing the classification, but also as a function of context like in the experiments by Labov. Like the AIs, humans might be influenced by the explicit wording. However, humans are able to recognize some parts in a text as purely ornamental. For instance, in the example provided by Liang et al. (2018) given above, the text about an aircraft is ornamented with the remark that the same aircraft had a scene in a specific movie. Humans would not consider such ornaments for classification. An AI does. Therefore, smartly constructed ornaments can be used to create adversarials.

4. Linguistic Aspects

Similarity of characters due to their visual nature, or of words due to sharing letters in many of the same positions, influences the processing of words and texts in human language comprehension, unlike in the same processing run by text classification AIs. These differences can be exploited by generating adversarials, as has been discussed above. We will discuss in the following how some linguistic aspects can contribute to this. We will focus on orthography/phonology, morphology, and pragmatics.

4.1 Orthography and Phonology

Weingarten (2011) discusses phonographic errors (in writing) in contrast to grammatographic errors. Phonographic errors occur if one substitutes a word with a sequence of letters that is pronounced like the target word but is spelled differently. If the error is a word, it is a homophone of the target word, but not a homograph (*"Mary Christmas"*). Phonographic errors can be used as adversarials. As an extreme example, let us assume that we have science fiction text snippets and want to assign each of them to a saga like Star Wars, Star Trek, Honorverse, Expanse etc. It is easy to assign the sentence *"During his training, Luke Skywalker saw a vision of his friends in danger"* to the Star Wars saga. However, a version with phonographic errors such as *"During his training, Lewk Skeyewolker saw a vision of his friends in danger"* might be problem for an AI. In contrast, a human would recognize the error and judge the writer as a jester (or as incompetent in spelling), but would not have a problem with the categorization. Substituting a "hot" word with a phonographic error might constitute a better adversarial than removing the word, since that is not always possible without changing a text's meaning. It might also be more effective than switching letters within the "hot" word since phonographic errors often have a larger Levenshtein distance to their target, and may thus withstand a preprocessing of the texts to be classified aimed at deleting typos.

4.2 Morphology

For a long time, preprocessing had been a smart idea to deal with morphological variations. In conventional, bag-of-words based classifiers (cf. Manning et al. 2008 or Jurafsky/Martin 2009), preceding current state-of-the-art DNN classifiers, words occurring in training and test data were primarily considered terminal symbols disregarding semantic or morphological relatedness. Highly inflecting languages such as German encode various information, such as case (in nouns and adjectives), person, tense and mode (in verbs) and number (in all these word classes), at the word-level, creating potentially dozens of word-forms for one lexeme. Thus, conventional classifiers based on word frequency and correlation between the appearance of word forms and target label disregard relations between e.g. singular and plural inflected forms of their base lexeme by design, distorting statistics about the relevance of terms for a given class and tampering with feature selection when creating the vector space for classification. Preprocessing of texts, in particular lemmatization (the substitution of all the morphological forms with the base form), countered those problems.

The advent of word embeddings with Word2Vec (Mikolov et al. 2013) and its successors mitigated the issue of apparently distinct but related word forms by projecting words into a vector space capable of encoding similarities on various levels, including, but not limited to, semantical and morpho-syntactical aspects. Given sufficient training data, a DNN text classifier learns to systematically disregard non-relevant (for the classification task) morphological variations (Claeser 2021). While certain word forms of relevant terms might be required, the presented lexicon does not necessarily need to be exhaustive, i.e. number marking as in "match" vs. "matches" might be irrelevant when it comes to assigning a text to the category "Sports". While previous generations of word embeddings such as Word2Vec and FastText (Joulin et al. 2016) conflated occurrences of word forms including possible homographs into a single unigram word vector, state-of-the-art transformer models such as BERT (Devlin et al. 2019) additionally represent potential context information in multiple hidden layers shipped as a refinable pre-trained vector space model. Circumventing the common out-of-vocabulary problem (OOV), BERT stores sub word units, morphemes such as the English "-ing", in addition to a fixed-size full-form vocabulary to resolve unknown inflections of lexemes represented in the dictionary.

Embedding-based deep learning language models and applications such as text classifiers might be considered more robust to adversarial attacks. However, in an interview about GPT-3 and language processing AIs (Küchemann 2020), Sina Zarrieß argued for morphological preprocessing at least with regard to texts in languages like Finnish. Why? Distributions of inflected word forms that follow Zipf's Law (Zipf 1949) tend to produce few or no instances of less common values in morphological categories such as the subjunctive mood in German ("Konjunktiv"). Consequently, while a DNN classifier might be trained to disregard the "tense" or "person" category values in verb forms as in "soll – sollte" ("should", 1st person singular present and simple past, respectively), it might be tampered with using the conjunctive form "solle". Manipulating morphological mechanisms such as the German Umlaut, which is necessary to incorporate aspects such as number in certain

German noun classes as in "Haus – Häuser" (house – houses), while facing little hesitation by a human classifier and leading to rejection of the term by a conventional classifier, might be mitigated to a certain degree by BERT's incorporation of unigram character representations. The exact extent of recent models' ability to cope with such modifications, however, is currently still under investigation. Finally, phenomena such as separable prefixes of verbs in a number of Germanic languages, such as German, Icelandic and, to a certain degree, even English, pose a challenge even to DNN classifiers. For example, in *"Tom hörte sich die Symphonie an"* (Tom listened to the symphony), the verb is *"anhören"* and the separable and displaced prefix is *"an"*. *"Anhören"* and *"hören"* (to hear) are semantically connected, but *"aufhören"* (to stop) like in *"Tom hörte danach mit dem Klavierspielen auf"* (Tom stopped playing piano afterwards) is not. So, in German, "hot" verbs might be substituted with a verb with such a prefix (or the phrases might be rearranged) so that a verb stem is considered by the classification which is not semantically related to the verb as a whole. Again, preprocessing, namely substituting all words with their base form (lemmatization), would suppress that problem.

4.3 Pragmatics

The most interesting linguistic aspect might be pragmatics. This can be illustrated by taking a look at GPT-3. In principle, GPT-3 takes a piece of text, the "prompt", and continues it. In their review of GPT-3, Marcus/Davis (2020) provided the following example:

Prompt:
You are a defense lawyer and you have to go to court today. Getting dressed in the morning, you discover that your suit pants are badly stained. However, your bathing suit is clean and very stylish. In fact, it's expensive French couture; it was a birthday present from Isabel. You decide that you should wear

GPT-3's continuation:
the bathing suit to court. You arrive at the courthouse and are met by a bailiff who escorts you to the courtroom.

Gwern (2020) argued that GPT-3's continuation is as it is since GPT-3 had learned the Gricean maxims (Grice, 1975), in particular, the maxim of relation (relevance): *Be relevant*: "Prompts should obey Gricean maxims of communication – statements should be true, informative, and relevant. One should not throw in irrelevant details or non sequiturs, because in human text, even in fiction, that implies that those details are relevant, no matter how nonsensical a narrative involving them may be" (Gwern 2020). The Gricean maxims explicate Grice's cooperative principle, the backbone of effective conversational communication among people. The principle and with it the maxims are incorporated into texts. For example, if in an Agatha Christie novel something from the past is mentioned, this always is relevant, either for the solving of the mystery or for introducing red herrings. That everything is relevant is the essence of the maxim of relation. In the example by Marcus and Davis, GPT-3 pays heed to the assumed relevance of the reference to the bathing suit and transfers it into its continuation of the text. The problem is that the maxim of relation does not always hold. Sometimes, people are not cooperative. Sometimes people would like to impress the hearer (or the reader), e.g. by adding some pieces of superfluous information that hint at the speaker's (or the writer's) huge and impressive knowledge. Above, we labeled respective parts of texts as "ornamental". These parts are not relevant but serve different purposes, e.g. to make the speaker look good. Humans are trained to recognize these parts as such and would not consider them for text classification or text continuation. As has already been mentioned, current AIs do not recognize ornaments and therefore "exploit" them for the classification and, obviously, also for continuation. Thus, to repeat our already achieved insight, adversarials can be generated as ornaments. However, tempering against such kinds of adversarials might be possible by "learning" to recognize text ornaments.

5. Conclusion

In our contribution, we discussed adversarials in the field of text classification. We referred to the mathematical approach on how to generate them and then focused on how to allow "utility-preserving". To do so, we took into account aspects of the human classification process as well as linguistic aspects. These examinations led to indications on how to generate adversarials against text classifications.

Goodfellow et al. (2015: 2) expressed their disappointment that DNNs in the field of image classification had not learned concepts, as demonstrated by the existence of adversarials. Adversarials also exist in the field of text classification (Liang et al. 2018; Xu et al. 2020). So, we may assume that text-processing AIs might also not have learned concepts. GTP-3 had learned to build sentences and texts in English and other languages that are grammatically correct. It can even answer questions correctly, although it fails to adequately deal with questions that include an empty definite description (Who was the Roman emperor last year?). Text-processing AIs can learn to use language adequately on the orthographic, the morphological and the syntactic level by building vector space representations of a language's symbols, the words, the phrases, and the sentences. However, to complete the "semiotic triangle" (Ogden/Richards 1923), the reference to the real world is missing. During lexical development, a child resorts to cognitive development (Piaget 1923). We would like to suggest that a language-processing AI is not capable of developing concepts, since it does not establish references to the real world for its representations of language symbols and therefore cannot establish these references, since it lacks cognitive development. Adversarials strongly illustrate that inaptness.

Figure 1

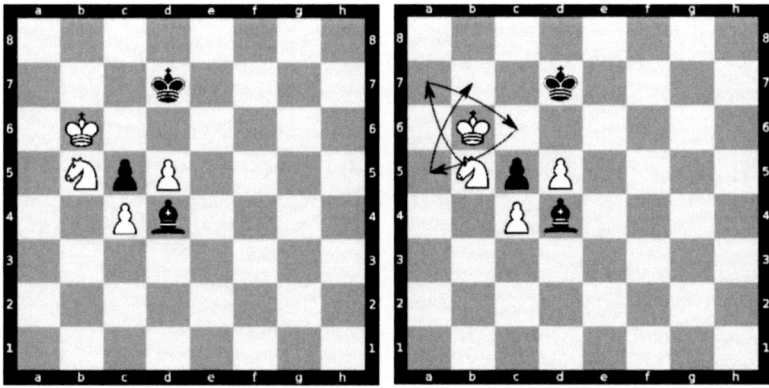

In order to substantiate our claim, we would like to point to one of the most awe-inspiring achievements of DNNs, their mastery of board games like chess. Adversarials can even be found within this area of strength as figure 1 shows. The figure (left) displays a position from the final of the Top Chess Engine Championship (TCEC), Season 14, November 17th, 2018 to February 24th, 2019. In the final, the engine Stockfish 10 won narrowly by 50.5 to 49.5 against Leela Chess Zero (Lc0) (Schormann 2019). In the position displayed, Leela, playing White, is to move. The position is easily won but

Leela failed. The position is an adversarial for Leela. So, why is the position won? Simple effect-based reasoning shows the following: (a) White will win if the black pawn on c5 falls. (b) The pawn will fall if the white horse reaches b7 since then the knight attacks the pawn and in addition prevents the black king from defending the pawn from d6. (c) White can move its horse from b5 to a7 to c6 to a5 to b7 (right figure) to take the pawn. (d) Black cannot prevent all this. Leela is not able to do effect-based reasoning. It also does not calculate trees of moves like chess engines of the period before Deep Learning engines did. Leela decides on elaborate pattern matching. Pattern matching favors positions in which one's own pawns are advanced as far as possible. Thus, Leela is fooled and moves its d-pawn to d6, but then victory is lost and the draw is certain.

References

Alain, Guillaume, and Yoshua Bengio (2016). "Understanding Intermediate Layers using Linear Classifier Probes." In: *arXiv.org*. URL: https://arxiv.org/abs/1610.01644v4, (4. Version von 2018).

Arras, Leila, Franziska Horn, Grégoire Montavon, Klaus-Robert Müller, and Wojciech Samek (2017). "'What is Relevant in a Text Document?': An interpretable machine learning approach". In: *PLoS ONE* 12, pp. 1–23.

Baehrens, David, Timon Schroeter, Stefan Harmeling, Motoaki Kawanabe, Katja Hansen, and Klaus-Robert Müller (2010). "How to Explain Individual Classification Decisions." In: *Journal of Machine Learning Research* 11, pp. 1803–1831.

Brown, Tom B. et al. (2020). "Language Models are Few-Shot Learners." In: *arXiv.org*. URL: https://arxiv.org/abs/2005.14165v4.

Brysbaert, Marc, and Tatjana Nazir (2005). "Visual Constraints in Written Word Recognition: Evidence from the Optimal Viewing-position Effect." In: *Journal of Research in Reading* 28, pp. 216–228.

Claeser, Daniel (2021). *Zur Rolle der Flexionsmorphologie in der automatischen Klassifikation deutschsprachiger Textdokumente*. PhD Thesis, Rheinische Friedrich-Wilhelms-Universität Bonn.

Devlin, Jacob, Ming-Wei Chang, Kenton Lee, and Kristina Toutanova (2019). "BERT: Pre-training of Deep Bidirectional Transformers for Language Understanding." In: *Proceedings of the 2019 Conference of the North American Chapter of the Association for Computational Linguistics: Human Language*

Technologies. Volume 1. Ed. by Jill Burstein, Christy Doran, and Thamar Solorio. Minneapolis, MN: Association for Computational Linguistics, pp. 4171–4186.

Goodfellow, Ian J., Jonathon Shlens, and Christian Szegedy (2015). "Explaining and Harnessing Adversarial Examples." In: *Proceedings of the 3rd International Conference on Learning Representations (ICLR 2015).* Ed. by Yoshua Bengio and Yann LeChun. URL: arxiv.org/abs/1412.6572.

Grainger, Jonathan, and Carol Whitney (2004). "Does the huamn mnid raed wrods as a wlohe?" In: *Trends in Cognitive Science* 8, pp. 58–59.

Grice, Herbert Paul (1975). "Logic and Conversation." In: *Syntax and Semantics.* Volume 3. Ed. by Peter Cole and Jerry L. Morgan. New York: Academic Press, pp. 41–58.

Gu, Tianyu, Brendan Dolan-Gavitt, and Siddharth Garg (2017). "BadNets: Identifying Vulnerabilities in the Machine Learning Model Supply Chain." In: *arXiv.org.* URL: https://arxiv.org/abs/1708.06733.

Gwern (2020). "GPT-3 Creative Fiction". URL: https://www.gwern.net/GPT-3 #expressing-uncertainty.

Haneczok, Jacek, Guillaume Jacquet, Jakub Piskorski, and Nicolas Stefanovitch (2021). "Fine-grained Event Classification in News-like Text Snippets Shared Task 2, CASE 2021." In: *Proceedings of the Workshop on Challenges and Applications of Automated Text Extraction of Socio-Political Event from Text (CASE 2021), co-located with the Joint Conference of the 59th Annual Meeting of the Association for Computational Linguistics and the 11th International Joint Conference on Natural Language Processing (ACL-IJCNLP 2021).* Ed. by Ali Hürriyetğlu.

Joulin, Armand, Edouard Grave, Piotr Bojanowski, and Tomas Mikolov (2016). "Bag of Tricks for Efficient Text Classification." In: *Proceedings of the 15th Conference of the European Chapter of the Association for Computational Linguistics.* Volume 2, Short Papers.

Jurafsky, Dan, and James H. Martin (2009). Speech and Language Processing: An Introduction to Natural Language Processing, Speech Recognition, and Computational Linguistics (2nd Edition), Upper Saddle River, NJ: Prentice-Hall.

Kent, Samantha, and Theresa Krumbiegel (2021). "CASE 2021 Task 2: Sociopolitical Fine-grained Event Classification using Fine-tuned RoBERTa Document Embeddings." In: *Proceedings of the Workshop on Challenges and Applications of Automated Text Extraction of Socio-Political Event from Text (CASE 2021), co-located with the Joint Conference of the 59th Annual Meeting of the Asso-*

ciation for Computational Linguistics and the 11th International Joint Conference on Natural Language Processing (ACL-IJCNLP 2021). Ed. by Ali Hürriyetğlu.

Küchemann, Fridtjof, (2020). "Nimmt uns der Computer die Sprache ab?" In: *Frankfurter Allgemeine Zeitung*, November 26, 2020. URL: https://www.faz.net/aktuell/feuilleton/debatten/die-informatikerin-sina-zarriess-ueber-sprachmodelle-wie-gpt-3-17070713.html.

Labov. William (1973). "The Boundaries of Words and Their Meanings." In: *New Ways of Analyzing Variation in English*. Ed. by Charles-James Bailey and Roger W. Shuy, Washington, DC: Georgetown Press, pp. 340–373.

Liang, Bin, Hongcheng Li, Miaoqiang Su, Pan Bian, Xirong Li, and Wenchang Shi(2018). "Deep Text Classification Can Be Fooled." In: Jérôme Lang (ed.), Proceedings of the Twenty-Seventh International Joint Conference on Artificial Intelligence (IJCAI-18), pp. 4208–4215 (arXiv:1412.6572v3).

Manning, Christopher D., Prabhakar Raghavan, and Hinrich Schütze (2008). *Introduction to Information Retrieval*. Cambridge, UK: Cambridge University Press.

Marcus, Gary, and Ernest Davis (2020). "GPT-3, Bloviator: OpenAI's Language Generator Has No Idea What It's Talking About." In: *MIT Technology Review*. URL: https://www.technologyreview.com/2020/08/22/1007539/gpt3-openai-language-generator-artificial-intelligence-ai-opinion.

Mikolov, Tomas, Kai Chen, Greg Corrado, and Jeffrey Dean (2013). "Efficient Estimation of Word Representations in Vector Space." In: *International Conference on Learning Representations*. Scottsdale, AZ. URL: https://arxiv.org/abs/1301.3781.

Ogden, Charles Kay, and Ivor Armstrong Richards (1923). *The Meaning of Meaning*, London: Routledge & Kegan Paul.

Piaget, Jean (1923). *La langage et la pensée chez l'enfant*, Neuchâtel: Delchaux et Niestlé.

Rayner, Keith (1997). "Understanding Eye Movements in Reading." In: *Scientific Studies of Reading* 1, pp. 317–339.

Ribeiro, Marco Tulio, Sameer Singh, and Carlos Guestrin (2016). "'Why Should I Trust You?': Explaining the Predictions of Any Classifier." *Proceedings of the 22nd ACM SIGKDD International Conference on Knowledge Discovery and Data Mining*. Ed. by Balaji Krishnapuram and Mohak Shah. New York: Association for Computing Machinery. URL: https://arxiv.org/abs/1602.04938.

Schormann, Conrad (2019). "Computerschach: Inoffizielle Engine-WM TCEC – Finale LC0 vs. Stockfish". In: *Rochade Europa* 4/2019, pp. 42–43.

Szegedy, Christian, Wojciech Zaremba, Ilya Sutskever, Joan Bruna, Dumitru Erhan, Ian J. Goodfellow, and Rob Fergus (2014). "Intriguing Properties of Neural Networks." In: 2nd International Conference on Learning Representations (ICLR). Banff, Canada. URL: https://arxiv.org/abs/1312.6199

Weingarten, Rüdiger (2011). "Comparative Graphematics." In: *Written Language and Literacy* 14, pp. 12–38.

Xu, Han, Yao Ma, Haochen Liu, Debayan Deb, Hui Liu, Jiliang Tang, and Anil K. Jain (2020). "Adversarial Attacks and Defenses in Images, Graphs and Texts: A Review." In: *International Journal of Automation and Computing* 17, pp. 151–178. URL: https://arxiv.org/abs/1909.08072.

Zipf, George Kingsley (1949): *Human Behavior and the Principle of Least Effort: An Introduction to Human Ecology*, Cambridge, MA: Addison Wesley.

Authors

Berkemer, Rainer, Prof. Dr., contributed the article "Learning Algorithms – What is Artificial Intelligence really capable of?". He is Professor at AKAD University and works in the fields of neural nets and fuzzy logic.

Claeser, Daniel, Dr., contributed the article "Let's fool that stupid AI – Adversarial Attacks against Text Processing AI". He is senior scientist at Fraunhofer Institute for Communication, Information Processing and Ergonomics FKIE and works in the fields of natural language processing (NLP) and machine learning.

Grottke, Markus, Prof. Dr., contributed the article "Learning Algorithms – What is Artificial Intelligence really capable of?". He is vice president of innovation and dual studies at AKAD University and works in the fields of digitalisation, family business, accounting.

Hartmann, Carsten, Prof. Dr., contributed the article "Transgressing the boundaries: towards a rigorous understanding of deep learning and its (non-)robustness". He is Professor of Mathematics at the Brandenburg University of Technology and works in the fields of applied probability, statistical physics and computational statistics.

Hartwig, Katrin, M.Sc., contributed the article "Trends in Explainable Artificial Intelligence for Non-Experts". She is a doctoral student in the department of Science and Technology for Peace and Security (PEASEC) at TU Darmstadt and works in the field of user-centered technical countermeasures to combat misleading information online.

Klimczak, Peter, Prof. Dr. Dr., contributed the article "Limits and Prospects of Ethics in the Context of Law and Society by the Example of Accident Algorithms of Autonomous Driving". He is head of the subject areas "Digital Solutions" and "Digital Infrastructure" in the Senate Administration for Education, Youth and Family (= Ministry of Education of Berlin) and an adjunct professor (außerplanmäßiger Professor) at the Brandenburg University of Technology. He conducts research on digital/social media, cognitive systems, and the use of artificial languages in media and cultural studies.

Kraljevski, Ivan, Dr.-Ing., contributed the article "Limits and Prospects of Big Data and Small Data Approaches in AI Applications". He is research associate at Fraunhofer Institute for Ceramic Technologies and Systems IKTS, Dresden. His scientific and professional interests include: speech and audio signal processing, speech recognition and synthesis, pattern recognition and artificial neural networks.

Kusche, Isabel, Prof. Dr., contributed the article "Artificial Intelligence and/as Risk". She is Professor of Sociology with a focus on digital media at the University of Bamberg and works in the fields of digital transformation, political communication and sociological theory.

Nowack, Kati, Dr., contributed the article "When You Can't Have What You Want: Measuring Users' Ethical Concerns about Interacting with AI Assistants Using MEESTAR". She is Senior Researcher at the Brandenburg University of Technology. Working at the intersection of cognitive and media psychology, she examines the influence of individual difference variables on the processes of computer-mediated communication, media selection and reception.

Özalp, Elise, M.Sc., contributed the article "Trends in Explainable Artificial Intelligence for Non-Experts". She is a doctoral student in the Department of Aeronautics at Imperial College London and works in the field of physics-aware machine learning.

Petersen, Christer, Prof. Dr., contributed the article "Man-Machines: Gynoids, Fembots, and Body-AI in Contemporary Cinematic Narratives". He holds the Chair of Applied Media Studies at the Brandenburg University of

Technology and works in the fields of media and cultural semiotics, materiality and technicity of media.

Pritzkau, Albert, Dipl. Inform., contributed the article "Let's fool that stupid AI – Adversarial Attacks against Text Processing AI". He is senior scientist at Fraunhofer Institute for Communication, Information Processing and Ergonomics FKIE and works in the fields of natural language processing and visual analytics.

Reuter, Christian, Prof. Dr. Dr., contributed the article "Trends in Explainable Artificial Intelligence for Non-Experts". He holds the chair of Science and Technology for Peace and Security (PEASEC) at Technical University of Darmstadt and works on the intersection of the fields of peace and conflict studies, cybersecurity and privacy as well as human-computer interaction.

Richter, Lorenz, Dr., contributed the article "Transgressing the boundaries: towards a rigorous understanding of deep learning and its (non-)robustness". He founded the machine learning company dida and is affiliated to the Zuse Institute Berlin as a postdoc in mathematics. He works in the fields of optimal control theory, Monte Carlo methods and machine learning.

Rieger, Stefan, Prof. Dr., contributed the article "Machine Dreaming". He is Professor for History of Media and Theory of Communication at IfM (Institute for Media Studies) at Ruhr-University Bochum and works in the fields of History of Science, Epistemology of Media and Virtuality.

Schade, Ulrich, Prof. Dr., contributed the article "Let's fool that stupid AI – Adversarial Attacks against Text Processing AI". He is head of research group "Information Analysis" at Fraunhofer Institute for Communication, Information Processing and Ergonomics FKIE and lecturer for "Applied Linguistics" at Rheinische Friedrich-Wilhelms-Universität Bonn. He works in the fields of applied linguistics and computational linguistics.

Tschöpe, Constanze, Dr.-Ing., contributed the article "Limits and Prospects of Big Data and Small Data Approaches in AI Applications". She is the head of the Machine Learning and Data Analysis Group at the Fraunhofer Institute for Ceramic Technologies and Systems IKTS and the head of the Cognitive Material Diagnostics Project Group at the Brandenburg University of Technology. Her research interests include artificial intelligence, machine learning, acoustic pattern recognition, intelligent signal processing, and technical processes quality assessment.

Winandy, Steffen, contributed the article "Let's fool that stupid AI – Adversarial Attacks against Text Processing AI". He is software engineer at Fraunhofer Institute for Communication, Information Processing and Ergonomics FKIE and works in the fields of cloud computing and scalable data analysis.

Wolff, Matthias, Prof. Dr.-Ing., contributed the article "Limits and Prospects of Big Data and Small Data Approaches in AI Applications". He is professor for Communications Engineering at Brandenburg University of Technology in Cottbus, Germany. His scientific and professional interests include: artificial intelligence, cognitive systems, speech dialog systems, quantum logic, and quantum-inspired AI methods.

Medienwissenschaft

Marco Abel, Jaimey Fisher (Hg.)
Die Berliner Schule im globalen Kontext
Ein transnationales Arthouse-Kino

2022, 414 S., kart., 48 SW-Abbildungen
30,00 € (DE), 978-3-8376-5248-2
E-Book:
PDF: 29,99 € (DE), ISBN 978-3-8394-5248-6

Martin Donner, Heidrun Allert
Auf dem Weg zur Cyberpolis
Neue Formen von Gemeinschaft, Selbst und Bildung

2022, 496 S., kart., 10 SW-Abbildungen, 5 Farbabbildungen
39,00 € (DE), 978-3-8376-5878-1
E-Book: kostenlos erhältlich als Open-Access-Publikation
PDF: ISBN 978-3-8394-5878-5
ISBN 978-3-7328-5878-1

Geert Lovink
In der Plattformfalle
Plädoyer zur Rückeroberung des Internets

2022, 232 S., kart.
28,00 € (DE), 978-3-8376-6333-4
E-Book:
PDF: 24,99 € (DE), ISBN 978-3-8394-6333-8
EPUB: 24,99 € (DE), ISBN 978-3-7328-6333-4

**Leseproben, weitere Informationen und Bestellmöglichkeiten
finden Sie unter www.transcript-verlag.de**

Medienwissenschaft

Sven Quadflieg, Klaus Neuburg, Simon Nestler (eds.)
(Dis)Obedience in Digital Societies
Perspectives on the Power of Algorithms and Data

2022, 380 p., pb., ill.
29,00 € (DE), 978-3-8376-5763-0
E-Book: available as free open access publication
PDF: ISBN 978-3-8394-5763-4
ISBN 978-3-7328-5763-0

Gesellschaft für Medienwissenschaft (Hg.)
Zeitschrift für Medienwissenschaft 27
Jg. 14, Heft 2/2022: Reparaturwissen DDR

2022, 180 S., kart.
24,99 € (DE), 978-3-8376-5890-3
E-Book: kostenlos erhältlich als Open-Access-Publikation
PDF: ISBN 978-3-8394-5890-7
ISBN 978-3-7328-5890-3

Olga Moskatova, Anna Polze, Ramón Reichert (eds.)
Digital Culture & Society (DCS)
Vol. 7, Issue 2/2021 –
Networked Images in Surveillance Capitalism

2022, 336 p., pb., col. ill.
29,99 € (DE), 978-3-8376-5388-5
E-Book:
PDF: 27,99 € (DE), ISBN 978-3-8394-5388-9

**Leseproben, weitere Informationen und Bestellmöglichkeiten
finden Sie unter www.transcript-verlag.de**